Praise for
Every Young Man, God's Man

"Every Young Man, God's Man pulls no punches in challenging young men to declare their loyalty to Jesus Christ early and not waver in a lifelong pursuit of His ways and plans. All important issues are explored with refreshing candor—from personal holiness to sexual purity to spiritual warfare and more. Every young man eager to make his life count will gain huge benefits from this book."

—JOSH MCDOWELL, author and speaker

"Every Young Man, God's Man does more than just warn young men of the dangers that lurk in the shadows of adolescence. It gives them hope that they can overcome and conquer their fears. Every chapter is filled with the kind of practical, down-to-earth advice that will arm young men against the assaults of sexual temptation, peer pressure, and isolation.… No overly simplistic solutions found here; just solid scriptural principles that create godly young men. My sons will read this book—very soon!"

—ROSS PARSLEY, associate pastor of New Life Church

"Kenny Luck has a brave and raw style that grabs you by the throat and, at the same time, gently moves you to want to change. He is able to talk about the dark, secret, and tough places that most guys would prefer to keep secret. He says things that others only think of saying with the clear intent to help guys experience God's love and power for their lives."

—DOUG FIELDS, pastor to students at Saddleback Church,
author, speaker, and president of Simply Youth Ministry

STEPHEN ARTERBURN
KENNY LUCK WITH MIKE YORKEY

WORKBOOK INCLUDED

Every Young Man God's Man

Confident, Courageous, and Completely His

WATERBROOK
PRESS

EVERY YOUNG MAN, GOD'S MAN
PUBLISHED BY WATERBROOK PRESS
12265 Oracle Boulevard, Suite 200
Colorado Springs, Colorado 80921

Details in some anecdotes and stories have been changed to protect the identities of the persons involved.

ISBN 978-0-307-45943-5
ISBN 978-0-307-55143-6 (electronic)

Published in the United States by WaterBrook Multnomah, an imprint of the Crown Publishing Group, a division of Random House Inc., New York.

WATERBROOK and its deer colophon are registered trademarks of Random House Inc.

Library of Congress Cataloging-in-Publication Data
Arterburn, Stephen, 1953–
    Every young man, God's man : confident, courageous, and completely His /
Stephen Arterburn and Kenny Luck, with Mike Yorkey
        p. cm. — (Spiritual integrity)
    1. Young men—Religious life. 2. Christian life. I. Luck, Kenneth L., 1964–
II. Yorkey, Mike. III. Title. IV. Series.
    BV4541.3.A77 2005
    248.8'42—dc22

                                                2004024720

Printed in the United States of America
2010

10 9 8 7 6 5 4 3 2 1

SPECIAL SALES
Most WaterBrook Multnomah books are available at special quantity discounts when purchased in bulk by corporations, organizations, and special-interest groups. Custom imprinting or excerpting can also be done to fit special needs. For information, please e-mail SpecialMarkets@WaterBrookMultnomah.com or call 1-800-603-7051.

This book is dedicated to Ryan Luck—my warrior friend and son.

*It is also devoted to the great-great-grandsons
of the young men in this generation who choose
to be loyal to Christ above all.*

contents

acknowledgments

from Kenny Luck

This book is the result of having the opportunity to be taught and mentored by strong godly men. At UCLA these men were Matt Booker and J. P. Jones. In my family, special thanks goes to my father-in-law and stalwart brother, Don Watson. In ministry, Rick Warren, Josh McDowell, Steve Arterburn, and Lance Witt have shaped my ministry by their very lives, words, and commitment to their Lord. At Every Man Ministries, Chris Hite, Phil Deol, Scott Plail, Tom Chapin, Chris Duncan, Chris Luck, Jim Waterhouse, and Danny Wallen have all sacrificed and fought for the worthy cause of reaching men for Christ. At Saddleback, my battalion of brothers answers the call with me in men's ministry and provides leadership for our church. God has used all of you to inspire, challenge, sharpen, and stretch my faith over the years so that His purpose for my life goes forward.

Special thanks to the CRAVE guys at Saddleback for letting me ask you some tough questions and for providing real answers so that your brothers around the world can better connect with the truth of God's Word.

The twenty-one-gun salute goes to Chrissy—thanks for all your sacrifices and support that allow me the freedom to pursue this ministry to men around the world.

Lastly, thanks to Cara, Ryan, and Jenna for loaning their dad to God on many nights and over many weekends so that men can come to know the God who made them and loves them as sons.

introduction

by Stephen Arterburn

I always wanted to be the father of a son—someone like you. No matter what you may have done or the trouble you have been into or the way you look or act, I would love being a father of a great young man like you.

One day I picked up a little boy named Carter who had been crying after he fell down. He looked at me after I hugged him and said, "You remind me of my dad." It was a great feeling to know that for a few moments I felt like a father to a little boy.

If you were my son, there are some things I'd want you to have: a bike and a skateboard and, when the time came, a car. I would want you to own all the cool stuff that cool guys have, including a surfboard, because if you were my son, you would be living right next to the ocean. I would want you to have great teachers, fun guy friends, and nice girlfriends you could be really proud of. I would want you to have a lot of things I did not have when I was growing up, and I would work hard to provide them for you.

Of all the things I would want you to have, though, one stands above the rest. If you had it, your life would be easier to manage. It would also make your life count. That one thing is *character*. To me character means believing in what is good and right and being able to live according to what you believe. A young man with character is consistent in what he does in public and private. He is one of the rare people who is more interested in what he gives than what he takes. People are better after being with him rather than feeling hurt or angry. The young man with character knows why he is on this earth and is working toward fulfilling his God-given mission. He knows he is called to be God's man and is doing whatever it takes to become God's man. He has a sense of direction and purpose that will not be sidelined by some selfish temptation to do or be less than he can be.

If you were my son, I would do my best to teach you to be your best. I would also help you understand that you are not perfect, and that over the course of your life, you are going to mess up and make mistakes—just like some of the best in the Bible made mistakes. And I would want you to know how to pick yourself up, put yourself back in God's hands, and proceed on down that road toward being God's man. I would help you accept the great and not-so-great parts of yourself. And I would do my best to help you accept those parts in others also.

> **The young man with character knows why he is on this earth and is working toward fulfilling his God-given mission.**

I regret that I won't have the opportunity to provide for you as a son. But here's something I have done: I've discussed many of the ideas in this book with Kenny Luck and encouraged him to produce this guide for your life—and what a great job he did! Kenny and I wish we could teach this book's content to you personally, but since we can't, we trust you will get fired up reading it on your own. Within these pages are the most important lessons a man can learn. They will steer you away from much grief, guilt, and pain in your relationships with God and people. They will guide you toward your true purpose on earth, and toward a life filled with love and many other good things.

So please read *Every Young Man, God's Man* slowly. And as you do, ask yourself how you can personally apply the principles taught here. Figure out ways you can make a few changes now that will impact your life forever.

Later, after you've finished reading the book, Kenny and I would love to hear from you. Tell us about your struggles and whether or not this book has helped. You can reach us at kennyl@everymanministries.com and sarterburn@newlife.com

I am confident that you will profit a great deal from what you read here. In fact I believe that *Every Young Man, God's Man* is going to help you become the man you truly want to be—the man your Creator wants you to be: God's man.

the man zone

The summer before my freshman year at UCLA, I came home one time after midnight to a dark house and sleeping parents. While my home was very quiet, my soul churned in chaos. I needed the safety and comfort of my bedroom to relax me. I sat on my bed and ran my right hand through my shoulder-length hair. While I had dismissed many things I didn't like about my life—going to church topped my list—I had one habit too ingrained to let go of: praying before I fell asleep. I guess this was my way to connect with God on my terms. After all, I was the "spiritual" party guy.

Most of the time, however, I would recite the same old prayers I had known my whole life. My lips would be moving, and I could hear myself speaking the words, but my heart and my soul were definitely checked out. I found these midnight prayers easy, comfortable, and safe. I'm sure to God I sounded more like a robot than a human being, but in my twisted thinking, I figured God wouldn't call my lack of sincerity on the carpet. Man, was I ever wrong.

That summer evening it was time for my nightly ritual. I got down on my knees at the foot of my bed and looked out at the star-filled Northern

California sky. I started with the Lord's Prayer *("Our Father, who art in heaven, hallowed be thy name…")*. Suddenly, I heard a voice inside telling me to stop. I thought, *What's up with this?* I started over, but I couldn't get out the memorized words that I had repeated thousands of times before. I didn't know what was happening, but I did know that my skin felt like it was crawling, which humbled and scared me. Instead of "Our Father, who art in heaven" coming out of my mouth, I heard myself whispering, "I want to see You… I want to see You."

Each time I said this, I felt a deeper and deeper presence filling the air around me. My body shook in response, and tears rolled down my cheeks like rivers. My emotion had been touched by the strong and fragrant presence of God.

For the first time in my life, I expressed to God what I really wanted more than anything—a real encounter with Him…just the two of us. I voiced a simple prayer—"I want to see You"—not to please my parents, not to impress friends, not to maintain some image, and certainly not to win His approval. What I said that evening was the true confession of a guy on his knees to a God who had been patiently waiting for me to get honest.

**Once you settle for less than God's best,
you start spinning your wheels.**

He didn't have to be patient since I had been acting like a hypocrite—an immature one at that. He knew I had been deliberately fooling myself, but He also saw someone who was experiencing turmoil regarding who Christ was. When I expressed a longing from deep within my heart—as simple as it was—He seized that measly effort to invade my room and bring me closer to Him as never before.

That night was a turning point. God reached out and touched me, and

I felt closer to Him as never before. I couldn't rationalize this experience away, I couldn't blame someone else for not living out what I believed, and I couldn't divorce myself from His will at my convenience any longer. Instead of judging me or punishing me, He threw His arms around me and said, "I forgive you. Now go and sin no more." God "unstuck" me spiritually as a young man, for which I'm grateful. What happened to me sounds a lot like what happened to David, who wrote this in the book of Psalms:

> He turned to me and heard my cry.
> He lifted me out of the slimy pit,
>   out of the mud and mire;
> he set my feet on a rock
>   and gave me a firm place to stand. (Psalm 40:1-2)

I had been stuck in the slimy pit of compromise. Once you settle for less than God's best, you start spinning your wheels. You may think you're gaining traction, but you're *not moving forward as a young man.* He's not going to point His finger at you while you rev your engine in the mud, saying "I told you so." God is more interested in you moving forward—but first you have to get all four wheels on the pavement.

This book is about you getting some serious traction in your drive toward spiritual significance with God. It's about becoming the young man God created you to be versus what you think you *ought* to be. This book is about facing the real fears keeping you from being *completely* His.

STAND UP NOW!

Through Every Man Ministries I have connected with thousands of younger spiritual brothers on college campuses and high-school settings for the last several years. What I have found is that you are just like me—battling the urges within and the forces outside to stay true to what you know deep down is right. The tension you feel is real spiritual warfare. *All* of us are at war against the Enemy of God, and we will have to fight against the dark side within that pulls us toward selfishness and away from our faith. Fear not, however, because this is our bond: we have common enemies and similar temptations.

Spiritually speaking, the confidence and courage to stand strong as God's man *now*—not later—is the challenge set before you. That means you will need an identity in and connection with God that is strong enough to risk rejection by others as well as delay gratifying yourselves. The biggest lie Satan can whisper in your ear is that you can *wait* to get serious about God and *delay* being spiritually responsible. I've met too many young people with this *mañana* attitude—that's Spanish for "tomorrow"— who feel they can get "serious" about their faith somewhere down the road. I even know one of those persons real well because that's *my* story.

There is no such thing as

harmless fantasies about women.

Whether you are on the courageous or not-so-courageous side of the faith battle, let me encourage you. Every Christian male I know has been there, but what I've found is that every day you put off taking spiritual responsibility for yourself, the harder it becomes. Believe me, there are a lot of guys in their thirties who learned lessons the hard way because they chose the "wide path leading to destruction" instead of "the narrow road." They passed up *years* that could have been loaded with God's blessing.

This book is an effort to help you see around the corner, avoid pitfalls, and experience God's best without regret or losses. I need to ask for you to put your faith in the battle-hardened wisdom of your "olda brotha" who has seen the Enemy do his dirty work, blowing up the lives of brothers your age who thought they knew it all. You're becoming a man, and that means you have to start thinking like one. Similarly, to become God's man, you have to think like one of His sons. To help you think like God's man, you need to think through the following statements that I've come up with. I call them "Kenny's Code." Read each one slowly, thinking about what each statement means to your heart.

Kenny's Code
- There is no such thing as "later" with God, only *now*.
- There is no such thing as being neutral with God—you can go only backward or forward.
- There is no such thing as playing both sides.
- There is no such thing as great results without sacrifices.
- There is no such thing as lies without consequences.
- There is no such thing as mixing God's values with others that are more popular.
- There is no such thing as being good on your own.
- There is no such thing as a real God without a real devil.
- There is no such thing as "I know better" when there's God.
- There is no such thing as harmless fantasies about women.
- There is no such thing as a disconnected and productive Christian.
- There is no such thing as a good "secret" that contradicts God's Word.
- There is no such thing as a good conscience without the Holy Spirit.
- There is no such thing as a relationship with God without communication.

- There is no such thing as growth without testing.
- There is no such thing as freedom without responsibility.
- There is no such thing as getting hurt by others and not needing to heal.
- There is no such thing as risking more for God and getting less back.
- There is no such thing as a bloody Savior and a lazy believer.

These are the bottom lines of this book. I wish these were my thoughts, but they are not. They are God's. They are His code for His followers. They are truth. They are unchangeable. They are a source of blessing or, if ignored, a source of judgment. They will save you a ton of pain and may even save your life—if you accept them in your heart *now*.

These bottom lines could have saved me a ton of pain. At one time, I was stupid enough to believe that I could play Christian and also play cool with the party and girl scene at school. I'll never forget one hottie telling me, "You are like the perfect blend of religious and cool."

There is no such thing as

a bloody Savior and a lazy believer.

I thought to myself, *Wow—what a great witness.* Ha! What a joke I was. One night I would hang out with my Christian friends at a Bible study, and the next night I would be laughing my head off at a huge beer bash with the "stoners." It's a good thing that I had friends praying that God would rattle my world and get me back on track. I needed my cage rattled, because there were parts of me that really liked the feelings of acceptance and the danger of dancing with sin. What I didn't like was the war raging within me, which made me miserable. But I never discussed those feelings with anyone.

The Man Zone

Let me share a little story with you:

> The young knight says to the king: "I love your daughter with all
> my heart and soul. I want to marry her."
>
> The wise king says: "Then go find a dragon and bring me its
> head. Then you may have my daughter's hand."
>
> The young knight asks: "Did I mention I have a large inheritance?"

We chuckle reading this story, but when you stop and think about it,
the wise king didn't want a flippant response to the condition that he set for
giving his approval to the match. What the wise king was really saying to
the young knight was this:

- Do you have the courage of a man, or will you run from your
  problems?
- Is there depth to your desire for my daughter?
- How bad do you *really* want my maiden?
- Will you change your tune under pressure?
- Will you face your fears and discover the man within?
- Will you risk everything?

Every caring father wants to know what lies beneath the surface before
he hands his priceless daughter over to what looks and smells like a gorilla.
He lays down a gauntlet to test what's on the inside. What about you?

> **Young man:** "I want to live for *You,* God. I love You. I want to be
> part of Your plans. Forever."

> **God:** "Are you willing to slay the dragon?"

The reason you have this book in your hands is because you're in the Man Zone now. The game has changed. Old ways don't cut it anymore. You can't laugh off your childish mistakes. You are maturing, which means you should be becoming serious about God. He's certainly getting serious about you. Before, He may not have held you accountable for some things, but now that you're becoming older, that's not acceptable to Him. Your future is at stake. Your mission for Christ—which only you can fulfill—could be hindered. You will be responsible for the choices you make.

**The game has changed. Old ways
don't cut it anymore. You can't
laugh off your childish mistakes.**

Don't blow off this important moment from God as if this was just a nice book your momma would love to see you holding. This is a life-and-death issue in the most serious and eternal ways. We're talking about a crossroads of character that will define your destiny.

> This day I call heaven and earth as witnesses against you that I have
> set before you life and death, blessing and curses. Now choose life, so
> that you may live and that you may love the LORD your God, listen
> to his voice, and hold fast to him. For the LORD is your life.
> (Deuteronomy 30:19-20)

Every great man in the Bible crossed through the Man Zone spiritually. Sure, many received help. Moses assisted Joshua. Jonathan aided David. David charged Solomon. The apostle Paul inspired and called out Timothy. Jesus told Peter he would be the man in Matthew 16:18. That's why I want to be that person who helps you step into the Man Zone.

On the field of battle the enemy lays down "suppression fire," which is intended to keep you pinned down so they can move their guys into a better position to kill you. In spiritual warfare Satan calls for suppression fire to distract you. He will work overtime to get your focus somewhere else. He may get you too busy to notice God or too tired to read your Bible or too comfortable in front of the television or computer to spend time with God. He'll do what it takes to keep you away from the Man Zone.

Fair Warning: continued reading from this point will involve serious distractions, temptations, internal conflicts, anxiety, fear, sexual thoughts, and any other available tactic. Why? Because the Enemy wants to limit you from becoming the man God wants you to be.

DRAW YOUR SWORD

I want you to lay your hand to your sword, draw it out, and stare the Enemy in the eye without flinching. God has got your back, and His goal is for you to drive the sword of His truth into the heart of compromise. He's looking for brave young men who will give their total loyalty to His kingdom:

> GOD is always on the alert, constantly on the lookout for people who are totally committed to him. (2 Chronicles 16:9, MSG)

There's another thing you need to be alert about, and that's where we're headed in this book. As you may already be aware, *Every Young Man, God's Man* is connected to a series that includes *Every Young Man's Battle.* That book was specifically written to address the sexual issues young men face, including sexual temptation, masturbation, and how to manage your mind and your body to honor God and women. If you are struggling most in the sexual arena, I urge you to read *Every Young Man's Battle. Every Young Man,*

God's Man goes beyond that struggle into other issues connected to living out your faith in *every* area of life, not just the sexual area.

God has got your back, and His goal is for you to drive the sword of His truth into the heart of compromise.

While sexual thoughts and behavior are the number one temptation, God did not create us to always be playing defense. Growth comes from gaining self-control in this area, which will help you think about God and His plans for you. Sexual self-control is a way to choose God's plan for your life, which will give a strong foundation for the future and a life full of His purpose.

In the chapters ahead, you'll learn:

- how to get unstuck in your spiritual walk
- how to have a total versus partial heart commitment to God
- how to face the truth about yourself, and then grow
- what attitude pleases God the most
- why blending your world with God's is not His plan
- how to manage the dark side within
- how to know who your friends really are
- the consequences of keeping secrets from God and others
- the power of total honesty
- how to overcome sin on a daily basis
- how to connect to God in His way
- how to use pressure and temptation for progress
- how to starve sin out of your life
- how to deal with major family or personal traumas
- how to keep your motivation to be God's man even when it hurts

You will be reading tons of stories about me and some of your fellow brothers that will help you see these principles in real time. Some are funny, some will scare you silly, but all are true. The best thing is that you'll relate to them and see that you're not alone.

Ready? Good. Keep your hands inside the car at all times, and make sure your seat belt is securely fastened.

You are now entering...the Man Zone.

getting the pose just right

In their book *Posers, Fakers, and Wannabes*, Brennan Manning and Jim Hancock introduce us to a character they call "The Poser." They argue that The Poser (a person who pretends to be someone he is not) lives in all of us. I saw a lot of myself in the following story in which Jim recounts the images The Poser created for him—images that would be accepted by other people:

> I first took advice from The Poser when I was faking my way through junior high school. I wanted to fit in. I was afraid of being left out. The Poser helped me appear better than I was (or worse if worse was better). He helped me conceal the truth from people I thought might judge me as harshly as I judged me. I kept taking his advice because, mostly, it worked.
>
> The Poser is the man of a thousand faces. He taught me how to construct a mask for any occasion from whatever I found lying around. With my musical friends I was all about whatever music they

liked. For my jock friends I was brooding and barely verbal. When I got with smart kids I bluffed my way through by recalling trivia and making up stuff (wait a minute…I still do that!). With The Poser's help, I managed to hold my own into high school, but it was hard, exhausting work. I went to church (spiritual face), I hung out with friends (wise guy face), I went out a little (sincere face). So many disguises, so little real fun, playing all those roles without knowing who I was. Or if I was anyone at all.

I was on an impossible quest, searching for my identity in the eyes of other people.[1]

Does Jim's journey into manhood sound familiar? It took him (and lots of young men) a while to figure out why he was such a social chameleon. Being The Poser was so natural he didn't even know he was posing! Although a Christian, his actions were dependent upon whatever crowd was around him, because The Poser created a new identity or "mask" for every situation. The problem with these multiple identities is that Jim could not develop any of them fully since he had to change costumes so often.

One of his identities was his "God Mask," but because of the competition for people's acceptance—versus God's—his identity in Christ was weak and useless. The same thing goes for us. When we lack a strong identity and don't know who we are, our ability to be loyal to anything or anyone is severely hampered.

Let me tell you about Brandon. At fourteen years of age he heard the message of God's love for him at a church camp. For the first time everything made sense to him. Brandon responded by heeding the speaker's

1. Brennan Manning and Jim Hancock, *Posers, Fakers, and Wannabes* (Colorado Springs: NavPress, 2004), 10-11.

call to come forward and give his life to Jesus Christ. His decision stuck—until he was confronted with the party scene in high school. Girls in their tube tops, raging hormones, pressure from buddies, and an invitation from Amanda to "go to the lake" caused Brandon to experience what I call "identity drift." Inside he was battling to keep his faith locked in a compartment away from his new—and very exciting—social life. Everything that reminded him of his commitment to Christ, including connections to Christian friends, faded into the background.

When we lack a strong identity and don't know who we are, our ability to be loyal to anything or anyone is severely hampered.

At a party Brandon listened to Amanda ripping those "born agains" she saw having Bible study at Starbucks. "Praise the Lord and hallelujah!" she mocked, and her passionate performance got a good laugh.

Brandon felt he should say *something*, so he uttered one of those "Yeah, ain't that the truth" comments, which effectively denied his identity as a Christian. He didn't feel good about it, so Brandon faked an excuse about having to go to the bathroom. He took that opportunity to step outside and look up at the full moon staring down at him. To Brandon it felt like God was staring him right in the face. Then a picture came into his mind, and it hit him like a ton of bricks: the campfire, the smell of smoke, the speaker, the warmth of God's love, and that full moon!

Brandon's true inner loyalty had been unmasked, and God had just called it on the carpet. Then another picture flooded his head—the cross at the campfire and Brandon nailing a note to it with a hammer and nail. The note contained the frivolous yet personal sins of a fourteen-year-old as well as his commitment to follow Christ his whole life. Seeing the moon that evening was as if God was saying, "Remember who you are."

FEARLESS LOYALTY

So many men, young and old, are caught between competing identities that divide their loyalty, just like Brandon. Maybe you've worn a mask or rationalized your faith away when it's been uncomfortable. If your inner loyalty and commitment to Christ are divided, how can you expect to overcome the fear of what other people think about your being a Christian? Moving into the Man Zone means having a radical inner loyalty to a person, not an abstract belief. It's having a clear and personal picture of Jesus Christ's passion for you on the cross and then letting your heart match His with love and loyalty. When you arrive at this kind of commitment, you will become more confident about bringing your faith into the open. Getting to that place will mean making a choice between Christ and everyone else.

To end boyish excuses, develop godly loyalty, and move into a solid identity requires manly honesty before God and people. So, I must take this moment and ask you a serious question about how you are going to live out your life. Ready?

WHERE IS YOUR LOYALTY GOING TO LIE?

Well? Do you have an answer? If you know who you are (God's young man), then you will not be afraid to identify with Him. If you can settle this now—before you leave for college or get out there on your own—you will experience a freedom like never before.

"How is that?" you ask.

Answer: simple—when your loyalties are settled, your decisions and actions will be easy. That's how it was for Hezekiah:

Remember now, O LORD, I pray, how I *have walked before You in truth* and with a *loyal heart,* and have *done what was good* in Your sight. (2 Kings 20:3, NKJV)

God had told Hezekiah that he was going to die, which would certainly get my attention. In response, Hezekiah dialed 911, and amazingly, he was granted a fifteen-year extension on earth! While Hezekiah knew God was all-powerful, he also knew that God was also a *rewarder* of those loyal to him, and that a "loyal heart" produced "what was good in Your sight."

How do you see yourself? What's your core identity that defines who you are and shapes your loyalties? Before you get into tough situations as a man, you have to get your identity settled and strong. Then you can focus on being who you are versus someone who oscillates between God Guy and Poser Guy, between Sunday Guy and Tequila Shooter Guy, or between Bible Study Man and Porn Studies Man. (These masked men show up out of nowhere, leave as fast as they arrive, and leave people asking the question, "Who was that masked man?")

To develop consistent loyalty and spiritual integrity, you have to make real choices under real pressure before you can experience real results.

The most successful, disciplined, and free people are those who know who they are. Exhibit #1 would be my cousins—yes, they're really my cousins—Wuv and Sonny with the band P.O.D. When I watch them perform on television or hear their new single on the radio, I see them as God's men who happen to be musicians. They had to work hard and sacrifice to get there, however. They practiced their instruments for years, stayed in fleabag motels, and survived on a diet of fast food for a shot at a contract with a major label, which they eventually got when they signed with Virgin Atlantic. Since then, P.O.D.—this stands for Payable on Death—has become one of the most successful Christian bands around.

Those at the top of their professions—Lance Armstrong, Shaun White, Kevin Garnett, Drew Brees, and Bono, to name a few—are totally sold out to what they do best. Lance stays in the saddle six hours a day, Drew studied for years the art of throwing the perfect spiral under pressure, Shaun endlessly adjusts his speed and angle for the perfect launches, Kevin shoots hundreds of free throws every day, and Bono and U2 practice their songs until they're sick of them. We see and admire guys who work on their sports or their crafts, but we *don't get* how it applies to our thinking about becoming God's man. How much training are you doing to become God's man? When you are doing zero training, you've compromised. You don't have a loyal heart.

What does it take to have a loyal heart?

An absence of fear.

I am in your space to remind you that your loyalty will be tested so your spiritual backbone can develop. God will put your spiritual commitment into arenas of testing to see what's there. He will help you get consistent and confident in making the right choices. When you do that—show loyalty under pressure—you will sense His approval and His pleasure:

> I know, my God, that you test the heart and are pleased with
> integrity. (1 Chronicles 29:17)

First, God will test your commitment to Him. It's just like great coaches who have their players practice under gamelike conditions. That way, when it comes time to deliver during a game, players will have the freedom to execute without the distractions of ignorance or fear. God knows this. To develop consistent loyalty and spiritual integrity, you have to make real choices under real pressure before you can experience real results. For instance, He will allow you to encounter alluring images of women (real or pixelated) to see what you'll do. He will allow you to choose whether you go out with a girl who doesn't share your faith in Christ. He's gonna see if you will respond differently than your school buddies who sleep with their girlfriends. God narrows your choices to make you into His man.

Second, God is pleased when you choose Him. You may not feel His pleasure when you're put on the spot by your friends, but you will know it later that night when put your head on your pillow. You can't hear the applause from heaven, but you may receive confirmation from a brother who was convicted by your stance. You may wonder why your youth pastor keeps harping about abstaining from sex, but you'll thank him on your wedding day. You see, every father is pleased when he sees his son loving the things and doing the things that he loves and does. Similarly, your heavenly Father is greatly pleased when He sees you undivided between what you believe and how you actually live and think.

Here's how it plays out later on. Once, my nine-year-old son, Ryan, and I were watching an NFL playoff game when the Victoria's Secret "angels" hit the screen with only their wings on. The remote wasn't nearby, so I immediately turned my head to Ryan and blabbered stuff like: "Hey Ryan, how's it going? How you doing? What's going on?"

I engaged him in conversation to draw my eyes—and his—away from the skin belonging to our fine-feathered friends.

He looked at me (okay, my ploy worked), and then he asked, "Dad, what are you doing?"

"Dude, there are some ladies on TV right now without any clothes on, and I don't want to look at any other woman that way except for your mom. So you can help me out by talking to me."

My son, who still thought girls have cooties, shrugged his shoulders. "Okay," he said.

Fast-forward two weeks later. Ryan and his younger sister are downstairs watching football, and I hear the same Victoria's Secret ad come on from my upstairs perch. I was just about to rush downstairs when I heard Ryan say to his sister, "Hey, Cara, how's it going? How you doing? What's going on?" You get the picture.

Think I was pleased? I was stoked! Think I felt God's pleasure? Up and down my spine! It happened because I wanted to remain loyal to God and bounce my eyes from sexy images and stay loyal to God and my son.

Fact time: each test of your loyalty gives you a chance to "win" spiritually, and each time you chalk up a victory, you gain increasing amounts of self-control, confidence, and clarity as God's man. Could you go for a little more confidence in your walk?

MORE CONFIDENCE

One of my part-time jobs in high school was working in a liquor store as a stock boy (my alcoholic father knew the owner real well). As I got older I worked behind the counter and rang up sales on the cash register. There was another benefit to working behind the counter: that's where we kept the "adult" magazines. When things got slow on Sunday afternoons, I had total freedom to rifle through those magazines—and I couldn't resist. (This happened before I got serious with God that evening in my bedroom.) I became hooked by this stuff—it was like nitroglycerin in my hands. Those sexy images took a heavy toll on my mind and heart.

Girls who didn't share my convictions about sexual purity gravitated to guys more than willing to play.

Still, I was determined in my new faith as a college freshman to fight this fight. I had my work cut out for me, though, because I was enrolling at UCLA, that bastion of babes, beer, and beach time. The nightlife in Westwood—well, let's just say that my Bruin pride believes there's nothing better. What a chick magnet! We're talking Babeville with the hottest-looking girls on your left, on your right, and dead ahead, but I was committed to honoring God and remaining loyal to Him. I made that commitment public; I let other people in on the fact that I was a Christian. I became active with other Christians on campus, not because I thought I was some super-hot Christian, but because I *knew* I wasn't a superhot Christian.

From the moment I said, "No thanks, that's not for me," and put my loyalty to Christ out in the open, that effectively removed me from the invitation lists to various parties. Girls who didn't share my convictions about sexual purity gravitated to guys more than willing to play.

My stand made me accountable for my faith in front of seventy other fraternity brothers, who watched me like a hawk, wondering when I would compromise. I didn't mind; in fact, I welcomed this healthy pressure because it felt like a godly reminder not to betray my stand. My fraternity brothers may have thought I was being strong, but the opposite is true: I was weak. So I had to rely on Christ to make my stand. Relying on Christ generated feelings of integrity within me, which bolstered my confidence to stand for Him.

The wisest man ever, Israel's King Solomon, made these points about integrity: "He who walks in integrity walks securely" and "The integrity of the upright will guide them" (Proverbs 10:9, 11:3, NASB). With undivided integrity:

- Choices are clear.
- There's no double life.
- There's no fear of getting exposed.
- You move beyond instant gratification.
- Feeling right replaces having to feel good.
- You maintain and deepen your connection to Christ.
- You experience God's rewards.
- You're less stressed.
- You get better at making right choices under pressure.
- You grow a spine for God. (That's what I needed most.)

HE LIVES IN YOU

Jesus Christ had an unbending and loyal heart for His Father. So why should any of God's men be surprised that the captain of our team would call us to develop such a heart for ourselves? Even His skeptical, conniving competitors had to admit that this guy was the real deal:

> Teacher, we know you are a man of integrity. *You aren't swayed by men, because you pay no attention to who they are;* but you teach the way of God in accordance with the truth. (Mark 12:14)

Jesus Christ:
- was free from the opinions of people
- broke the "rules" when God's Word called for it

- went against His culture confidently
- did not apologize for His faith
- accepted rejection as part of the deal
- lived for an audience of one

This same Jesus lives in *you*. One day Jesus surprised a big group of his followers by saying, "Why do you call me 'Lord, Lord,' and do not do what I say?" (Luke 6:46). What Jesus was saying was this: "Are you on the team or aren't you?" He was attacking the thinking that a man could name Him as his leader ("Lord") yet still live a life opposite of what his leader valued. It's obvious why this doesn't make sense, yet so many men try to live this way anyway. Jesus wasn't interested in winning a popularity contest or getting on the good side of a girl. He was not going to be played.

All of God's men—even the strong ones—struggled to be loyal. They knew they couldn't do it on their own, so they fought hard to stay committed. God wants you to live a life loyal to Him, but it starts with a loyal heart.

If that's your desire, then you can pray the same prayer the most famous God's man ever prayed:

> For you are great and do marvelous deeds;
>> you alone are God.
> Teach me your way, O LORD,
>> and I will walk in your truth;
> *give me an undivided heart,*
>> that I may fear your name. (Psalm 86:10-11)

David needed to go to the next level that God was calling him—the place of total loyalty and commitment. A place where his walk was solid and true. God is calling you to that same place because an undivided life starts with an undivided heart.

Our next stop in the Man Zone is about having guts—the spiritual guts to get out of your comfort zone and make changes in who you are and what you do. What you'll discover is that God loves you too much to leave you unchanged.

do the hard thing

I recently asked a room of young men, ages seventeen to twenty-one, to take an anonymous survey that contained the following question: what are the top three battles you face as a younger man?

One hundred percent of them—every guy in the room—wrote that sexual temptation, lust, masturbation, or porn topped his list. When I asked the guys to tell me why they lost battles with temptation, all of them took advantage of the survey's anonymity to reveal why sexual temptation got the better of them:

- They failed to choose the way out that God gives them.
- Their personal time with God eroded over time.
- They felt disconnected from other Christian guys.
- They rationalized their behavior by saying, "God will forgive me."
- They had no genuine accountability.
- They experienced loneliness and isolation.
- They had a lack of discipline, which made it easier to give in to temptation.
- They exercised no self-control, preferring instant gratification.

- They discovered that the visual pictures in their minds were strong.
- They remained apathetic toward the consequences.

I also asked these young men to describe ways that helped them win some battles against sexual temptation. Here's what they said:

- They could talk about their struggles with someone else.
- They felt close in their walks with God.
- They were confident about the prospect of "better things" coming as a result of obedience.
- They recalled Scripture in their minds.
- They feared getting caught.
- They knew that God showed them an alternative—a way out.
- They talked to God in the midst of their temptation, asking for His help.
- They stayed "active" in better pursuits.
- They remembered God is with them.
- Their desire to honor God was stronger than their desire to sin.
- They wanted to grow in Christ.
- They underwent less stress without sin in their lives.

Several expanded on their answers, including this young man:

When I am alone with my temptations, I choose pleasure. Feeling like I'm all alone in it makes the situation worse and causes me to be spiritually lazy. On the other hand, when I am with friends or can interrupt the temptation with a phone call, prayer, exercise, or some-thing else, then that interruption keeps me out of the situation.

Sound familiar? In your head you may know what you *should* be doing, may know exactly what God desires, and may understand what situations spell disaster. What every one of these guys struggled with was consistency, because consistency required doing the hard thing over and over until they gained the character to defeat sin in their lives.

Here's my point: you are not alone when you admit your battle with sexual temptation, and you are not alone if you fail.

Mark, for example, knew exactly what God's plan for sex was, but he rationalized and debated with himself about the whole idea of remaining pure. Once the debate began in his mind, he worked through various scenarios regarding his girlfriend, Kelly. Like a kitchen faucet with a slow leak under the cabinet, Mark began allowing certain things to happen. For instance, their good-bye kiss went from a peck to a full-on session of deep kissing. He figured that was okay because everyone still had their clothes on. He hadn't *really* stepped over the line physically, so he viewed this as acceptable behavior for an unmarried young man.

Then, at a beach party, people began leaving late that night, and Mark knew that this would be a wonderful opportunity to be alone with Kelly. This meant saying no thanks to an invitation to join friends at a nearby Denny's for a late evening—or early morning—breakfast.

One hundred percent of them—every guy in the room—wrote that sexual temptation, lust, masturbation, or porn topped his list.

Kelly hesitated, however, saying something about feeling hungry, but Mark wasn't interested in hearing that, because he had other things on his mind. Instead, he blurted out some lame excuse about how he didn't have any money, sending the guys off with a quick, "See ya."

Kelly never realized he had talked her into a compromising situation that offered both parties little or no chance to escape. Back in the beach parking lot, her boyfriend led her to the backseat of his car, and within an hour he had snatched Kelly's virginity away unceremoniously. Kelly partici- pated in the act, but there was nothing to celebrate. Regret and resentment now dominated her feelings toward Mark. The secrecy and manipulation on Mark's part, combined with her own weakness, made her angry at her- self and at him.

Consistency required doing the hard thing over and over until they gained the character to defeat sin in their lives.

Mark got what he wanted, but as their relationship became more strained, he didn't care for her vibe. *Everything* became so uncomfortable, so the only alternative in his mind was to eliminate the cause of the dis- comfort by throwing the relationship away. Within two weeks they mutu- ally agreed to break up, which was fine with Kelly, because she felt their relationship had become shallow and dominated by sex. In her mind she had been used and manipulated by Mark, and the mystery about making love to her future spouse had been robbed from her.

What heartache on both sides! A great relationship and a potentially greater future imploded because Mark allowed a small compromise to fes- ter in his heart. He knew, as the aggressor, that he took things too far when he and Kelly french-kissed for a long time, but he rationalized his behavior by thinking he could handle the ramp up in getting physical.

Mark's rationales came in the form of little excuses—everything was okay because he liked her, she wanted it just as badly as he did—but at the end of the day (and night), they were excuses. Making excuses is what little boys engage in—not God's men. Sure, it's not easy to stay pure, which is why I feel that honoring a commitment to God and to your future wife to remain sexually clean is the stuff of men.

God's men have a long-range plan. God's men think through questions—tough questions. Have you ever asked yourself:

- Why can't I grow past sexual temptations and thoughts?
- Why am I not getting closer to the standard I know is right?
- Why do I keep repeating the same mistakes over and over?

**Making excuses is what little boys
engage in—not God's men.**

If you are asking yourself these questions, then you are searching for the one thing that separates men from boys—character. Character is the stuff inside you that causes you to act one way or another when you face a moral dilemma. It's what you do when nobody else is looking. Character is required:

- to delay gratification
- to prevent free falls into sin
- to overcome feelings in the moment
- to reject lies quickly
- to face sin head-on
- to trust good impulses more than bad ones
- to be honest with others about weaknesses
- to get consistent
- to rise again after a fall
- to apply wisdom
- to honor Christ

I believe that being a Christian and having character are not the same thing. When God entered your life, you instantly inherited many things. You were forgiven of all your sins, you became a child of God, and you were placed spiritually in heaven with Christ—to name a few of more than thirty different blessings that come to a believer the moment he believes in Jesus Christ. A fundamental change in your character traits (who you are and how you react under pressure) was *not* on the list. God has chosen to bring us character only when we decide to do hard things that require faith in His way. And doing hard things is like weeding a garden, or in the days before machines, plowing new ground.

PLOWING NEW GROUND

Becoming a man involves doing some very uncomfortable spade work, which means turning the soil. This is one of the hardest parts of manhood for younger brothers to embrace. Why is that? For the most part, parents have shielded them from making spiritually and emotionally tough decisions themselves.

**Kinda commitments, which require no character,
are synonymous with compromise.**

When you don't have to face emotionally tough decisions, you get used to going through life making half commitments. Stuck between adopting values you learned growing up and establishing your own identity and convictions, the Enemy wants you to water down what should be strong commitments. He even wants you to feel it's an expression of individuality to:

- kinda go to church
- kinda read God's Word
- kinda stay away from sexy R-rated movies or Internet sites
- kinda not get wasted at parties
- kinda date girls with a commitment to sexual purity

- kinda stop masturbating
- kinda share your faith
- kinda connect with other Christians
- kinda be accountable to other guys

Kinda commitments, which require no character, are synonymous with compromise. In that sense, they actually take you backward as a man. You may have made some of these half commitments yourself because it felt more comfortable that way or gave you an excuse to be irresponsible—there's less guilt and less discomfort that way. Whatever your case, God never said His role in our lives was to make us comfortable. In fact, God says real manhood will cost you some sweat:

> I said, "Plant the good seeds of righteousness, and you will harvest a crop of my love. *Plow up the hard ground of your hearts, for now is the time to seek the LORD,* that he may come and shower righteousness upon you." (Hosea 10:12, NLT)

God's man Hosea was speaking to a group of spiritually immature men in Israel. He used their knowledge of farming to explain God's work in their lives and how they could be productive for him. The picture he painted was the all-too-familiar one about hard work and sweat paying off at harvest time. Any good Israelite knew that a fruitful yield started with the condition of the soil. Hard soil was bad, and soft soil was good. Hard soil offered little chance of taking the seed, while tilled land yielded a crop—perhaps a bountiful one. The farmer had to do the hard work (breaking up the unplowed ground) to get the results.

Hosea's metaphor works today as well. If you want to be God's man on the outside, you've got to pull out the jackhammer and get to work on the inside. For you, the decision spiritually might look like:

- making a commitment not to masturbate as a habit
- telling a buddy about your desire to be sexually pure
- making a contract with your girlfriend not to tempt each other sexually (being specific and honest)
- having accountability partners
- not spending fruitless hours playing video games
- finding and committing to a weekly Bible study with other guys
- serving others in ministry
- not drinking alcohol
- sharing your faith in Christ instead of hiding it
- rededicating yourself to God's purposes
- waiting on God to answer your prayers versus manipulating circumstances to get the results you want
- seeking out an Internet accountability partner so that porn is not an option for you
- telling the truth to someone close to you
- looking at girls as *His*—not *yours* to play mental games with
- listening to and respecting your parents' wishes
- telling your youth pastor something about you that no one knows about—then asking for his help and counsel

Plowing up the hard ground means doing something uncomfortable that will stretch your faith. It means deciding to do what real God's men (versus posers) do—facing their fears. It involves tension and risk and will cost you something, usually your pride.

To Jesus Christ our lives are like fields He has purchased that need to be worked. He will point out one field to you at a time. Once you have worked that field of change into productive acreage, He will move you to the next weed-infested plot. The thing about weeds—which I view as attitudes and actions that choke His plan to produce fruit in us—is that these weeds can easily grow back if you are not careful. Tilling weed-infested soil means going after the roots, digging deep, and exercising persistence. The key is not to give up and trust God when it's taking longer than expected to change a behavior pattern.

> **Plowing up the hard ground means
> doing what real God's men (versus posers)
> do—facing their fears.**

Take my struggle with masturbation. Before I was a Christian, I became very comfortable with this practice as a way of feeling good, especially when I felt lonely. After I became a Christian, this practice didn't magically disappear overnight, even though I knew that it wasn't God's best.

I would have to say that this "weed" was one of the toughest to eliminate completely from the fields of my sexual life. Every time I stepped into a shower, I felt like an alcoholic stepping inside a rollicking happy hour, where I could see the bartender mixing a margarita and setting out a bowl of warm tortilla chips. I couldn't pass up the opportunity. This temptation chased me every day over the next fifteen years of my Christian life, despite my attempts to cultivate self-control.

One of the most difficult things I have ever done was to talk about this habit with the men in my Bible study. It was also one of the best things I ever did. When I confessed my situation to my brothers, God gave me the strength to say no to the flesh and say yes to His Spirit in the moments of testing. He knew it took guts for me to give up my "dirty little secret." He knew it required faith and humility because I risked rejection for a stronger walk with God.

Confronting weaknesses in your character early on will set the stage for a strong walk later. If I had allowed my habit to persist—as well as all the mental gymnastics that went along with justifying my sexual behavior—my adult life would look radically different today. For me, masturbation was a compromise of God's best, and I knew I was lying to myself when I thought, *Everyone does this* or *It's okay because I'm not married yet.*

That type of thinking, when allowed to remain in your character as an older man, will be deadly to your future marriage and family because what you're really doing is becoming good at selling out your faith for an intense, pleasant feeling. This is all about self-control, and if you can exercise self-control now, then that character trait will greatly strengthen your ability to be God's man for your future wife and family. Trust me when I say that cutting out masturbation before I got married has helped me to *stay* married.

When you resist change, however, God has other ways to get our character in order, and those usually involve His calling a time-out on your plans. God can forge character by allowing difficulties, delays, or even the consequences of your choices to act as His agents of change. The Bible is filled with examples of His making men uncomfortable so He could teach them something about character. Just ask these guys:

- Joseph was stuck in an Egyptian jail for thirteen years before he became the number two man in Egypt.
- Moses lived in the desert for many years before God asked him to deliver the Israelites.
- David lived like a fugitive and was hunted like an animal before he became the greatest king of Israel.
- Jonah had an "Aha, I got it God" experience inside the stomach of a huge fish.

- Job endured catastrophes and testings.
- Paul was physically blinded by his encounter with Christ.

The point of all these male biographies is that God *uses* hard times and uncomfortable situations to mold and shape our characters in ways that no other circumstance would. Just as the repeated heating, pounding, and cooling of metal forges the strongest steel, God wants your character strong so you can fulfill His purposes on earth. He loves you too much to allow you to remain immature, untested, and weak as a man. Most important, He knows that you cannot produce in greatness for Him what you do not possess in character.

Maturity is recognizing that sometimes you need to do the very thing you don't want to do to become the man you need to be.

He also knows that younger men have a hard time trusting Him with certain things—especially with sex. He's watched a few billion lusty stallions get creative in this area, observed how they create wiggle room with His will, and have tried to paint His clear instructions gray. He knows exactly how you think. He knows all the mind games that testosterone produces in men. He knows all your dreams. He knows you want intimacy with another person. But He also knows that hooking up with a girl and physically gratifying yourself *at this time* will not make you a man, prove anything, or make you happy.

Life, as you'll see, is so much more than a thirty-second blast of sexual energy. That's why the first stop in getting sexual character for all young men is to pick up the "brother" book in this series called *Every Young Man's Battle*. If you really want to make an impact, get a bunch of guys you hang with to start a group and go through it. Now *that* takes guts!

THE PAYOFF

You can't necessarily expect immediate results when you choose to do the right thing. In fact, my experience over the years has shown me that God takes His time, even though I think I already have learned my lesson or am *sure* that I'm ready to be responsible.

That's why way too many of my younger brothers miss God's ultimate blessing—they are simply too impatient. They give up too early, too easily in the name of fun, because they are demonstrating the emotional and spiritual development of a twelve-year-old. Maturity is recognizing that sometimes you need to do the very thing you don't want to do to become the man you need to be. God's men have this perspective:

> But God is doing what is best for us, training us to live God's holy best. At the time, discipline isn't much fun. It always feels like it's going against the grain. Later, of course, it pays off handsomely, for it's the well-trained who find themselves mature in their relationship with God. (Hebrews 12:10-11, MSG)

A NO MEANS NO

When I was a college sophomore and a new Christian, I was slow in understanding that I would be better off avoiding girls rather than embracing them. Since I didn't have the self-control to manage a serious relationship without muddying the waters sexually, I had no business having a girlfriend. Fortunately, my fraternity Bible study, classroom studies, and intramural sports kept me plenty busy and out of trouble at UCLA. That's why meeting Heather right before the end of the spring quarter caught me by surprise. She was cool and Christian. *This,* I thought, *will be different.*

We dated a month before the school year ended, and then I was off to Europe on a missions trip. Throughout my travels in Spain, France, Germany, and Switzerland, I kept a journal and entered the lovesick infatuated musings of a guy who I would probably slap silly today. I guess all sorts of romantic feelings bubbled inside me while I was serving the Lord in Europe. I *really* looked forward to coming home and exploring this new frontier of dating a Christian. No matter who you are, it's nice to think there is someone on the other side of the world waiting just for you.

**For the first time in my life, I was not
on the hunt for a relationship.**

While I was romanticizing this on the cobblestone streets of Europe, Heather was wisely concluding in Los Angeles that I was not the relationship for her. Not long after I touched down at LAX, she *ended* it. Talk about shock and awe. "But...but...but..." was all I could come up with. Discovering that our relationship was over before it began was something I didn't take too well. I kept wondering, *What are You up to, God?*

I chewed on that one for a while until I arrived at the conclusion that if God wanted this relationship to happen, nothing could have stopped it. He clearly said no. Deep down, this made me feel a little better, and I decided that relationships were not His purpose for me at that time. I concluded that God wanted me to invest my energies in:

- my walk with Him (versus a girl)
- school (what a concept!)
- ministry to unsaved UCLA students (there ya go)

For the first time in my life, I was not on the hunt for a relationship. It was during this down time, this period when I focused on what God wanted me to do, that I caught the eye (and later the heart) of a girl who saw me saying yes to God. Yep, I got the girl in the end—a UCLA cheerleader no less—but it was *after* I accepted God's no by faith, figuring He had His timing and a special person waiting out there for me.

God wants your respect, obedience, and trust when He says no to certain activities or relationships.

As a young father, I have to admit that I say no every now and then just to see how my kids react. Will they respect me? Obey? Sometimes I ask to see if they will go with my plan just because it's me who's asking. Deep, deep down, I hope and pray that I get the right response to my direction—especially when I know it's hard for them to swallow a no in the short term. Cara, Ryan, and Jenna know that listening and following Dad's direction is almost always the best way to go. The reason why is that they know what I love more than obedience is *rewarding* obedience with over-the-top blessings. Obeying and respecting my verbal commands will come back to them in a much bigger blessing later that day, the next day, or when they really have a need.

So how do you react when you hear God saying no to you?

God wants your respect, obedience, and trust when He says no to certain activities or relationships. To think and act this way, however, requires a step of faith, a belief in Him, and a peace-filled hope that His plans and timing are the absolute best. What God is doing is asking for your trust and obedience *now:*

> Trust GOD from the bottom of your heart;
> > don't try to figure out everything on your own.
> Listen for GOD's voice in everything you do,
> > everywhere you go;
> > he's the one who will keep you on track.

> Don't assume that you know it all.
>> Run to GOD! Run from evil!
> Your body will glow with health,
>> your very bones will vibrate with life!
>>> (Proverbs 3:5-8, MSG)

God's young man replaces running from good with running from evil. God's young man replaces trusting in his feelings with trusting in his Father. God's young man replaces lip service with active listening and obedience. God's young man replaces limiting God's influence to certain parts of his life with giving God everything happening in his life. God's young man risks letting God be in control and manage him freely. What this means is:

- saying no to oral sex when your friends are saying yes
- saying no to double standards when your "Christian" friends are tempting you to join in the fun
- saying no to looking at sexually explicit Web sites when your whole dorm floor is doing it
- saying no to lying to your parents when it's the only way you can go where everybody else is going

You get the point. God's young man says no to temptation so that he can say yes to God. If there's a no from God, then there should be a no from you, too.

Part of being able to forsake comfort for godly character has to do with knowing *who* your heavenly Father is and how He loves to reward you. Maybe you feel God has got you pinned down on something. Maybe He's got you wondering what His will is for you. Or maybe you just don't *feel* like towing the line on a particular temptation. That's normal! You are not a robot, and God doesn't expect you to swallow everything He throws your way with a smile. Sometimes God's will *feels* like a cruel joke—even sucks, if you're honest. But in that moment of struggle between choosing God's plan or your plan, God's young man pauses to consider *who* is doing the asking.

**God's young man says no
to temptation so that
he can say yes to God.**

One of the most important things Jesus wanted men to know about God the Father is that He is a loving dad. I didn't know what that meant while I was growing up, so when it came time to trust God when I first became a believer, I trusted myself and my instincts rather than God, because that's what I was used to. But over time—and a lot of painful consequences later—I began to get it. God was not a fun-killer, a puritan, or a policeman. He was just a dad—a wise one, a trustworthy one, a maker of men, and a rewarder of sons who choose His way instead of the way their feelings might dictate.

These are the moments God wants to make a man out of you. This inner transformation happens when you choose the way that will test your character more. When you pass the test, you will change, your relationship with God will deepen, and you will discover what it means to be like Christ. The promise will become a reality:

> When I was a child, I talked like a child, I thought like a child, I reasoned like a child. When I became a man, I put childish ways behind me. (the apostle Paul, 1 Corinthians 13:11)

Manhood is about making new decisions—mature ones that rely more on our faith and less on our feelings. As we'll see in the next chapter, this decision process must be guided and shaped by embracing and acting upon the truth.

mind games

Being honest with yourself is difficult.

I know. I hadn't forgotten how I was before I became a Christian. Back then I had perfected the art of lying to myself. I found it easy to be dishonest when it was in my interest. For instance, when I worked at the convenience store on long Sunday afternoons, I helped myself to candy bars and beef jerky from the display shelves without paying. Instead of thinking, *That's stealing!* I rationalized my actions by saying to myself, *They make so much money off these things.*

I always lied to my parents about my whereabouts on weekends because I wanted to hang with my friends and not come home when my parents wanted me to come home. *I'm not doing anything bad,* I thought, instead of recognizing that I was speaking a flat-out lie about my plans to Mom and Dad.

After vowing never to use marijuana because I was an athlete, I willingly smoked dope because I thought I was in such good shape that it wouldn't hurt me. Then there was the time I bought cocaine for my senior prom, saying to myself, *This is only for a special occasion.* That sounded a lot better than *You're using illegal drugs and could mess up your life!*

My appetite for pleasure and fun controlled my life. Why should I say no to what I wanted to do? I was young enough, insecure enough, and lonely enough *not* to listen to the voice in my head questioning some of my decisions. While I am ashamed to reveal everything about my BC (before Christ) days, they reveal a fundamental truth about me: when it was in my interest, I was a pro at playing mind games to get what I wanted when I wanted it.

I wish I could say that the mind games stopped *after* I became a Christian. The fact is, that part of me still remained in my character. After all, I was good at telling lies—I had practiced for years. So for me to become good at something else—like telling the truth—also took some practice. I wasn't aware that God, however, who was in charge of my training program, would be the one teaching me how to be honest.

SELF-TRICKERY

I bet you've rationalized a few things. You wouldn't be normal if you haven't. It's easy to do. All you have to do is repeat one of the following excuses:

- *I deserve this.*
- *No one will ever know.*
- *I am not hurting anyone.*
- *My friends' parents let them.*
- *That's just the way I am.*
- *Parents just don't get it.*
- *Everyone I know at school does it.*
- *Technically, it's not having sex.*

- *It's better than getting a girl pregnant.*
- *God wants me to have fun.*
- *This will be the last time.*
- *After college, I'll stop.*

We love to excuse our wrong behaviors. We love to justify our weaknesses. We love to minimize the damages. We love to rationalize our sin. We make fun of those who are being good. We blame our parents, our teachers, or the cops. At one time or another I used these mind games on myself. I'm sure I believed what I was saying at the time, although I was twisting logic for selfish purposes.

Danny used these same mind games when he complained to Ashley that she didn't really love him. When they started dating four months earlier, he respected her virginity. He bought into the "true love waits" motto. But as he daily fantasized about her, the whole virginity thing became less attractive to him. He resented the firewall she had installed regarding physical intimacy.

> **For Danny, purity had gone from a standard that honored God to a mind game of technicalities, loopholes, and rationalizations to get Ashley to compromise.**

Danny's mind became one track—and it was no longer on God. He wanted to touch her more, explore her more, kiss her longer, and hug her deeply. It was like he tossed his moral bearings overboard; that's how focused he was on her body, which was built very well. He imagined what she looked like with her top off when they kissed, which only revved his motor higher. But he felt her resisting his advances to go a little further each time they got into heavy kissing.

"You love me, right?" he asked after one extended session on the couch in her living room.

She nodded her head, which rested against his chest.

"If two people are in love, what's wrong about expressing that love?" he asked.

Danny didn't hear her answer. A little head was doing all the thinking—and it wasn't the one mounted to his neck and shoulders. So he tried a different tack. He asked her if she could go "down there" to take some of the pressure off. He said it wasn't the same as having sex. It's what couples who weren't married did. For Danny, purity had gone from a standard that honored God to a mind game of technicalities, loopholes, and rationalizations to get Ashley to compromise.

Ashley knew what she was being asked to do, so she made some excuse. Then she confided in Danny's best friend Brian about how he was acting. "Could you talk to him about it?" she asked. "Tell him that if he doesn't back off, I don't want to date him anymore."

At the beach that weekend, Brian and Danny went surfing in the early morning. Afterward, when they were back in the parking lot, changing out of their wetsuits, Brian casually asked, "How's it going with Ashley?"

"Why? You interested?" Danny laughed.

"No, dude. Nothing like that. It's just that you guys are serious."

"You're right," Danny lamented. "It's not the same, though. She is such a prude sometimes."

"What do you mean?"

"She doesn't want to fool around—at all!" Danny protested.

"Well, maybe she's right on this one, bro." Brian said, recalling his discussion with Ashley.

"What are you talking about?" Danny was getting agitated.

Brian took a deep breath and let it rip. "Sounds like it's all about you getting off. Problem is: it's not just about you. It's about her commitment. It's about God. You know the deal on this one, bro. God's not gonna re-write that part of His Word so we can fudge. He's got reasons."

"Oh yeah? Give me one good one."

"Obviously, you're not ready to listen if I told you one," Brian said.

Danny ran his right hand through his sun-bleached hair. "What do you mean?" he asked.

Brian kept pouring it on. "If you can blow off your commitment to God so easily now," he said, "how can you expect to keep your commitment to her if you guys get married? That's what she's thinking in the back of her head, man! No self-control now, no self-control later. It makes her doubt you."

Having his sheets pulled made Danny feel uncomfortable. "You sound like that psychologist on *Oprah,* dude."

Brian raised his hands and shrugged. He had him. Danny was caught—not by Brian, but by God. The mind games were over for now.

All of us will stand before God one day and have to account for our actions today. You want that day to be a great one. He won't accept your bogus excuses for why you traded in your commitment to Him for cheap physical thrills or moments of gratification. What will you say to the Lord—the same Lord who reads all your thoughts and exposes your mind games? That's why, when facing a moral dilemma, you have one of two ways to go: either face up to the truth or run from God. What will it be for you? Choosing to live your life by the truth or by lies?

TRUTH IS NOT THE ENEMY

When certain situations arise, young men keep truth at arm's length because they still want to dance with sin. Depending on how you look at things, truth can be perceived as:

- an enemy of fun
- an enemy of certain adrenaline rushes
- an enemy of cool
- an enemy of acceptance by those you want to like you
- an enemy of sexual gratification
- an enemy of your plans to deviate from your faith for an evening
- an enemy of a guilt-free high

The worst habit a young man can get into is telling himself lies that give him enough wiggle room to continue participating in activities that he *knows* are harming his relationship with God and others. The deception goes like this: *If I avoid the truth (or suppress it temporarily) about what I'm doing, I can keep doing what I'm doing.* This sort of thinking leads to actions that:

- divide your allegiance
- drive you into sin
- distance you from God
- disconnect you from godly accountability
- damage your witness for Christ

The best habit you can get into is seeing how God's purposes for bringing truth to your life are all about *you!* He's doing this because he loves you. He may be telling you things you may not *want* to hear, but they are things that you *need* to hear to become God's young man. The fact is that He can't help Himself—He *is* the truth. So how do you know when God's speaking His truth to you? It's God talking when:

- you are not free to pursue sin like you used to
- you are forced to pause and think about consequences
- you are uncomfortable for all the right reasons
- you want to run away from the message
- you don't want to take responsibility for your actions
- you feel uncomfortable or anxious about a behavior

- you are approached by someone you respect with concerns
- you remember a clear insight or biblical command that speaks to the behavior

Jesus described these moments of truth as opportunities to "see the light"—times when men will either move toward God or run from God:

> The light from heaven came into the world, but they loved the darkness more than the light, for their actions were evil. They hate the light because they want to sin in the darkness. They stay away from the light for fear their sins will be exposed and they will be punished. But those who do what is right come to the light gladly, so everyone can see that they are doing what God wants. (John 3:19-21, NLT)

Our actions reveal our true heart and our maturity in Christ. When Jesus shows up on your porch with some truth about your present direction, an attitude that needs adjustment, or an action that needs to be addressed, how do you react?

- Do you slam the door of your mind to His voice of truth? Or do you open it wide?
- Do you respond with just promises to change? Or do you take action?
- Do you fear being exposed as a poser? Or do you see yourself as a sinner just like everybody else?
- Do you lie to yourself? Or do you take responsibility?
- Do you hide the real you? Or do you let others see you as you really are?
- Do you keep doing what you want? Or do you start doing what God wants?

See the difference? One guy says "whatever" by his response. The other guy says, "That's me! What do you want me to do now, Jesus?" When God turns the mirror of truth on one of His young servants, a boy will flee, but God's young man will turn and face it. A boy fears the realities that his destructive behavior is causing. But a courageous young man of God weathers the storm of discomfort in his gut, listens to what he's being taught, and moves into the Man Zone.

THE KNOT IN YOUR STOMACH

His parents were right, but Tom could not admit that. He fought them tooth and nail about getting a summer job to pay for *his* car insurance, *his* gas, and *his* car repairs. His mom and dad told him that since he was not taking summer school classes, the next three months would be a great time to find a part-time job to cover his car-related expenses.

Something in Tom couldn't admit that his parents were right, however. He had other things on his mind—like sleeping in and hanging out with his friends.

When he described his fight to his buddies, he was surprised that everyone didn't see his side. One friend said, "Dude, your old man chipped in over half the money to buy that metallic blue Honda CRX in the driveway, and then he bought you those chrome rims as a car-warming present. Your dad is awesome. I don't think he's asking too much."

But most of his friends thought Tom's parents were hassling him. "Yeah, I don't know any parents who made their kids pay for *anything* while they're still in school," said one.

Tom pressed his case at the dinner table one night. "Mom, you said that as long as I was in college, you and dad would take care of stuff like this," he stated, kind of like a lawyer making an opening statement.

"I think that's a bit of a stretch," his father interjected. "She meant room and board, Son, not the costs of owning a car. Mom and I think you should be taking on some of the financial responsibilities that come with growing older. If you don't want to, then maybe the freedom of having your own car isn't the right thing."

"But, Dad…"

"I want you to think about it. We think that since you're not taking summer classes, you can do some work around the office and earn some cash to take care of your expenses. That's all we're asking. I want you to pray about that."

Playing the God card brought the discussion to a close. Tom muttered something about thinking about it and excused himself to visit Justin. *I'm outta here,* he thought.

Sometimes accepting the truth is hard because change requires action, which can produce tension.

He unlocked the front door to his CRX, got in, and turned the key. Something made him pause before he backed out of the driveway—something deep inside. He took a long breath and stared at the picture windows fronting their home. He could see his parents sharing a dessert and coffee. They were being more than fair. Even though the timing of their request caught him off guard, he knew they were right. He didn't need to pray about it; what he should do was clear to him. He turned off the ignition, walked back inside, and did what God wanted him to do—apologize to his parents and ask his dad when he could start working in his office.

Sometimes accepting the truth is hard because *change requires action,* which can produce tension. I'm talking about that knot in your stomach when a problem or issue connected to you has to come out into the open.

I can understand why there are times that you don't want to hear the truth. It messes up your plans and timing. Other times, it's difficult to face your faults, and the cost of owning up to them is shame—that painful feeling that arises from guilt. When you are ashamed of your actions, you can only go one of two ways with this feeling—you kill the messengers or take responsibility and change. Facing up to the truth can feel like your losing something. In Tom's case, his carefree summer was going out the window, but Jesus was calling him to change, honor his mom and dad, and face the truth with courage. Sure, he had a huge knot in his stomach walking back into that house, but he had the wisdom to recognize that was God in his gut! So he decided to gamble on that tug calling him to do the right thing.

When faced with a situation like Tom's—when your sheets have been pulled and your flaws exposed—Jesus advises us to do what's counterintuitive and unnatural. He says to take the hit: "For whoever wants to save his life will lose it, but whoever loses his life for me and for the gospel will save it" (Mark 8:35).

Cuts to Heal Versus Stabs to Kill

My brother-in-law Christian (yes, that's his real name) is the chief of surgery at a Sacramento hospital. He's an amazing guy blessed with iron nerves, and his skilled hands are great with a blade. Mountains of thank-you cards and a flood of presents every Christmas are tangible reminders that his patients appreciate his gift. Think about it: they love him for cutting on them! It sounds funny to say that, but they realize his cutting is an incision to heal, not a stabbing to kill. His postoperative patients are grateful for helping them live healthier lives free from cancerous tumors, breast lumps, ruptured appendixes, or torn hernias.

God sometimes exacts surgical cuts on aspects of your personality to bring you toward better spiritual health. Your willingness to go under the knife requires faith in the surgeon and an expectation of a healthier life with God.

In a moment of truth—when you want

to run from reality or run from God—

He says, "Don't run! Take my hand. It's okay.

I want to take you to a new place."

Christian may be a great surgeon, but cutting on people is not his best quality. I admire how he educates his patients and calms their fears while leading up to an operation. The way he explains things puts their minds at ease and makes them believe that this procedure is routine and that everything will be just fine. In the same way, God also extends His hand to calm our fears:

> But I'll take the hand of those who don't know the way,
>   who can't see where they're going.
> I'll be a personal guide to them,
>   directing them through unknown country.
> I'll be right there to show them what roads to take,
>   make sure they don't fall into the ditch.
> These are the things I'll be doing for them—
>   sticking with them, not leaving them for a minute.
>   (Isaiah 42:16, MSG)

In a moment of truth—when you want to run from reality or run from God—He says, "Don't run! Take my hand. It's okay. I want to take you to a new place."

I call that place the Next Level.

The Next Level

When God brings the truth to you, your acceptance has great rewards. You feel closer to Him, like part of the team, when you get with the program He's recommending. If you shine Him on, however, and reject the truth, God cannot connect with a young man who disregards the truth and lies to himself. Remember: His character won't allow it.

One time Jesus told a lady giving Him the runaround that "the *true* worshipers will worship the Father in spirit and *truth*, for they are the kind of worshipers the Father seeks" (John 4:23). Want to connect with God at the Next Level? You can do it by getting honest with yourself. Ask yourself these questions:

- Am I being honest with *myself* regarding my spiritual commitment to Christ?
- Am I being totally honest with *God* about my life?
- Have I been honest with *others* about my spiritual life and struggles?
- Am I willing to hear the truth from God and other brothers about my spiritual direction?
- Will I do what they say?

Openness and honesty always lead to a closer connection with God—and with other people. Living a lie creates distance in these relationships.

Scott had been playing God for a fool. He was leading his youth group on Friday nights, recruiting others for a mission trip to Mexico, and getting into "deep" discussions about the Lord with the other guys in his "Huddle." Week after week, Scott was like a rock, and his youth pastor was pretty excited about having a strong and honest guy in leadership. Once, in a guys-only discussion, Scott was courageous enough to discuss his struggles with sexual temptation, which made it safe for other guys to talk about stuff they had never shared before.

Scott wasn't honest about one thing, however: his Internet browser was loaded to the gills with superexplicit porn sites. *That,* he thought, was something he had to keep to himself. Then Scott's participation in his Friday Huddle fell off, and when his youth pastor called his cell phone to see how he was doing, Scott didn't return his calls. When he and his youth pastor finally touched base, Scott said he was sorry for missing the Friday Huddles, but school and weekend soccer tournaments had taken over his schedule.

Openness and honesty always lead to a closer connection with God—and with other people. Living a lie creates distance in these relationships.

Everyone saw less and less of him until the youth pastor received an urgent call from Scott's dad, who said he needed some help talking to Scott. It seems that Scott had been making phone calls to some 976 numbers—where he listened to live girls talk dirty and how they wanted to do certain sexual acts on his body. Scott needed a credit card to participate, so he used his father's credit card number, which wasn't real smart since Dad would find out sooner or later. It turned out to be sooner, because the next credit card statement was inflated to the tune of three hundred dollars!

Scott foolishly thought he could live a double life—a life for God and a life chasing sexual thrills at the same time. What he found out is that God does not bend His will or play to our self-deceptions. Instead, he discovered that God will out us, if necessary, to get our attention and refocus our hearts and minds on Him. If only Scott had exercised more honesty in his Huddle. He later said that there were several times when he felt like his deep, dark secret would leap out of his throat, but fear kept that secret locked inside.

Your relationship to God hinges on your being honest with God—and others—about what's really happening in your life. Stop playing mind games that pollute your relationship with Christ. When God confronts you with the light of the truth, you *should* feel uncomfortable. Use that discomfort to realize that God is calling you to another level of honesty and closeness to Him. You are moving into the Man Zone when you desire to know—and act—upon God's truth. As Jesus said, "I was born and entered the world so that I could witness to the truth. Everyone who cares for truth, who has any feeling for the truth, recognizes my voice" (John 18:37, MSG).

**When God confronts you with the light
of the truth, you should feel uncomfortable.**

As you will find out in the next chapter, recognizing Jesus's voice is one thing, but taking Him at His word and leaving the results to Him is another. In fact, it can be downright scary.

you know better

"Kenny, take a look," my friend Benji said, pointing to the driver's side door. What I saw rocked my world that Sunday morning—a smashed-in quarter panel on my car. "What are you going to do?" he asked.

It was the summer before my freshmen year in college. My friends and I had found a dirt parking lot perfectly suited for making "doughnuts" with our parents' cars. We slammed on our accelerators and then jammed on the brakes while yanking the steering wheel so that our cars would spin in big circles. We cranked up the music and laughed our heads off.

Then it happened. My car—actually, my mom's—kissed a railroad tie. While it was just a "touch," I ended up denting the driver's side door. Now I was in deep linguine.

My first impulse was practical—save my own skin! I had several hours to do *something* since my parents were gone that morning, so Benji and I drove Mom's car to "Auto Row" to see if any dealerships were open. No luck—all we saw were signs saying Closed on Sundays. I was about to give up hope when I spotted Stevens Creek Auto Body at the end of a long alley.

In the distance, I could see a guy working under a car. He was my first glimmer of hope.

After explaining my deep doo-doo dilemma, the mechanic agreed to help me escape the wrath of Godzilla, otherwise known as Dad. Benji and I wheeled Mom's Capri with the crushed quarter panel into the operating room, knowing that I was placing my future in the hands of a complete stranger named Ole (a Scandinavian name pronounced Oh-lay). I knew nothing about bodywork, but what I witnessed over the next few hours scared the living daylights out of me.

First, Ole drilled holes in the dented door to try to pull it out, but that didn't work.

Next, he filled the dent with Bondo, a pasty mixture of water and powder. He spread the Bondo into the two-foot-long dent like peanut butter on fresh bread. The mixture went on sloppy, but it dried quickly and out of shape.

Ole then sanded the dried Bondo, which proceeded to take off some of the original paint on the door panel. "Not to worry," he said. "We'll paint over it."

"Can you match the color?" I asked. The Capri was a bluish-green hue.

"Sure, but I'll have to go to an auto parts store," he said. We accompanied him and watched Ole purchase two *different* shades of spray paint, which raised my blood pressure. I questioned him about using two different colors, but he said he planned to *combine* the colors to achieve a color match. *Oh, mama!* I thought. *I'm dead meat now.*

For almost three hours I was a mess. My face grimaced with each step of the process. I couldn't bring myself to trust this guy. With each step he took, he looked like he was doing *more* damage to the car, not repairing it. I wondered if this guy *really* knew what he was doing because:

- He didn't look like the sharpest tool in the box.
- His body shop methods didn't make sense. After Plan A (pulling the dented door panel out) didn't work, he was going to Plan B (using Bondo and spray paint).
- When he bought two cans of spray paint with colors that didn't match the color of Mom's paint job, I really questioned his abilities. He also didn't appear that confident to me.
- He said it would only cost me $75. How good could he be?

Then Ole started displaying the master's touch. He sanded the Bondo-filled door until it looked like a perfect match of the old driver's door, and then he started laying down alternate layers of paint. My doubts turned to hopeful confidence. It turned out that he knew *exactly* what he was doing the whole time (I later learned he worked exclusively on Porsche body repairs), so the repair on the Capri turned out perfect. For an added bonus, he saved my sorry seventeen-year-old rear end.

The way I saw it at the time, though, I was putting my future into the hands of another person. That felt very risky! I certainly didn't trust him to make Mom's car look as good as new, but Ole did. I had to let go and give in to the process, even though I doubted his skills to fix my problem. Fortunately, Ole knew better than to listen to someone as ignorant as me.

These days, there are times when I feel the way Ole must have felt about me. I will have a young guy bring his problems into my "shop" and ask for help. He has usually dented more than a door panel: he has crashed into a tree because he was blinded by his sin. Now that his life has been wrecked, he's asking what can be done. I know what he should do—get back on God's highway, but that means driving in a manner that will keep him on the straight and narrow.

For some, staying on God's highway makes them uncomfortable. They don't like being confined to a route God has laid out for their lives. But their discomfort can be a good thing—a sure sign that an inner spiritual battle is raging for control of their lives.

I believe that when you wreck your life, your pride will *drive you,* your fear will *deter you,* or your faith will *direct you.* Let's take a closer look at these three possibilities.

Pride Says to God: "I Know Better"

I often see many young men respond to God's plan with youthful pride—an "I know better" attitude that is the equivalent of trash-talking. Think about what happened to me at that auto body shop. What if I said, "Hey Ole, can you step aside and listen while I give you a few pointers on how Mom's car should be fixed? After all, I've been driving for a whole year. Let me show you how a *real* pro gets it done."

Their mind-set and actions seem to say:
"Thanks for coming along for the ride, God,
but I'll take the wheel from here."

You're probably saying, *Yeah, right.* Actually, the best thing I did that morning was shut my pie hole and let Ole do what he does best.

Or think of your favorite hobby, sport, or kind of music. Who do you think is the top dog—that one person excelling above the competition in that sport or field? Got him (or her) in your head? Now, picture *yourself* stepping into his world and telling him how he can do his thing *better.*

My friend Paul is a good road racer, but I could never imagine him giving Lance Armstrong tips on how to attack the L'Alpe d'Huez in the Tour de France. I play in a men's soccer league, but that doesn't mean I can fly over to England and clinic Thierry Henri (the leading goal scorer in the

English Premier League) on how to strike the ball sweeter. My buddy Danny is a killer surfer, but he wouldn't dare paddle up next to Kelly Slater and tell him what waves to drop in on. No, we give the pros plenty of room because they're *better* than we are. Better yet, we would listen closely if they deigned to give *us* a few tips, right?

These scenarios may seem far fetched, but *this is exactly how the majority of young men act toward God.* They are light-years apart from God when it comes to wisdom, yet they fling their "wisdom" around like *they* spoke and created the heavens and the earth. In fact, their ignorance makes them dangerous to themselves and to others. Their mind-set and actions seem to say: "Thanks for coming along for the ride, God, but I'll take the wheel from here." They would never utter those words, of course, but their *actions* say otherwise. I can just imagine God scratching His head in amazement when people shine Him on.

Here is what the Lord, the *Creator* and Holy One of Israel, says: "Do you question what I do? Do you give me orders about the work of my hands?" (Isaiah 45:11, NLT). What areas of your life do you claim to know better than God:

- Do *you* set your own sexual boundaries versus respecting God's mind on the matter?
- Do *you* decide which areas you'll allow His influence to shape your lifestyle or where the off-limits signs will be posted?
- Do *you* selectively obey some commands and ignore others?
- Do *you* believe it's okay for you to believe one thing and live and act another way?
- Do your actions show that you question His wisdom?

When my daughter, Jenna, was six, she liked to say to her brother, "You're not the boss of me, Ryan!" What Jenna was saying was that Ryan would not control her actions but rather, "*I* am the boss of me!" Jenna had a right to be skeptical of her older brother, because his motives toward his sister were not always noble—and at times were highly questionable. Granted, at nine years of age, he didn't know better.

Unlike Jenna, however, you do not have the right to be skeptical with God because He *does* know better. Don't forget that He spilled His own blood for you to prove that He can be trusted.

If you continue to resist God, He has ways of showing you that you don't know better. That's what happened to a guy named Naaman in the Bible. He was a hotshot Syrian general who was powerful, commanding, and successful. Underneath his armor, however, his body was racked by a skin disease called leprosy. On the outside—shining armor and victory. Underneath and on the inside—sores and shame.

Don't forget that He spilled His own blood for you to prove that He can be trusted.

When his maid told Naaman about a God's man named Elisha who could heal him, Naaman immediately suited up, withdrew a hefty amount of money from the bank, and set off for Israel. His simple, direct plan: "I pay, and the sores go away."

But it wasn't that easy. More important, God wanted to heal more than Naaman's ghastly skin condition—He wanted Naaman to learn humility. So instead of accepting Naaman's cash, Elisha told the general that he had to expose himself by taking a bath in the Jordan River—not once but seven times! Talk about humbling. Here's what Elisha's messenger said to Naaman: "Go, wash yourself seven times in the Jordan, and your flesh will be restored and you will be cleansed." The thought of showing the world his shameful condition (leprosy back then was like having AIDS today) caused Naaman to go ballistic. He said, "*I thought* that he would surely come out to me and stand and call on the name of the LORD his God, wave his hand over the spot and cure me of my leprosy" (2 Kings 5:10-11).

The bottom line of Naaman's temper tantrum can be found in the two words *"I thought."* He thought God's plan to heal him would be custom-fitted to his plan, which, most notably, did not require any humility before God or man. *I thought* is the language of pride and reflects a lack of knowledge and respect about who God is and how you should relate to Him.

**Naaman's stubbornness
almost cost him his miracle.**

The good news is that Naaman had awesome friends who corralled him and said that swimming in the Jordan River might be the best course of action if he wanted to realize this miracle. They prevailed upon Naaman to switch mental gears:

> So he went down and dipped himself in the Jordan seven times, as the man of God had told him, and his flesh was restored and became clean like that of a young boy.
>
> Then Naaman and all his attendants went back to the man of God. [Naaman] stood before him and said, *"Now I know* that there is no God in all the world except in Israel." (verses 14-15)

In snowboarding terms, Naaman did an old-fashioned 180. *"Now I know"* reflects his new appreciation for God's position and a recognition that He knew better. Naaman's stubbornness, however, almost cost him his miracle. His story should make every young man think hard about his reaction to God's instructions.

To help you move forward with God and experience His miracles in your life, ask yourself these questions:

- Am I doing it His way or my way?
- How does God want me to handle this?
- What does God's Word tell me to do?
- What are my godly brothers saying?

Only two things would keep you from asking yourself these questions—ignorance or pride. Neither trait will get you into the Man Zone with God.

Fear Says: "I'll Miss Out"

The second common way that people respond to God is when they think, *If I do it your way, I'll miss out.* The fear of missing out causes young men to reserve certain areas of their lives away from God's purpose. I've seen this kind of thinking in countless counseling sessions, which convinces me that this kind of thinking is guilt-producing, unproductive, and painful in the lives of my younger spiritual brothers.

Jeremy feared that he would miss out on the college experience if he didn't explore the party scene. Shortly after unpacking in his college dorm, he was invited to cruise fraternity row during rush week. No one knew that Jeremy had been a Christian since he was eight years old—and he wasn't about to reveal that information. Why? Because he was making a calculated decision of whether he should step outside of God's plan for his life.

So Jeremy jumped at the chance to experience the party scene first-hand, and he also offered to drive so that he could further ingratiate himself with his newfound buddies. Four rush parties and six tumblers of beer later, Jeremy turned the ignition and slammed his Toyota 4Runner into gear. The time was 2:00 a.m.

It would be the last time Jeremy ever got behind the wheel of a car.

Four hours later Jeremy's parents were awakened by a social worker at the University Medical Center. *"We regret to inform you that at 5:12 this morning, your son expired following a multivehicle car accident..."* Jeremy thought he was missing out, but now his parents are missing out on a son.

Nate felt like he was missing out because the last three girls he asked out all said, "No thanks. I think I'm washing my hair Saturday night." Feeling depressed and lonely, he did a Google search and was quickly connected with a beautiful, shapely girl who was definitely not saying no out there in cyberspace. Her home page gave him a knot in his stomach—and a twitch below his beltline. Image after image ratcheted up the intensity, and the stranglehold tightened. The Evil One whispered: "She's safe because she will never say no to you. She won't ask questions, and she doesn't mind if you stare. That's what she's there for. And no one will ever know. She's accessible any time you want."

> They felt like they were missing out
> on something—a feeling, a thrill,
> a connection, an experience—that God
> simply would not know how to provide.

Nate's hand felt like it was glued to his mouse. He felt scared and excited at the same time, knowing that this stuff was from the pit of hell, but he felt too compelled to turn his eyes away or click out of there.

Fast-forward three years and thousands of point-and-clicks later. It was a big day for Nate—he was getting married to Jennifer after his college graduation. The good news is that he hadn't slept with his future bride while they were dating, but the bad news is that he continued to date the "blondies" on the Net.

His wedding night was supposed to be *the* over-the-top sexual experience, but when it came time for him to make love to his new wife, he wasn't physically able to consummate his marriage that night. He couldn't get it up! Her body…well, let's just say it didn't stack up real well compared to his girlfriends on the computer screen. He needed their sexy images to satisfy himself, not his wife's less glamorous body. As you can imagine, their marriage got off to the worst start possible.

Jeremy and Nate were followers of Jesus, but they felt like they were missing out on something—a feeling, a thrill, a connection, an experience—that God simply would not know how to provide. These two guys both swallowed the same lie—if you seek first the kingdom of God, then all these things will be taken *away* from you. Jeremy's independence, his disconnection from family and Christian friends back home, and a curiosity about the party scene beat his faith down and built up his fear regarding God's ability to meet his needs.

As for Nate, he was one of the millions of young men who fear being lonely and unloved, so they look for it in the digital eyes of women without heartbeats. He didn't know that pornography would be more powerful than a hit off a crack pipe. He didn't know that cybersex releases real chemicals into the brain that methamphetamines can only mimic. He didn't know that he was training his body to react to pixelated images of naked women at the expense of his future sexual relationship with his bride. When he felt the presence of the Evil One, he was afraid to mention his problem to anyone at his Christian college and, above all, to his parents.

Make no mistake, when you fear you will miss out on something—and respond by compartmentalizing certain areas of your life away from God—you *will* miss out:

- You will miss out on His best.
- You will miss out on His character.
- You will miss out on intimacy with Him and others.

- You will miss out on the freedom that only responding in faith can bring.
- You will miss out on the eternal blessings God promises those who choose faith over fear.

In other words, you will miss out on life the way it was intended to be. My message to you is this: move against your fear today and send a different message to God. That message should be: *Lord, You win,* which is the third way you can respond to God.

Faith Says: "You Win"

I really get into March Madness, that month when NCAA basketball goes crazy with excitement. I think the reason I love watching games on television is the energy—the hopping-high teams and their face-painted fans. Whenever my UCLA Bruins qualify, I hang on every shot and every whistle. Many of the games go down to the last possession of the ball.

Every college or university in the sixty-four-team tournament believes it has a chance of getting to at least the Sweet Sixteen. Every year, though, it seems like a Cinderella team shocks the sporting world and earns a trip to the Final Four.

Sometimes in these heavily fought battles, one team earns such a big lead at the end that there's a moment of surrender in which *both* sides know that the game is over. It might be a fifteen-point lead with a minute to go, or a seven-point lead with seconds left on the clock. After forty minutes of pushing, shoving, yelling, fouling, swishing, blocking, cutting, passing, running, screening, shooting, picking, charging, and scoring, the team that's down realizes there is no way it can overcome the point deficit with the few seconds left in the game. So it surrenders.

It's easy to recognize this moment. The team that's ahead will dribble the clock out at half court while the other team forgoes putting any pressure on the dribbler. Everyone knows that the losing team has resigned to its fate even though there is time left on the clock. Laying off the ball communicates to other team:

- You guys were better today.
- We are not fighting you anymore.
- You are advancing to the next round.
- We surrender to our fate.

In a sense, this is what our third response to God should be all about: you can't compete against God's will and expect to win anymore. Continuing to fight the outcome won't make things better, but it might make things worse. When you surrender, you're deciding to let God's will prevail—to let Him win so that *you* can move forward as a man. And while it's unnatural for highly competitive athletes to concede victory, it requires humility to say, "You know better, Lord."

You can't compete against God's will and expect to win anymore.

That's what powerfully independent and strong men have done throughout history when they wanted to experience God's plan to the fullest. King Nebuchadnezzar was one of those proud men who, after seven maddening years, finally acknowledged God's complete control of his life and his kingdom. He stopped competing with God's will and said, "You win, God":

I, Nebuchadnezzar, looked up to heaven. My sanity returned, and
I praised and worshiped the Most High and honored the one who
lives forever.

> His rule is everlasting,
>> and his kingdom is eternal.
> All the people of the earth
>> are nothing compared to him.
> He has the power to do as he pleases
>> among the angels of heaven
>> and with those who live on earth.
> No one can stop him or challenge him....

Now I, Nebuchadnezzar, praise and glorify and honor the King of heaven. All his acts are just and true, and he is able to humble those who are proud. (Daniel 4:34-35,37, NLT)

How are you responding to God today?

Is it in pride?

Pride says: *I know better.*

Is it in fear?

Fear says: *I know my needs better.*

Is it in faith?

Faith says: *You know better.*

So much rides on your decision because, as we'll see in the next chapter, the competing voices of culture are not going to let you rest.

battle, don't blend

In the hit film *Lord of the Rings: The Return of the King*, the hero Aragorn (played by Viggo Mortensen) faces a nasty dilemma. An epic battle is looming between the good men led by Aragorn and an evil force led by Sauron. After making a titanic effort to recruit more good guys, Aragorn learns that he is outnumbered and outflanked by bad guys waiting for the go signal to overrun his standing army.

Elrond, a man who can see into the future, meets with Aragorn to suggest a potential solution. His idea is to appeal to an army of ghostly "spirit" mercenaries who exist between the living and dead in a state of shame and dishonor. They are a cursed, ugly, and unruly legion of men who have a nasty habit of killing any mortal who ventures onto their mountain. Recruiting them would be next to impossible for any man—but Aragorn is not any man. First, however, he must accept his identity and live it out responsibly. Elrond and Aragorn discuss the matter in this way:

Elrond: You're outnumbered, Aragorn. You need more men.

Aragorn: There are none.

Elrond: There are those who dwell in the mountain.

Aragorn: Murderers. Traitors. You would call upon them to fight?! They believe in nothing! They answer to no one.

Elrond: They will answer to the *King of Gondor!* [Elrond reveals the sword of Andúril and presents it to Aragorn—it is the signature sword of the king.] Andúril—Flame of the West. Forged from the shards of Narsil. [After an intense stare at this legendary sword, Aragorn accepts and unsheathes it.]

Aragorn: Sauron will not have forgotten the Sword of Elendil. The Blade that was broken shall return to Minas Tirith.

Elrond: The one who can wield the power of this sword can summon to him an army more deadly than any that walks this earth. Put aside the ranger. Become who you were born to be.

Aragorn can continue to live as the "ranger"—a nomad loyal to no one who turns his back on his responsibility. Or he can accept his true identity as king and change the tide of war. One choice is compromise. The other is to take a strong stance.

TAKING A STRONG STANCE

When it comes to the spiritual battle raging inside your soul, Jesus Christ will ask you to *let the ranger go*—that side of you that does not embrace your true spiritual identity and responsibilities. When war lurks at your front porch, one side—one set of values—must prevail. If you don't know it already, you're fighting for that set of values right *now*.

**When war lurks at your front porch, one side—
one set of values—must prevail.**

A true God's young man must abandon the middle ground and determine, in his own mind, that he cannot peacefully coexist with his enemies. This pattern of taking a strong stance is well illustrated in the Bible for us to clearly see. Think about:

- Moses (representing the will of God) versus Pharaoh (the will of man)
- David's anger toward the giant who mocked God—Goliath
- King Hezekiah and how he made a radical break from the evil ways of his father, Ahaz
- Elijah and his showdown with the prophets of Baal
- Daniel's stance against the pagan practices of the Babylonian culture
- Jesus's battle with Satan's temptations in the wilderness
- Peter and John's courageous stand for Christ before the Sanhedrin (the same body that condemned Jesus to death)
- The believers in Revelation who have "defeated him [Satan] because of the blood of the Lamb and because of their testimony. And they were not afraid to die" (12:11, NLT)

Changing into God's young man requires a change in your perspective about spiritual warfare. You can no longer dismiss it, deny it, or deflect your responsibility to engage it. Instead, you must forget the notion that you can play both sides without taking it in the shorts every now and then. In other words, you cannot *blend* God's purposes with opposing purposes and practices. Specifically, you are warned not to blend with what the Bible describes as the "world":

> Stop loving this evil world and all that it offers you, for when you love the world, you show that you do not have the love of the Father in you. For the world offers only the lust for physical pleasure, the lust for everything we see, and pride in our possessions. *These are not from the Father. They are from this evil world.* And this world is fading away, along with everything it craves. But if you do the will of God, you will live forever. (1 John 2:15-17, NLT)

To God, the world represents the popular culture around you—a culture that runs counter to your faith. It is heard in the voices that say:

- There's no right or wrong.
- There's no absolute truth.
- There's no such thing as evil or the devil.
- Whatever works for *you.*
- You gotta trust your senses.
- Who's to say that any lifestyle is wrong?
- Money is power. And more money is more power.
- You control your future.
- Indulge yourself.
- Impress others.
- Don't play it safe.

The world wants to define what's normal for you—and it will if you let it happen. Just flip on MTV, study the newest Abercrombie & Fitch catalog, or check out the latest run of *Bachelor.* What the world values isn't hard to pick up. The world will always emphasize feelings over commitment, a free spirit over character.

I remember a time when my official "religion" was having fun. I didn't want anybody to get too serious with me because that would interrupt my—you guessed it—fun. All my friends belonged to the same denomination of church as I did, which made for great...fun. We would start plotting during lunch at school on Monday what we'd do on Friday and Saturday nights. Our agenda was pretty simple: how are we going to have... yeah, baby...fun?

The world will always emphasize feelings over commitment, a free spirit over character.

The reason we were so into having fun was because our home lives bit the big one. Fun was a welcome salve, especially when you were either the son of an alcoholic dad, an abusive dad, a divorced dad, or a stepdad who took no interest in you. No one talked about this heavy stuff, but we knew one thing—our merry band of brothers was soothing medicine to our fragmented lives.

Our whole mission was to let loose, have fun, and play around. That's why all of us bought into every experience the world had to offer. But when we became high-school seniors, we were getting tired of the party and girl scene. It was just stale. In fact, I remember tape-recording a late-night conversation at my kitchen table with some of the guys. Out of the blue I asked my friend Pat, "What would you do if Jesus Christ were here right now?"

"I would fall down and worship him," he said. Hello! None of us were evangelists or even had a serious faith, but look what popped out.

There's a saying *en vino veritas,* which means truth in wine. It suggests that when people drink, they lose the inhibition to bottle up what's going on inside. You heard the longing that was in my heart—to experience Jesus Christ. Pat's response reflected his heart too—he wanted to be a worshiper.

I share this with you because the other side may look appealing, but everyone experiencing the world really wants what you have—a relationship with God. What we had in the world before knowing Christ was a cheap substitute that left us more thirsty for the water that "will become in him a spring of water welling up to eternal life" (John 4:14). I blended with the world, as an unbeliever, by default. It was my only option. When I became a Christian, I realized having fun was not my purpose. Having a relationship with Christ was. Fun was just a pain reliever.

Jesus's point: battle—don't blend.

It does not matter whether you came to know Christ at seven or seventeen. If you know Him—you've got all the fun you need. You don't need the world. In his last meeting with his disciples before going to His death, Jesus wanted to make one thing about the world perfectly clear to His men. He told them:

> If you find the godless world is hating you, remember it got its start hating me. If you lived on the world's terms, the world would love you as one of its own. But since I picked you to live on God's terms and no longer on the world's terms, the world is going to hate you. (John 15:18-19, MSG)

Jesus's point: battle—don't blend.

THE GOAL: CHRISTIAN AND COOL

I entered my fall quarter at UCLA fresh off the salvation train. I was a newbie Christian carrying around hefty baggage from an old life that needed to be dumped. One duffel bag that I schlepped around was my need for acceptance. I was like many of the guys I talk to today—and perhaps like you: not totally secure in God's love and acceptance of me, insecure in myself, and trying real hard to be cool so people would like me.

On the one hand, I had this new faith that I was totally excited about. On the other, I had a sophisticated cool radar constantly monitoring what people around me were doing or what they liked. Once I locked on to a solid reading of their cool, I focused my energies in that direction until I achieved the targeted levels of acceptance or approval.

I joined a fraternity not long after I arrived on the Westwood campus, where I did everything in my power to fit in—except to drink or take drugs. While I avoided those behaviors, I did plenty of others things to fit in: I dressed exactly like everyone else, adopted the fraternity handshake, spouted the lingo, and called my fraternity brothers by their house-given nicknames. I joined my fraternity brothers in the gym, where we sculpted our bodies so that we could attract the Tri Delts. The fact that I developed rock-hard abs to wow young women that I didn't plan to date (since they were non-Christians) doesn't make sense today, but that was what I was thinking back then, because the world said people were impressed by hard bodies.

I fooled a lot of people who thought I was spiritually mature since I could readily quote a passage of Scripture to any pertinent issue.

That's not how God thinks. "Don't you realize that friendship with this world makes you an enemy of God?" the Lord of the universe asks. "I say it again, that if your aim is to enjoy the world, you can't be a friend of God" (James 4:4, NLT).

I wish I had memorized that verse when I was at UCLA. You see, I was a Scripture memory whiz back then because I thought that was a sure-fire way to impress the people in my campus Bible studies. Whenever a heavy topic got raised or someone in the study had a problem, Scripture Man came to the rescue: *"That's a bummer you got cut from the Bruin football team, Rich, but Romans 8:28 tells us, 'We know that in all things God works for the good of those who love him, who have been called according to his purpose.'"*

I fooled a lot of people who thought I was spiritually mature since I could readily quote a passage of Scripture to any pertinent issue. What I did, however, was blend the right behavior with the wrong motive. I studied, memorized, and quoted the Bible to get people to ooh and aah over how spiritual I appeared to be instead of memorizing Scripture for my edification. I blended the worldly value of narcissism (look at me, look at me) with memorizing God's Word.

I look back at that time of my life and shake my head. But I thank God that He demonstrated patience with me until I matured enough to set aside the ways of the world. But what about you? Are you straddling the fence? Or do you hop down on the world side of the fence every now and then so that you can be cool with your friends? If so, here are some ways you become more a friend of the world than a follower of Christ.

You Look at God's Forgiveness like a Credit Card Advance

A couple of years ago, Zach dropped by a high-school youth group with his friend Eric, and the music kept him coming back. He liked what he heard enough to go on a Mexico getaway with the youth group that summer. On a hot, breezy night outside Tijuana, he expressed his desire to know Christ personally for the first time. Zach's decision was validated as he got plugged into a Bible study and started helping in the children's ministry. This was not the same guy.

Then Kurt, Zach's college pastor, heard about a houseboat trip on the Colorado River that Zach took with some of his old party friends. Instead of cracking open Bibles, they cracked open some longnecks and got wasted. Kurt asked Zach to join him at a burger joint to discuss the lost weekend over a double-double and some fries. Zach wasted no time in coming clean. He said that he definitely left his Christianity at the dock that trip.

Zach used God's forgiving heart like a credit card, taking a cash advance on forgiveness.

When Kurt probed a little further about his floating bar weekend, however, Zach pushed back pretty hard. "Listen, I've known some of these guys my whole life. They are my friends," he said. "We were having a good time. That's all."

"Zach, I don't care about them. What about you? Was this something you think was all right to do as a believer?" Kurt pressed.

"God has forgiven me. Why can't you? What's the big deal?"

Zach used God's forgiving heart like a credit card, taking a cash advance on forgiveness. Do you think you can swipe your credit card of forgiveness every time you're in debt with God? If so, you have the wrong attitude of what it takes to be God's young man.

You Compartmentalize Your Behaviors

Steve and Brad are pretty tight—as friends and as accountability partners. A year ago Brad 'fessed up to Steve that he clicked 'n' picked his way through an Internet porn gallery, something he used to do with great regularity before he became a believer.

When Brad became a Christian, things went well for the first six months. He developed friendships with other believers (including Steve), enjoyed his newfound relationship with Christ, and walked through life with the confidence of his salvation. Just one little thing: he still liked looking at naked women on the Net, which he knew did not please the Lord.

That's when he came clean with Steve.

Brad was Super Joe Christian away from his bedroom, but once he sat down in front of the monitor, he stayed seated for a full meal.

Steve, who understood how vulnerable Brad was making himself, had the impression that his friend would tell him about any continuing problems in this area. Brad never told him that his problem with computer porn was worsening, or that he still hadn't installed any blocking software, as he promised.

Meanwhile, Brad put on a happy face, continued to show up at Bible studies and Sunday night church services on his college campus, and made plans for a summer missions trip to Africa. What Brad was doing, however, was compartmentalizing his sexual life away from God.

Brad was Super Joe Christian away from his bedroom, but once he sat down in front of the monitor, he stayed seated for a full meal. While he had made a clear decision to live God's way, Brad had put God on hold in this area of his life. He liked being a Christian when he was with Steve or with other believers, but he also liked the sexual high he received from the sexy images his laptop provided.

I tell young guys all the time to imagine they are married. "Then picture yourself going to your wife after the vows, the wedding, and the honeymoon, and saying: 'Sweetheart, I love you. I love being connected to you in every way. But at least once a week, I would like to sleep with another woman.'"

You say the same thing to God when you tell Him you love Him, want to be with Him, but you still want those evenings free to chase after some cybertail. That's what happens when you compartmentalize a part of your life away from Him.

You Allow Your Feelings to Dominate Decision Making

Many young Christian men are slaves to their feelings. They have trained themselves to say yes to every whim or desire that pops into their heads. They see something cool at an electronics store, and they have to buy it. Someone says they know about a great party in the next town, and off they go. They sit next to a top-heavy girl at lunch, and they have to masturbate that night. The idea of pausing and actually considering the consequences of their decisions is somewhere out there on Pluto. These young men have never disciplined themselves to delay gratification, but they have mastered giving in to impulses. The Bible describes the young men who act on impulse like this: "I saw among the simple, I noticed among the young men, a youth who lacked judgment" (Proverbs 7:7).

The world's goal is to get you to join this fraternity of losers who can't say no.

Those who lack judgment don't think. They act on impulses and feelings, satisfy their appetites, and return to God's graces thinking they will suffer no consequences for their actions. The world's goal is to get you to join this fraternity of losers who can't say no.

The world's values are like poisonous mustard gas to God's young man. Inhaling them into your spiritual life brings about painful and often fatal consequences for your faith. God warns His followers to avoid the toxic nature of this world by guarding against corruption:

> Anyone who sets himself up as "religious" by talking a good game is self-deceived. This kind of religion is hot air and only hot air. Real religion, the kind that passes muster before God the Father, is this: Reach out to the homeless and loveless in their plight, and guard against corruption from the godless world. (James 1:26-27, MSG)

Don't Delay, Obey

The Southern California office of Every Man Ministries is adjacent to the Cleveland National Forest, home to assorted wildlife ranging from mountain lions to rattlesnakes. The creatures I feel most sorry for are the squirrels, since they seem to be easy pickings for hawks that swoop in and snatch them up into the air for a quick snack. The squirrels have also not figured out that standing on paved roads is a great way to end up as road kill.

One morning while I was driving into work, I saw a squirrel standing in the middle of the road. From five hundred yards away, he looked like he was eating something, oblivious to the world. When I was about four hundred yards, he popped his head up and noticed my car. At three hundred yards, he assumed the sprint position. At two hundred yards, he took a few steps away from whatever he was munching on but returned for another bite. At one hundred yards, he did the same thing. At one hundred feet, he was still filling his cheeks right up until the moment I flattened him like a pancake. As Freddie Mercury of the rock band Queen would put it: "Another one bites the dust."

When I got to the office, I scribbled a thought down on a Post-it note that I have never forgotten to this day: *Don't delay the instinct to obey.*

The key to beating the world is prompt obedience to the voice of Christ in your life.

The decision by that squirrel to delay scooting to safety cost him his life. His action reminded me of the same mistakes I have seen so many young men making. They delayed obedience, figuring they still had plenty of time. They intuitively knew danger was lurking, but they feasted—or drank or did drugs—up until that moment when their worlds came crashing down. They were used to taking their cues from the world rather than from God's Word.

The key to beating the world is *prompt obedience* to the voice of Christ in your life. Jesus said to guys, "You know these things—now do them! That is the path of blessing" (John 13:17, NLT).

NO IS A GOOD THING

When it comes right down to it, becoming God's man means learning to say no to the world. When you say no to the world, you are saying yes to God and a closer relationship with Him. When you say yes to the world and its values, you're saying no to a close relationship with God.

Sometimes your buddies want you to say yes before you even have a chance to think. This means you have to figure out what you're going to say *before* you get asked to do something. What will you say when you're out driving with some friends, and your buddy pulls into the parking lot of the strip club? What are you going to do? What will you say? Are you going to battle or blend?

Looking at adult entertainment is saying yes to the world. Downloading porn-blocking software from www.xxxchurch.com is saying yes to Jesus. Not telling anyone about your penchant to surf adult Internet sites is saying yes to the world. Confiding in a buddy and saying he can look at your Internet history anytime is saying yes to Jesus.

When you say yes to the world and its values,
you're saying no to a close relationship with God.

Going off to school and hanging out exclusively with non-Christians is saying yes to the world. Going off to school and seeking out other Christians is saying yes to Jesus.

Checking out ladies in their low-cut jeans with their thong underwear is saying yes to the world. Bouncing your eyes away is saying yes to Jesus.

Trying to get your girlfriend to go to second or third base with you is saying yes to the world. Calling a time-out and setting boundaries is saying yes to Jesus.

Blowing off a buddy when he's in trouble or shares a need with you is saying yes to the world. Taking the time to listen and offer concrete help is saying yes to Jesus.

Loving God means not blending with the world moment by moment. It's seeing the connection between obedience and a closer relationship to Him. It's seeing other needs above your own. It's saying no to indulging yourself with sin. It's being real and honest rather than being a poser. It's caring more about what God thinks and less about what people think.

If you want to be God's young man, then you battle more and blend less with the world around you. You may have to risk losing the world, however, to gain rank as God's young man, according to Jesus: "Whoever wants to save his life will lose it, but whoever loses his life for me will save it. What good is it for a man to gain the whole world, and yet lose or forfeit his very self?" (Luke 9:24-25).

What Jesus means here is that saying no to the world is saying yes to him.

The battle doesn't stop with the world around you, as we'll see in the next chapter. You have got another enemy that is even more elusive, cunning, and subtle in a deadly sort of way. That enemy is camping at your bathroom mirror every morning because he's *you*.

the dark side

Growing up, I took part in powerful battles between the forces of good and evil. In my neighborhood:

- Cowboys fought Indians (certainly not politically correct today).
- G.I. Joe gunned down Hitler's Nazi army.
- Spider-Man arrived at the scene of a crime…just in time.
- Batman gave the Joker, the Riddler, and Catwoman knuckle sandwiches.
- Johnny Quest foiled evil plots.
- Speed Racer destroyed the various "devils" of Daytona.
- David brought down Goliath hard.

I always chose to be the good guy when playing with my brothers and friends. I guess back then, when I was just a little squirt, my mind was free of emotional and spiritual conflicts. I simply wanted to be on the good—and winning—side, where truth and justice always prevailed. With age, however, I discovered a few things:

- The good guy doesn't always win.
- Loyalty can be bought.

- The real world isn't so black and white.
- Real-life heroes make bad choices (think Pete Rose).
- Temptation and conflicts of the soul are real.
- There's a dark side to life.

The "dark side" was made famous by the *Star Wars* trilogies and epitomized by the infamous character Darth Vader. While he and the other *Star Wars* characters are thoroughly the stuff of Hollywood, the saga's core theme reflects a biblical reality, which is this: every man has a dark side, something pulling him to do the wrong thing. This force inside him wages war against his noblest intentions.

I believe this dark side phenomenon makes every man a potential double agent—capable of doing the very worst even when he desires the very best. That's why the Bible makes it clear that the enemy you *really* need to be watching out for is *you*.

For instance, have you ever:

- experienced the dark force making you look like a total dork?
- sensed the other you taking over your mouth and spewing criticism on those you supposedly love?
- heard the voice that says "go for it" when you know you *shouldn't* go for it?
- let your body take control and lead you down the wrong path sexually?
- noticed how your dark desires know when and where to strike so as to create the most damage?

A friend expressed his situation this way: "I realize I don't have what it takes. I can will it, but I can't *do* it. I decide to do good, but I don't really do it; I decide not to do bad, but then I do it anyway. My decisions, such as they are, don't result in actions. Something has gone wrong deep within me and *gets the better of me every time*. It happens so regularly that it's predictable. The moment I decide to do good, sin is there to trip me up."

My friend feels controlled, manipulated, and lied to by the dark side. You can tell by his words that he feels helpless against this powerful inner enemy. Every time he wrestles, he gets pinned. His intentions are good, but his legs get cut out from underneath him whenever he tries to follow through. His dark side is so inbred, so powerful, and so deceptive that he feels like a boxer trying to escape a flurry of right hooks and left uppercuts.

You may know my friend. His name is Paul—the apostle. Nearly two thousand years ago, he put into words how everyone feels when the dark side takes over our lives and our actions.

**Every man has a dark side, something
pulling him to do the wrong thing.**

Paul labeled this our "sin nature," and the previous description is found in Romans 7:18-21 (MSG). It's good to know we are in good company when it comes to this battle because we *all* are at war with our dark side.

The goal of God's young man should be to get the upper hand on this powerful foe. Paul didn't just lament his helplessness—he used the tools God gave him to free himself from living a life of contradiction. He knew that to prevail in this war, intelligence on the enemy was key.

EXPOSING YOUR DARK SIDE

Sharks have always fascinated me. That's why I love it when the Discovery Channel sponsors Shark Week. I hate to admit this, but I find watching unsuspecting seals getting caught off guard by these finned eating machines thoroughly fascinating. The shark's breathtaking acceleration as he swoops in for the kill is both morbid and beautiful at the same time. After witnessing this underwater mayhem unfold, you see with your own eyes that sharks are very good at what God created them to do.

What gets a shark going is the smell of blood. One whiff activates its predatory instincts, senses, and physical responses. We cannot deny that sharks are:

- *Predatory:* they hunt down other animals for the purpose of killing them.
- *Persistent:* they will follow the scent of blood for miles to find their prey.
- *Powerful:* they will leverage their physical assets of sharp teeth and muscle to overwhelm their victims.
- *Precise:* their calculated timing is deadly.
- *Purposely deceptive:* they often attack from underneath their victims to avoid detection.

In your journey with God, I know you feel the dark side lurking like a shark beneath the surface of your life. The dark side inconspicuously swims in the waters of your character, hiding in your thoughts and dropping ideas into your mind that run counter to God's plan. The dark side contradicts what constitutes sin by muddying the waters so you cannot make out the clear instruction of God's Word. Your dark side is patient until it's time to strike.

When I started my freshman year at UCLA, I met some other Christian guys at a coffeehouse on campus for Bible study. Talking about the Lord and learning more about Him got my day off to a great start. From there I usually went off to class or hustled over to Wooden Center (the gym) to play some hoops or lift weights. Life was good.

I certainly felt high on God and high on life, especially the latter after playing a couple of hours of spirited basketball. Then I would walk back to my dorm and cool down before taking a shower. Once I stepped in the shower stall, however, the dark side was waiting for me. More often than not, a good day, a good Bible study, and some good hard-nosed basketball succumbed to a good old-fashioned ambush.

Your dark side is patient until it's time to strike.

What happened is that the dark side loved to take that feeling-good-about-myself mood and spin it into a bad thing. Whenever a lot of good energy would go out, the dark side would seize that moment and whisper, *You deserve a reward,* as I entered the shower stall—right when I was feeling on top of the world. That's when the dark side would exploit that pride and get me to sin.

Go for it dude, he would continue. *Help yourself to a dollop of shampoo... Fantasize about that Delta Gamma who sat next to you in class... It will feel great... No one can see you... You are safe... It will feel good... Imagine her with her top off... You worked hard today... Reward yourself with something good—now.*

Somehow the dark side knew exactly when to strike, knew when I would be most open to the temptation to masturbate, knew the girls on my radar screen, and above all, knew my weakness in this area. More times than I care to admit, I was a goner.

That's because my dark side was in control.

The Mission of the Dark Side

The first step to defeating the dark side is to acknowledge its presence. Jesus exposed it when He warned: "The spirit is willing, but the body is weak" (Mark 14:38).

Your dark side is integrated into your very being, much like a double agent trying to take you down from the *inside*. Your sin nature, or spiritual dark side, is constantly tempting you to do things you shouldn't be doing as God's young man. When you give in to its lies, the resulting lifestyle leads to pain in your relationship with God and His people.

Surveys I've taken with young men reveal that they sense the dark side in their practice of masturbation more than anything else. These guys feel like they are literally sleeping with the enemy and have formed an unholy partnership with the dark side. Virtually all of them say that this partnership brings nothing but grief and guilty feelings. They say that they always feel like failures afterward.

My goal is to make you a wise fish.

Why are these feelings universal? Because the dark side dominates their minds and their wills. Even though they read in the Bible about the freedom they have in Christ, they wonder why they go through life feeling like slaves.

That's because the dark side is a strong opponent. He sends lies your way—lies that he hopes will soften your resolve. He knows how to tempt you because he *is* you—at least the old you. He's got the complete toolbox of falsehoods at his disposal and knows all the lines. The irony is that he always paints your number one temptation as the number one solution!

The Bible says the dark side baits us like bigmouth bass: "Temptation comes from the *lure* of our own evil desires" (James 1:14, NLT). The lure sure looks like the real thing to a fish, but it's actually a barbed steel hook that, once swallowed, ain't coming out till the fish is flopping in the boat and gasping for air.

The difference between us and fish is that we're supposedly smarter. We should recognize lures for what they are, and when one pops in front of our eyes, we should ignore it and swim away from the temptation. If you're not good at spotting the lures the dark side dips in the waters of your life, you will get reeled in, gutted, and consumed. My goal is to make you a wise fish.

You Are a Brother

A friend told Josh that Austin was sleeping with Jessica. Josh immediately called Austin and asked if they could meet. Austin's response: "I've got no time to meet this week." It was obvious to Josh that the issue wasn't about time but about priorities—and God wasn't a priority for Austin. Neither could Josh accept Austin's rationale for his sin, so one time when he spotted his friend on campus, Josh walked right up to him. Austin, who was clearly surprised, knew why his friend wanted to see him, so the first words out of his mouth were, "I am not like you, Josh." This was followed by the next beauty, which was, "And you're not my dad."

> "But God can't go from being a big part of your life to a small part unless you're making space for the wrong things."

Josh just smiled and shook his head—letting Austin feel the stupidity of his little outburst.

"You're right," Josh replied after a long pause. "You are not me, and I am not your dad. But I am your brother—in Christ. I know you don't want to hear that right now because you can't be doing what you're doing with Jessica and still be tight with me or God. I don't care if you push me away, avoid me, or never see me again. But God can't go from being a big part of your life to a small part unless you're making space for the wrong things."

"So now I am into 'wrong things'?" Austin said defensively as he made a quoting gesture with both hands.

"Dude, you got a Bible," Josh fired back. "You know what we covered at that summer retreat with Reggie. You remember what he said about sex. You know, dude. You know."

Austin didn't want to hang. Walking backward, he retreated from Josh, saying, "I'll catch you later, man."

How does a guy go from being committed to Jesus just three months earlier to acting like this? Simple: he believed the dark side (his sin nature) within him, a dark side that said, *She likes you, man. She'll go further if you ask. You will love it. God created men and women to do this exact thing. You don't have to listen to Josh. You're an adult—act like one. Life is short. You may never get this chance again.*

Austin bit down hard on the big lure that his dark side floated out there. No surprise when he got reeled into sexual sin. Little did he know that his relationship with God would go sideways, as well his relationship with Josh. He had subconsciously kept them both at arm's length to make having sex with Jessica less emotionally conflicting. Now the joy is gone from his life, and he's stagnating in a septic tank of lies and false promises. This was the goal of the dark side all along.

The dark side loves remaining anonymous, unnamed, and hidden. The dark side even appreciates that I haven't capitalized his name! On top of that, he doesn't like the fact you're even reading this! His ability to influence your life rests on one thing—staying disguised and keeping his cover.

The dark side doesn't have to influence your actions, though. You can beat him at his own game by committing to a campaign of exposing him constantly. You do that by figuring you have two types of people living in one body, and your Spirit-filled nature has to suppress the dark side—or else.

Will you still feel the dark side's urgings to sin?

Yes.

Will you be tempted to lash out in anger when confronted by others?

Absolutely.

Will you still feel the pull to give in to your sin nature?

Definitely.

But now, at least mentally, you will be more aware of what is happening to you. You won't write off your commitment to Jesus Christ so easily. That's what happens when you know you are in a war: you become more aware of your enemy.

Now that you're better prepared for those lures that the dark side casts your way, you're ready for the next step: becoming vocal to defeat your adversary.

"May I Have Your Attention, Please?"

Remember those obnoxious morning announcements you heard over the classroom intercom, followed by the Pledge of Allegiance? Then there were those *unexpected* announcements—the ones that came in the middle of fourth period. They usually started with some kind of beep, letting everyone know that a subject of school-wide importance was about to follow.

No matter where you were or what you were doing, the world would stop for a few brief seconds, and everyone would get really quiet. The absolute worst thing that could happen for me was to hear the following words over the loudspeaker: "Will Kenny Luck please report to the office? Kenny Luck, please report to the office immediately."

Whenever that happened to me (true confessions time), I stood up and felt like I was wearing nothing more than a jock strap and a wan smile as I trudged out of the classroom toward the school office. I mean, I felt *exposed.*

Fast-forward to a time when I was in my twenties. Ever heard of the *Girls Gone Wild* videos? I hope not. What happened is that I was lounging on the couch late one night, flipping through channels, when I came upon this infomercial about girls taking off their clothes. *Girls gone wild*, right? Right at that moment, the dark side popped a lure into my head that said: *Can you believe that, dude? Look at her. She's hot. Check that pair out. And guess what? Nobody'll know that you're here all by yourself.*

For the dark side it was not

business as usual anymore.

But something very different happened that evening—I didn't bite down on the lure! I had been talking about this exact same stuff with some other guys, and we said that when something like this happened, we should get mad at the dark side. That night I blurted *out loud,* "That's a lie!" Then I hit the off button on my remote, and that was it.

Game over. No more *Girls Gone Wild* tempting me. I'm telling you that doing that was a huge step in my journey toward becoming God's young man.

For the dark side it was not business as usual anymore. He had been his normal lying self, but that night I exposed his lies and embarrassed him. It's like I was just waiting to pull the trigger on his antics. That's why I zapped the *Girls Gone Wild* infomercial into oblivion.

That taste of victory was sweet. Since then, I've learned that one of the biggest things the dark side hates is being exposed *verbally.* Yep— sounds silly, but you've got to verbally expose and confront him. You do this by calling on the carpet the tempting thoughts the dark side puts in your head.

You might be thinking: *Is Kenny telling me to talk to myself when I'm tempted?* You got it! That's exactly what I'm saying. When you express a thought verbally to the dark side, it stops being a mental negotiation; you change the playing field completely. What you're doing is *confronting* the dark side when you give voice to thoughts such as:

- *That's definitely not God's plan.*
- *Explain this one to Jesus.*
- *This will not help a thing.*

When your dark side wants you to bite into a big honking sin, you have to call it what is—an attempt to deceive you. The longer you linger around a lure, the more likely you'll bite. That can be fatal to you. God's young man operates by one rule when it comes to lures: don't let them dangle—get out of there. "Kisses from an enemy do you in," God says (Proverbs 27:6, MSG).

When your dark side wants you to bite into a big honking sin, you have to call it what is—an attempt to deceive you.

After you call the dark side on the carpet, you call out the Scripture to keep him away. You gotta prepare for temptation by learning to identify when it happens, quoting the Scripture that deals with it (one that you've committed to memory), and speak it out loud the moment your dark side tempts you. Psalm 37:30-31 says, "The mouth of the righteous man utters wisdom, and his tongue speaks what is just. The law of God is in his heart; his feet do not slip." If we can talk ourselves into doing the wrong thing, we can certainly talk ourselves into doing the right thing! Spiritually, this means loading the magazine of your heart with God's Word and pulling the trigger with your mouth by speaking it into your situation.

Here are some pertinent examples:

- When Jenny Zahati (a.k.a. "Jenny's a hottie" for you slower readers) is flaunting her chest, and you want to have a mental happy meal, remind yourself that your duty is to "love God…with all your mind" (Matthew 22:37).
- For you guys who struggle with masturbation, we've all been there, right? If you step into the shower and you sense the battle, call out a Scripture like, "So I say, live by the Spirit, and you will not gratify the desires of the sinful nature" (Galatians 5:16).
- When your mom or dad asks for your help with something around the house, remember Jesus's words in Matthew 20:28: "The Son of Man did not come to be served, but to serve."

NO MERCY

After you expose the dark side by verbally calling out the sin and the Scripture, you pin down the sin by *speaking to God* and asking for His support and help. It's like a cop who wants to handcuff a bad guy, and he asks his partner to come over and hold the guy down so that he can finish cuffing him.

The dark side loves it when you lose your poise, but you don't ever have to panic if you know the Lord.

What rocks a young guy's world is not knowing what to do when the shot clock on his temptation ticker is winding down. Panic often sets in. The dark side loves it when you lose your poise, but you don't *ever* have to panic if you know the Lord. God says simply, "Talk to me." Don't be fancy— send up a signal flare to God:

- When you are tempted sexually, pray: *Son of Man, have mercy on me.*
- When you are in the middle of a heated discussion and don't know what you'll say next, pray in your mind: *Lord Jesus, have mercy on me.*
- When you're feeling lonely and depressed, pray: *Lord Jesus, come to me* or *Lord Jesus, help me.*

The point is this: "GOD's there, listening for all who pray, for all who pray and mean it. He does what's best for those who fear him—hears them call out, and saves them" (Psalm 145:18-19, MSG).

God gave us our mouths to be used as weapons to defeat the dark side. When we begin to use them for this purpose, Darth Vader doesn't stand a chance.

hot gates

In 480 BC, King Xerxes of Persia led his army of 150,000 fighting men and 600 ships across the Aegean Sea to conquer Greece. When the Greeks caught wind of his plans, a general named Themosticles (pronounced Them-ost-i-klees) designed a plan to stop the invasion at the narrow mountain pass of Thermopylae (pronounced Therm-op-oh-lee). Also known as the Hot Gates, Thermopylae guarded the entrance to central Greece.

Themosticles' reason for making a stand at Thermopylae lay in its terrain—a narrow mountain pass about sixty feet wide. The mighty Persian army had to funnel through that narrow gap, which presented the much smaller Greek forces a decidedly home-court advantage. So when the masses of Persian soldiers approached the Thermopylae pass, the Greeks were waiting to pounce on them.

The defense of Greece at the Hot Gates was led by the proud and menacing King Leonidas, who hailed from the Greek city of Sparta, home of the feared Spartan army. When Leonidas arrived at Thermopylae, Xerxes sent him a message: *Lay down your arms or see your vaunted army destroyed.*

The Persian king was sure the Greeks would not have the stomach to take him on after seeing the ranks of his impressive army.

Leonidas's terse reply: "Come and take them," which was the BC equivalent of saying, "Bring it on, dude!" Obviously, Xerxes was not acquainted with the Spartan never-say-die mentality.

From the age of seven—the age when Spartan boys began training for war—the Spartan creed had been drilled into Leonidas's head: conquer or die. In other words, the Greek king wasn't about to let Xerxes' forces march into Athens unopposed. The Persian invaders would have to pass through the Hot Gates of Thermopylae and pay the toll in blood.

I've seen how important it is to bottle up the Enemy at various hot gates—or what I call spiritual strongholds—so that larger battles don't have to be fought.

Xerxes was furious with Leonidas's reply. The Persian king ordered his generals to let it rip: flood the pass with as many troops as they could and take down that arrogant Spartan king and general. This was personal.

What Xerxes did was send a majority of his men to their early deaths. It turns out that Themosticles was right: the Hot Gates was the perfect place for the vastly outnumbered Greeks to resist the huge Persian army. For three days 10,000 Greek soldiers held 150,000 Persians at bay—until they were betrayed! A Greek traitor showed Xerxes a roundabout way over the mountain, which changed the battle completely.

A division of the Persian forces swept around and attacked the Greek forces from the rear. Leonidas responded by withdrawing all of his troops to foil the surprise attack—except for his personal guard of three hundred elite Spartan soldiers. When the battle reached Leonidas, the Greek general was one of the first killed, but his soldiers surrounded his body and fought to the last man. Their courageous stand allowed the rest of the Greek army to make an organized retreat to southern Greece, where they lived to fight another day. And it also inspired the proud Greek nation to carry on the fight with equal courage.

The significance of the Spartan stand at the Hot Gates of Thermopylae is taught at nearly every war college. While three hundred Spartans fought off thousands, the Greeks evacuated Athens and relocated their people, their army, and their navy to make a last stand at the island city of Salamis. This time around, better positioned and prepared, the Greeks defeated the Persians at the battle of Salamis. Military historians agree that if the small band of Greeks had not made its courageous stand at Thermopylae, the outcome would have been far different. Defending such a seemingly small space saved an entire nation.

As I work with younger men, I've seen how important it is to bottle up the Enemy at various hot gates—or what I call spiritual strongholds—so that larger battles don't have to be fought. How you defend those hot gates determines how the next ten to fifteen years will play out. The Bible warns you to position your forces "so that when the day of evil comes, you may be able to stand your ground, and after you have done everything, to stand" (Ephesians 6:13).

We'll take a look at how you best position those forces in the rest of this chapter.

EITHER RESISTING OR YIELDING

Kevin is on fire for God, or so people say. From the outside, you'd have to admit there's a lot of evidence to support the claim. He's made all the right connections in the campus ministry office and serves on the spiritual life committee at college. Kevin faithfully leads a Bible study for underclassmen and organizes the chancellor's prayer breakfast for faculty and student leaders. Close friends say that Kevin is as solid as the marble statue of the college's founder in front of the student union. The reality is that Kevin is about as solid as a papier-mâché statue standing in the rain.

Kevin fed freely but inconspicuously when feasting his eyes on the curvy bodies of his sisters in Christ.

When Kevin was a freshman taking a computer science class, he partnered on a project with Carl. Both guys stumbled across a favorite left on one of the school computers, which opened a sexual Pandora's box. After sipping porn for a couple of months, off and on, Kevin began mentally slobbering over the pretty girls he saw on campus. The deceitful voice of the Enemy suggested that this was anonymous and safer. Kevin fed freely but inconspicuously when feasting his eyes on the curvy bodies of his sisters in Christ. Anyone wearing a tight-fitting top, tighter-fitting jeans, and open cleavage received the "missile lock" treatment from the eyes behind the sunglasses.

Kevin never imagined anyone catching on to him, but she did. She was older, not a Christian, and not a student at the university. She was a flirtatious waitress at a nearby diner, and when she served him his pigs-in-a-blanket combo that morning, he knew he was smitten by her winsome smile and unbelievable build. When he finally mustered the courage to ask her out, he didn't think she would say yes, but she did. He never expected her to invite him over to her apartment, but she did. He never imagined such a "sweet" girl so willing to offer herself on her bed, but she did.

Kevin never thought that he would be so unprepared to resist. What he had done was dismiss his defensive forces at the hot gates because he thought he could handle whatever the Enemy would throw at him. The defeat has been costly; ten years later, Kevin's still dealing with the fallout from his tragic choices.

It Can Happen to You

Satan loves to thread the needle and slip through a slim pass to gain a foothold in your life. Give him credit where it's due: he knows where the openings are. The Enemy is known for his schemes, which means he studies game film on you just like a Division I coach will look for holes in his opponents' defenses. The Enemy is always doing reconnaissance on you. If given half a chance to stroll into your life, he can exploit a hot gate in no time and quickly overwhelm you. Kevin's lusting may have seemed like small stuff in the beginning, but it was the opening the Enemy needed. Once his initial thrust was not rebuffed, he ordered a full-scale attack on Kevin when the waitress came into his life. You know the outcome.

A hot gate that Satan might look for is one in which he can overwhelm your thoughts first, knowing that behavior will follow. The Schemer knows that if he can get a guy like you *not* to mount a vigorous defense at the hot gate of sexual fantasizing, he can take over a young man's life rather boldly. Once the first deception is not resisted, he pours more lies into your mind, which softens you up for his planned invasion.

Each mental happy meal he indulged in brought the Enemy's victory closer and closer.

If the Enemy encounters no resistance at the thought level, he puts a lot of energy toward the next hot gate by solidifying his position with a physical bond. In Kevin's case, the physical process of visually feeding on his sisters in Christ had a direct consequence; eventually it led him to an emotional and physical attachment with someone else. Each mental assault takes its toll and invests Satan with more power so that after a while temptation will *feel* irresistible. To take a cue from Kevin's story: each mental happy meal he indulged in brought the Enemy's victory closer and closer.

Hot gates must be places where you resist and make your stand—not yield. For instance:

- Dave rationalizes his drinking as his Christian "liberty." *Yielding.*
- Chris keeps copies of *Maxim* in his apartment bathroom. *Yielding.*
- Tim says that oral sex with his girlfriend is, technically, not having sex. *Yielding.*
- Brian says he doesn't need to download accountability software even though he has admittedly sipped porn on the Internet. *Yielding.*
- Sean totally plagiarized major sections of his sociology paper so that his sociology teacher would give him an A. *Yielding.*
- Scott maintains that it's fine to privately counsel high-school-age girls alone as a college intern at the church. *Yielding.*
- Matt keeps missing his accountability group because he doesn't like being asked hard questions about Sandy and him. *Yielding.*
- Jeff spins the Mazatlan spring break trip by telling others that it's fully chaperoned when it's not at all. *Yielding.*
- Darren doesn't see what a big deal it was to invite the guys over for an *American Pie* marathon movie night. *Yielding.*
- John is bagging on a summer missions trip because he sees it as a way to hook up with Lindsey this summer. *Yielding.*
- Robbie's personal theology allows for a personal Savior but not the devil. *Yielding.*

ARE YOU SERIOUS ABOUT THE DEVIL?

Many young men I meet have not squared their lifestyle with a major spiritual reality: the literal existence of Satan—the devil. They have swallowed his greatest lie—that he doesn't exist or that he isn't someone to waste your time worrying about. Since most pay him no heed, he's never enjoyed more success with younger men. After all, why defend a hot gate if there is no real Adversary? Why position, prepare, or persistently resist him when you believe there's no Tempter?

Young men who think this way have no stomach to fight because they've gone soft spiritually and are more concerned with blending in with their friends. Jesus did not allow this attitude among His followers. In fact, He laid it out in plain language when it came to spiritual warfare. He identified Satan as "the father of lies" whose exclusive mission *right now* is to "steal and kill and destroy." Look up the passages in John 8:44 and 10:10. Jesus's own words to His men regarding the devil's aim is unequivocal and can be counted on as good intel on the Adversary.

Willingly giving ground to the devil is stupid, because once territory is surrendered, it takes three times the effort and energy to win it back.

Not defending a hot gate from Satan's rush means that you are accepting a lie or participating in an activity you *know* is not God-approved. Willingly giving ground to the devil is stupid, because once territory is surrendered, it takes three times the effort and energy to win it back. No, it's best to beat him at the gate and never let him develop any momentum against you.

Remember the Spartan battle cry? *Conquer or die.* That pretty much summed up their do-or-die commitment. What about you on the issue of sexual self-control? What's your war cry? This is your Thermopylae, you know. The world, the flesh, and the devil act as arrogantly as Xerxes ever did. They've slaughtered so many millions throughout history that they can't imagine that you'd ever fight back.

That's why you should expect Satan to send wave after wave of tempting thoughts and situations your way during the next several years. But like Leonidas and his men, your ironclad commitment to a strong resistance *now* will secure the best possible future for you with God, with your future wife, and with your future children.

DEFENDING A HOT GATE

You cannot defend a hot gate without God's Holy Spirit. He has the power and direction to work with you in the area of self-control against rogue thoughts and behaviors. (We will dive deeply into this partnership in chapter 13). But you can start this process right now by cooperating with God's Spirit in four specific ways:

1. *Turn the radar on.* The Bible says, "Be self-controlled and alert. Your enemy the devil prowls around like a roaring lion looking for someone to devour," according to 1 Peter 5:8. If you've ever seen zebras on *Animal Planet* drinking water from a pond, you'll notice that while their muzzles may be dipped in the water, their eyes are glued to the bushes. They know a lion could suddenly pounce on them from out of nowhere, so they never let their guard down. You need to cast a wary eye toward what the Enemy could do to you—especially when he's camouflaging himself.

2. *Turn to God and ask for strength.* You must talk to God directly about your hot gate issue. The Bible guarantees a response from Him if you faithfully ask for His help in your personal spiritual battles: "He gives us more and more strength to stand against such evil desires," says James 4:6 (NLT). The bottom line—wage war in prayer. Prayer is like mortars and suppression fire. As in any conflict, two guns are better than one, so meet and pray with a friend.

3. *Turn to your fellow soldiers.* Some of the best advice ever given to a young God's man was this: "Flee the evil desires of youth, and pursue righteousness, faith, love and peace, along *with those who call on the Lord out of a pure heart*" (2 Timothy 2:22). See what's going on here? You say no to temptation by saying yes to another brother in Christ who's heading the same way.

4. *Resist.* Here's God's promise to those in the resistance movement: "Resist the Devil, and he will flee from you" (James 4:7, NLT). This means putting your feet, your words—and whatever action is necessary—into motion as soon as you sense the Enemy's presence. These actions allow God a powerful opportunity to enter the situation.

Here are some things you can do when temptation comes your way:

• You leave.
• You dial the cell number of a friend and check in.
• You call out Scripture.
• You throw magazines like *FHM* into the trash.
• You look the other way.
• You tell your Bible study about your "close encounter of a sexual kind."

Tony did what few guys have the guts to do. He chose to tell his Bible study about his struggle with lust and masturbation. And Tony was a stud!

He was known as the guy who passionately worshiped, who'd witnessed to the guys on his high-school soccer team, and who had told others that he was committed to sexual self-control.

When Tony looked up, there were trails

of tears on his face. You could hear a pin drop.

"My life is not clean right now."

Here's what happened. He was hanging out with some of the guys in his Bible study, and the discussion turned to a leadership conference he had attended. It seemed that the main speaker talked about spiritual integrity and the importance of being undivided between what you believe and how you really live your life. An important component of spiritual integrity was maintaining accountability with those you trust, said the speaker.

When he saw his buddies the next time at their Bible study, Tony eased into the discussion by quoting from 2 Timothy: "If you keep yourself pure, you will be a utensil God can use for his purpose. Your life will be clean, and you will be ready for the Master to use you for every good work" (2:21, NLT).

There was a long pause when he finished. He looked down at his shoes for a long moment, and everyone saw him breathe deep and gain his composure. When Tony looked up, there were trails of tears on his face. You could hear a pin drop. "My life is not clean right now," he said. "I read this verse because I want to be someone God can use."

Tony explained the conviction he felt at the leadership conference while at the same time crossing the line with his eyes on the Net—and in his dating relationship with Kathy. He announced to the group that starting this day he would retake his lost ground. "Pray for me," he asked his buddies. "Pray that Kathy and I will install the right boundaries on our relationship."

No one had *ever* seen that much guts. Their group was never the same after that burst of candor. Tony's honesty raised the bar for the whole group. The group decided that morning to break into pairs for accountability and make a group covenant for sexual integrity.

Just like the Greeks' valiant stand at Thermopylae, the Enemy won a skirmish but lost the war when Tony repented and resisted his temptations with courage. He inspired his band of brothers to fight back against Satan's devious suggestions.

Keep in mind that there's more at stake than what you can see right now.

The most courageous act a young man can take is *deciding to fight*. With Tony and his friends, he never knew that one act of spiritual courage would impact so many. Very often one act of obedience to God is the margin of victory or defeat for guys needing a push to go forward. We will never know the overall significance of our stand until *after* we make our personal stand to defend the hot gate of sexual temptation, just as the Greeks couldn't immediately grasp the significance of the Spartan stand at Thermopylae.

You must adopt the war cry and fight. You may not know all the consequences of your battle now, but you can be sure that those in your future will benefit from your godly courage—your future wife, the children you will have, and other fellow soldiers. Keep in mind that there's more at stake than what you can see right now.

Don't yield ground to the Enemy. Hang in there and do what's right, which is a form of obedience, a topic that will be the focus of our next chapter.

are you picking and choosing?

On June 6, 1944, the U.S. Army and the Allies stormed the beaches of Normandy, France. If you've ever watched the History Channel or thumbed through history books detailing what happened on "the longest day," then you have an idea of how massive this military invasion was. Operation Overlord was the largest air, land, and sea assault in world history—the biggest one-day invasion in the annals of warfare.

I found my heart racing and my body getting supertense when I viewed *Saving Private Ryan,* Steven Spielberg's epic depiction of D-day and the subsequent battles in the Normandy area. I agree with reviewers who declare that *Saving Private Ryan* is the most realistic war film ever made. The film is rated R for its realism—not raunch. Although certain scenes are drenched in blood and the violence is intense, I recommend that all young men see it sometime, because *Saving Private Ryan* is the real deal—not some Xbox shooter game.

One hundred fifty thousand *real* men belonging to the Allied forces

(U.S., British, and Canadian) crossed the choppy English Channel and were dropped into hell on earth. German pillboxes manned by machine-gunners on the bluffs overlooking Utah, Omaha, Gold, Juno, and Sword beaches picked off thousands of eighteen- and nineteen-year-old soldiers. If your regiment was in the first assault wave, you had about a fifty-fifty chance of surviving the first hour. That's why guys getting ready to land were puking, praying, and preparing for the worst.

"There is a way that seems right to a man, but in the end it leads to death."

Put yourself in that Higgins boat with thirty other men as you approached the beachhead. Look around you. Fifteen of your buddies will end up being buried under white crosses and Stars of David in French soil. As your landing craft gets closer, German cannons open up, and the sounds of war cause the adrenaline in your body to skyrocket. Suddenly your boat ramp drops, and you scramble into a hail of gunfire. The water was supposed to be three or four feet deep, but you step into a crater hole, and now you're scrambling to get your helmeted head above the surface. You manage to gain a breath, but it's tough sledding since you're weighed down by sixty pounds of gear on your back. You strain with everything you've got for the shore, but exploding mortar rounds impede your progress. After ten minutes of slogging, you throw yourself on the beach—exhausted, confused, bewildered, and scared out of your wits because the American soldier lying next to you lost his head—

Then you see him—the beach master. He's the guy they told you to find when you made it to the beach. He's a hard-boiled navy guy whose job is to guide you along a path cleared of mines so that you make it to the sand berm and cover. He's waving and pointing you in a certain direction.

"Follow those guys," he screams above the din. You look to see some buddies moving in that direction. It's your first glimmer of hope. *Thank God for the beach master,* you think. They told you in training to listen to these guys if you wanted to live. *Follow his direction.*

Fifteen minutes have passed since the war started for you. You have jumped, swam, crawled, and scampered two hundred yards to cover. Half your unit is dead, but the beach master is pointing you toward safe cover, where you can join up with a group of soldiers from the Twenty-ninth.

You follow the beach master's directions to a T and meet up with your new buddies. Your new platoon leader gathers you all together to give you instructions. That's when you notice that he's holding a helmet filled with some guy's brains! His steely eyes glare at every man standing around him in a semicircle. "This is what happens to guys who don't listen to the beach master," he growls. "This whole area is mined. Go where you are told."

He didn't need to say anything more. Apparently the guy whose brains now filling the helmet thought he could break rank and pick his own route—choose his own path to safety. He had been told what to do, but he simply failed to heed the instructions he was given. What that soldier did reminds me of a warning in the Bible: "There is a way that seems right to a man, but in the end it leads to death" (Proverbs 14:12).

SELECTIVE OBEDIENCE KILLS

The story of the soldier who died by not listening to the beach master is true. The lesson is so profound that it nails about 95 percent of the struggles I encounter with younger men: *selective obedience to God's instructions.* What does selective obedience look like?

- You hear what *you* want to hear.
- You reject or discount what's not in sync with *your* personal desires.

- You replace God's clear instructions with *your* own plan.
- You act out *your* own plan.

Sometimes God's commands don't fit in with your "flow," your image, your friendships, or the lifestyles that go with them. So you set aside His directions because you want to be free to do what you want rather than what God wants. But just like the soldier who didn't listen to the beach master, your freedom will be short-lived. I guarantee you that the negative consequences of your decisions will catch up with you.

When they selectively obeyed God's instructions, they were taken to the woodshed for a good old-fashioned butt whipping.

All men I know have felt the punishing blows that selective obedience brings. It doesn't matter who you are or what you want to become. The Bible is full of stories about great kings who could not bring themselves to complete obedience. On several occasions, good kings could not resist the impulse to fudge on God's clear instructions regarding the worship of pagan gods among His people. Allowing their subjects to build pagan shrines or "high places" among the people of God was the equivalent of erecting a statue of Osama Bin Laden in downtown Manhattan.

In God's eyes, the building of shrines to pagan gods was totally offensive, and every king *knew* this. So while they might not be good kings, God judged their reigns on how they dealt with the issue of idolatry. Then you had situations with kings who would destroy the idols and then felt free to sin in other ways. These kings were timeless poster children for every man who thinks that God has no problem with selective obedience. This is how some of these men are remembered in the pages of Scripture. Pay attention to my italics, which are added for emphasis:

The LORD said to Jehu, "Because you have done well in accomplish-
ing what is right in my eyes…your descendants will sit on the throne
of Israel to the fourth generation." *Yet* Jehu was not careful to keep the
law of the LORD, the God of Israel, with *all* his heart. *He did not turn
away from the sins of Jeroboam,* which he had caused Israel to commit.

In those days the LORD began to reduce the size of Israel.
(2 Kings 10:30-32)

Joash did what was right in the eyes of the LORD all the years
Jehoiada the priest had instructed him. *The high places, however,
were not removed;* the people continued to offer sacrifices and burn
incense there. (2 Kings 12:2-3)

He [Azariah] did what was right in the eyes of the LORD, just as his
father Amaziah had done. *The high places, however, were not removed;*
the people continued to offer sacrifices and burn incense there.

The LORD afflicted the king with leprosy until the day he died.
(2 Kings 15:3-5)

You get the picture. These were good guys—God's men—doing lots of
good things, except for going all the way with their obedience. When they
selectively obeyed God's instructions, they were taken to the woodshed for
a good old-fashioned butt whipping. God got fed up with these guys, so
He shut them down and exiled them to countries who loved evil practices
more than they loved God. God's assessment of these guys and the people
who followed their lead went like this:

They followed worthless idols and themselves became worthless.
They imitated the nations around them although the LORD had

ordered them, "Do not do as they do," and *they did the things the
LORD had forbidden them to do....* So the LORD was very angry with
Israel and removed them from his presence. (2 Kings 17:15,18)

All could see that God's instruction was *very clear.* But these men obeyed
God selectively, and their stupid pride cost them and many others their
freedom. On a more personal level, God was totally hurt.

THE PICKING AND CHOOSING SYNDROME

Let's look at the case histories of three guys your age who are following in
the footsteps of those kings from yesteryear.

Case 1: Silence of the Lamb

Brad was comfortable being a Christian and comfortable with the ladies. He
was smart, not very athletic, but blessed with his mom's searing blue eyes
and his dad's six-foot-three-inch DNA. At nineteen, who could ask for
more—he was a dating machine.

**Her magnetism made Brad skip over one
small thing—she was not a believer.**

When Brad met Jennifer, he was immediately attracted to her cover-
girl looks and impressive build. She was not, let's say, shy about putting her
God-given beauty on display, and it seems every outfit she wore was designed to get a rise. Her magnetism made Brad skip over one small thing—
she was not a believer. He did think about it but treated those thoughts like
smelly socks—he threw them into his mental hamper and quickly forgot
about them.

Each Saturday night when they were together, a thought would cross Brad's mind: *Talk to her about your faith.* He also felt like he needed to let her know about his convictions regarding sex. He never opened his mouth. Meanwhile, as they kept getting closer, Brad continued to clam up about God.

Case 2: The Fangs Come Out

Jamal loves his band. They play regular gigs at churches in Los Angeles. He is the front man—singing lead vocals, getting the crowd into the concerts, and ministering to the audience. He knows his Bible and dedicates his Sundays to volunteering in a ministry to kids.

Jamal, who told me that his life goal is to serve the Lord and do His will, cannot talk to his parents without what he calls his "fangs" coming out. His parents trigger something inside him for some reason. Even though he is respectful to every other adult in his life, he is defiant and disrespectful to his own mom and dad. "Same ol', same ol'," he says, like it's just another day and his behavior toward them is normal.

Case 3: Faking It and Paying the Price

Mike is an impressive young guy. He also knows how to make an impression on his parents. Listening to his folks talk about him suggests a spiritual maturity way beyond his years. As a dad, I only hope that my son would be as centered in Christ.

One morning in Starbucks I ran into Mike's mentor, a guy named Phil, while picking up my Frappuccino. Phil and I share Mike's father as a mutual friend, so it was natural to talk about Mike. That's when Phil's face clouded over, and he started shaking his head. He looked at me and said, "Paul and Donna [Mike's parents] have absolutely no idea what he's up to." Phil went on to detail several conversations he had with Mike about his physical relationship with Laura and how he was putting himself out there as a guy working out his faith even though he was sleeping with his girlfriend.

———

Brad is silent about his faith when he should be opening his mouth. Jamal's mouth goes from bringing good news to spewing hot lava on his parents. Mike is a joke—believing he could simultaneously host the Holy Spirit while getting naked with his girlfriend. Each young man is called to a higher standard, but in each case God's clear instruction was set aside like dirty laundry and rationalized away. Each young man picked and chose when and where he would be God's young man and when and where he would don that mask. Each young man bent God's Word and muted the Holy Spirit to follow his feelings.

They practice what I call 80/20 obedience, and the problem is that the 20 percent will always take you down. Brad, Jamal, and Mike are exercising freedoms in their faith without checking with God or His Word. They are inviting a trip to the woodshed, and it won't be pretty:

Every word of God proves true. He defends all who come to him for protection. *Do not add to his words,* or he may rebuke you, and you will be found a liar. (Proverbs 30:5-6, NLT)

The veteran Paul told the young God's man Timothy about guys who serve their own interests and who "love pleasure rather than God. They will act as if they are religious, but they will reject the power that could make them godly. You must stay away from people like that" (2 Timothy 3:4-5, NLT).

The bottom line about 80/20 guys is that their love for God is an act. They consistently put the 20 percent over their love for God. They are like the 80/20 kings of the Old Testament who allowed the high places to exist under their watch when God had said they had to go. Add it all up, and it's easy to make the argument that your 20 percent is an idol as well.

They practice what I call 80/20 obedience,
and the problem is that the 20 percent
will always take you down.

Young men know what God says about sex outside of marriage, but they keep unzipping their pants anyway. Sons know when they are ripping apart their mom and dad's values only because *they* want to sin—not because their values are wrong. Guys know when they are acting cool to get the acceptance of their friends or their girlfriends because, deep down, they know what separates them from other friends is *not* acting like them. They are being cliquey and know that Jesus would never go for it.

When a young man who has a strong relationship with God is tempted to become an 80/20 guy, *he does what God would have him to do.* Over. Done. No-brainer. He doesn't back off from his 100 percent commitment.

That's the goal, men. You practice choosing God and not adding your spin to His Word, even if it is less comfortable or costs you a relationship. You do this because you know that more than the obedience, God loves to reward your trusting His way with huge blessings.

PAST CARING

Let me tell you about a guy who knows how to avoid selective obedience. Nelson is a soccer guy—a very successful player and now the coach of female high-school players. Nelson tells me that his biggest struggle as a single young man is masturbation and lusting after being around good-looking babes on the soccer field. It's quite okay to struggle. It's not a sin to be tempted. But it is a sin to RSVP to the temptation and mentally taste the delectable hors d'oeuvres. Nelson knows this, which is why he's seeking ways to tip the scales in his favor by loving God with all his mind and strength.

"Almost all of the soccer coaches I know are single guys, which makes it hard to be God's man," he told me. "You travel to tournaments in Las Vegas and other cities. It gets lonely because they're girls and you're a guy, and when you get lonely, it usually spells trouble. For many coaches, these trips offer good opportunities to explore the wild side."

Nelson said what really helped him was opening up to a father of one of his players. "This dad is a Christian man," he said. "I respect and admire him because I see how he lives out his faith at these tournaments. He's not down in the bar tying one on with some of the other parents. Instead, he's hanging out with the kids at the pool or watching a DVD with his daughter and family in the hotel room. Anyway, I asked him to keep an eye out for me on the road, you know, adopt me as a son when we travel so that I don't get myself into trouble. I didn't want to do this, but knowing me, I had no choice if I wanted to feel right before God. I had to give someone else permission to be in my life to help me avoid sin."

Nelson does not pick and choose
which parts of God's commands
he will adopt and incorporate into his life.

By looking for ways to put himself out there as a follower of Christ, it makes things a little easier, in a strange sort of way. He talks about his faith, sees the relationships he has with players and families as a ministry, and tries to teach soccer and good values to the girls. Acting on his faith this way has propelled a young man into the adventure of the battle. He's not shy about having his Bible open around his players, though he never pushes his faith on them or makes anybody pray before games.

I know that Nelson's partnership with the Holy Spirit—the voice inside that tells him to do what God wants—and his steady diet of God's Word keep him away from developing 80/20 habits with his faith. Nelson does not pick and choose which parts of God's commands he will adopt and incorporate into his life. If he's not sure what to do, he checks the Word first, talks to the soccer dad who's mentoring him, or calls me. In other words, Nelson has put himself out there on purpose, and by going for it, he's freer.

No One like Him

Our ancient spiritual brothers who passed the test of obedience all had their spiritual gut check. They had to face the discomfort that full obedience brings—much like test pilot Chuck Yeager enduring incredible noise and violent shaking before hitting the calm air of mach 1. Our ancient spiritual brothers fought their fear of what others would think. They battled weaknesses in their own character and faith. Some battled huge spiritual opposition. King Hezekiah of the Old Testament overcame them all at the ripe old age of twenty-five! Check this out:

> [Hezekiah] did what was right in the eyes of the LORD, just as his father David had done. *He removed the high places,* smashed the sacred stones and cut down the Asherah poles....
>
> Hezekiah trusted in the LORD, the God of Israel. There was no one like him among all the kings of Judah, either before him or after him. He held fast to the LORD and did not cease to follow

him; he kept the commands the LORD had given to Moses. And the LORD was with him; he was successful in whatever he undertook." (2 Kings 18:3-7)

Like I said, Hezekiah was a young man. He saw how his father, King Ahaz, and the other kings handled things. He took notes on his palm (leaf) pilot. He learned from their mistakes and was determined not to imitate their style of selective obedience. When you read how the Bible describes this God's young man, several things should pop out:

- His focus was not on what people thought.
- He went after the most troubling area of disobedience (idols).
- He was praying and talking to God ("trusted the Lord").
- He was not budging ("holding fast").
- He did not selectively obey ("kept all the commands").
- His commitment made him stand out ("no one like him").

When he risked wholehearted obedience, God sent a tidal wave of blessing his way.

Hezekiah stormed the hill and took it. When other kings backed off, Hezekiah didn't hesitate. When the rumor mill kicked in, he looked toward the face of his heavenly Father, where he saw a thumbs-up sign. When others questioned God's Word, he risked taking every word seriously. When he felt isolated, he chatted up God. When he put himself out there, he got noticed for all the right reasons—by God and by man. When he risked wholehearted obedience, God sent a tidal wave of blessing his way.

In this way King Hezekiah was most like the King of kings:

Christ's *one act of righteousness* makes all people right in God's sight and gives them life. Because *one person disobeyed* God, many people became sinners. But because one *other person obeyed* God, many people will be made right in God's sight. (Romans 5:18-19, NLT)

Neither Hezekiah nor Jesus found obeying God a cakewalk, but what an awesome example of men who went for it. They went for it not because they psyched themselves up or were pressured, but because they humbled themselves before God.

This quality, lacking in so many young men, is the subject of the next chapter.

are you Gumby or Superman?

When I was growing up, cartoons and shows for kids were very different from what they are today. For action, I liked watching *Super Friends*. This was my dream team of action heroes: you had Aquaman, Batman and Robin, Flash, Wonder Woman, the Wonder Twins, and ten other characters who each possessed unique superpowers that they employed against the bad guys. My favorite Super Friend was the captain of this indestructible outfit—Superman.

Superman could do just about anything—like blowing air across the room and freezing a villain in his tracks. Everything bounced off my super-hero, who had titanium skin. No matter what Lex Luthor or Braniac threw at him, Superman survived every bullet, every car crash, every assault, every missile, and even every stray meteor from outer space. Nothing was a match for his hard body. Superman was unbendable, unbreakable, and impene-trable. Objects that hit the Man of Steel disintegrated, exploded, bent, or slumped while his six-pack abs, ballet tights, and wavy black mane remained unruffled. Whenever I played with the kids in the neighborhood, I chose to be Superman because the Man of Steel *always* came out of his battles unhurt and unchanged.

On the other end of my TV Land spectrum were the educational shows. There was a guy in a red sweater named Mr. Rogers and his make-believe friends, King Friday and Lady Aberlin. Stage left was the *Sesame Street* gang of Big Bird, Elmo, Grover, and Oscar the Grouch teaching me numbers, spelling, and how to get along. Finally, there was a green clay action figure named Gumby and his horse (also made of clay) named Pokey. Their adventures always delivered a life lesson, and Gumby acted just like his name sounded: while he always planted both feet on the ground, his head was somewhere in the clouds.

Gumby's show was one of the first shows to use a new art form called Claymation, a complicated and time-consuming process in which the creators slightly move clay figurines one iota at a time to produce an image of lifelike movement. Gumby's creator, Art Clokey, chose clay because of its malleability. "Clay changes every time you touch it," he said. "You push it and mash it, and a lump turns into something, just like magic." This process made Gumby look and feel very different from other shows on television. I liked this program so much that I actually had my mom go out and buy me a Gumby doll, er, action figure. (If you tell anyone, I'm going to kill you.) What I liked about my Gumby doll was changing his shape to fit my imagination at the time. He could do—or be—anything I wanted.

I identified with Superman and Gumby for different reasons. I think part of me wanted to be a superhero while another part of me definitely had my head in the clouds. Pretty weird combination, if you think about it. One guy was indestructible. The other was soft and bendable. The Man of Steel tried to never get bent out of shape. The green figure made of clay *always* was being handled and changed to become real to me (the viewer). Superman always prevailed over the bad guys in the end. Gumby, on the other hand, always had his heart changed by the end of an episode—in victory or defeat.

FLEXIBILITY AND HUMILITY REQUIRED

Even though it pains me to say that Superman and Gumby have long since gone off the air, I see the characters of these two figures reflected in the attitudes of young men everywhere. The hearts of supermen, as I call them, are spiritually made of steel in their attitudes toward God. The *S* on their chests stands for *self,* although it could also stand for *stubborn* or *stiff* as well. These guys, for one reason or another, are inflexible in their attitude toward God. They will let all sorts of bad things happen to them instead of listening to God's direction. But in God's eyes, these guys are not superheroes; they are superzeros because of their prideful, unyielding attitudes.

**When I look at young men who make a
successful transition into becoming God's
young man, one quality stands out above
all others—flexibility to the will of God.**

Does God still work with these men of steel? The answer is yes, but as you know, steel is not easy to work with. Try bending it over your knee sometime. The heart of steel must be heated in the fire and pounded or molded into shape by trials, difficulties, and pain. Though the process is hard for young men, God is an excellent blacksmith. He knows what it takes (even if it takes years) to mold His men into the image of Christ. To the young men hard of heart, He says get ready for surgery on the soul:

I will give you a new heart and put a new spirit in you; I will remove from you your heart of stone and give you a heart of flesh. And I will put my Spirit in you and move you to follow my decrees and be careful to keep my laws. (Ezekiel 36:26-27)

At the other end of the spectrum are the Gumbies—guys flexible and bendable to the will of God. They might get twisted around or bent out of shape from life, but they trust the hands shaping them and their characters. They are willing to be handled like clay in the Master's hands. Like Gumby, they change their shape or their direction every time they allow God to reshape their hearts and their lives—especially in the rough times. They let God squish, push, press, and mash because they know that's best for them. When I look at young men who make a successful transition into becoming God's young men, one quality stands out above all others—flexibility to the will of God.

To produce real results in his spiritual life, a young man has to make a trade: the *S* on his chest for a chance to be just a lump of clay in God's hands. That's not easy. In fact, to become flexible and moldable in God's hands requires an attitude rare among young men—humility. Whenever I see humbleness in a young man, I see flexibility to God's will. The two go hand in hand and are the true superpowers of God's young man. The Bible teaches that humility is the one attitude younger men must pursue if they really want to fly spiritually: "Humble yourselves, therefore, under God's mighty hand, that he may lift you up in due time" (1 Peter 5:6).

Jesus said, "Learn from me, for I am gentle and *humble* in heart" (Matthew 11:29). The reason he points to this attitude in Himself is because He knows that it's a quality that makes a relationship with God really work. Think about it. A humble attitude toward God:

- saves you from the grief and pain that selfish pride creates
- helps you accept God's will when your prayer goes unanswered for some reason
- makes you search for God's purpose in a circumstance instead of getting resentful
- guides your heart toward decisions consistent with God's plan
- brings you more closeness with God
- frees you to serve others instead of demanding service
- allows you to worship more authentically
- enriches prayer with a proper reverence
- makes you a better learner
- helps you to come back after stumbling

You can say that King David was one of the most Gumbyesque persons in the Bible. What a great model for us. God said, "David son of Jesse is a man after my own heart, *for he will do everything I want him to*" (Acts 13:22, NLT). When God asked David to do something, there was no debate—he was clay in God's hands and adjusted his attitude accordingly. As easy as that sounds, don't think for a minute that it was some magic dispensation of God's Spirit upon him or a special anointing. David simply understood that there was a God and he wasn't Him! You could say that he was blown away:

> When I look at the night sky and see the work
>   of your fingers—
>   the moon and the stars you have set in
>   place—
> what are mortals that you should think of us,
>   mere humans that you should care for us?
>   (Psalm 8:3-4, NLT)

THE GREAT DIVIDE

As a new believer at UCLA, I remember being surrounded by a lot of "mature" Christians. I heard many of them pray and ask God to make them more humble, and I remember thinking how noble they were to ask God for humility. Their prayers, however, spurred more questions in my mind:

- How will they know when they get it?
- What does "humble" look like?
- Does this mean letting everybody take cuts in line in front of you?
- Does this mean never saying thank you if you get a compliment? dressing down? not combing your hair? not calling attention to yourself?

After asking myself these questions, I reasoned that praying for humility may not be the way to get it after all. Besides, if they got what they asked for, wouldn't they take pride in their humility? There must be a better way. Then I asked myself: when am I personally humbled?

Answer: When someone is bigger and better than I am at something.

When am I personally humbled? When someone is bigger and better than I am at something.

I immediately thought of a few times when God put me in my place. I recalled the time I visited a deserted beach and stared out at the vast coastline and endless expanse of sea. Then my mind jumped to the time when I traveled up the chairlift in Sun Valley, Idaho, looking at a 360-degree panorama of snowcapped mountains. I remember flying through valleys of enormous red-tinged cloud formations during a sunset approach into Denver International Airport. And then there was the time I mountain-biked down the summit of 11,053-foot-high Mammoth Mountain and felt like I was riding through someone else's yard (namely, God's). Those are the moments when I see how big and powerful He must be and how small and insignificant I am. I see David's point in real time: who am I that that He should even think of me?

When a man recognizes this God gap, there is only one way he should respond: silence. King Solomon understood the great divide between man and God. He advised wise men in this way: "God is in heaven and you are on earth, so let your words be few" (Ecclesiastes 5:2), which is another way of saying, God is bigger and better, so keep your ears open and your mouth shut!

- You may be smart, but He is smarter.
- You may be accomplished, but He made the universe.
- You may be helpful to others at times, but He carried the sins of the world to a bloody death on a cross.
- You may feel responsible for your successes, but He gave you every skill you possess.
- You may be a nice guy, but He loves and forgives infinitely.
- You may be the master of your universe, but He is master of the entire universe.

Trust me on this one—you will never need to pray for humility as much as you will need to remember your place. So the next time you feel like bragging, put a cork in it, listen to Him, and learn the ways of the Creator. Coming face to face with the reality of who He is and who you are should lead you into the only constructive attitude possible—humility. God Himself says that recognizing the great divide leads to a knowledge of and respect for Him:

> So that from the rising of the sun
> to the place of its setting

> men may know there is none besides me.
> I am the LORD, and there is no other.
> I form the light and create the darkness,
> I bring prosperity and create disaster;
> I, the LORD, do all these things.
> (Isaiah 45:6-7)

Positionally, God is in charge over what He makes—case closed. He's been calling the shots since the beginning of time, and He expects us to recognize that and give Him the freedom to direct our lives. Sure, it's humbling to get worked on, but in God's case, we should relax. God is always one up, and we're always one down. That should be enough, but we're human, so we often keep forgetting stuff like this. It helps to remember the depth of the love behind His power and His position. This makes every God's man *want* to be flexible in His hands.

IT MUST BE SOME MISTAKE

Hard rock music is in my blood. I can't pass up a tasty lick on an air guitar when I rumble through the house or using my steering wheel as a drum set when a big beat comes on the radio. I'm a headbanger at heart who grew up listening to AC/DC, Ted Nugent, Queen, Van Halen, the Steve Miller Band, and the Rolling Stones. These days I gravitate to hard rock Christian bands, and one that I've been following is a raw group called Seventh Day Slumber. Their songs and their music is not your normal diet of pop music or fad worship. They deliver gut-wrenching vocals, hard-driving rock guitar, and pounding percussion that gets your head bouncing. A song off their 2003 album *Picking Up the Pieces* grabbed me by the throat. It's called "My Struggle." The lyrics, written by Joseph Rojas, reveal a man who's fighting

some demons in his life, including lots of sin and baggage from his past
that keep him from believing the simple truth—that God loves him:

> Must be some mistake
> Cuz I am not worth the price you paid
> With every passing hour
> I convince myself that you saw something in me
> I can hear them still,
> As the whispers laced with hatred fill the room
> I guess I am wasting my time, how could you love
>> a man like me?

> Lord, I need your strength
> Cuz I am weak and falling to my knees
> And who is on my side?
> Cuz I can't tell my friends from enemies
> I am filling up with hate,
> Bitterness controls the air I breathe
> What am I fighting for? Or do you have a plan for me?

> Must be some mistake
> Cuz I am not worth the price you paid

When I first heard this song, I thought of Jesus's story about the prodigal son. The son blew it big time, and he returned to his dad with his tail
tucked safely between his legs. Nothing like being broke and smelling like
the hind end of a pig to wipe out whatever pride you had left. Broken and
humiliated, the prodigal son reached the edge of his father's estate, looked
up, and saw his father running toward him with a big grin on his face. His
first thought had to have been: *He's coming to me? Must be some mistake.* By

any standard, no oddsmakers would have bet on the reunion going down like this. But that's how it happened:

> But while he was still a long way off, his father saw him and was filled with compassion for him; he ran to his son, threw his arms around him and kissed him. (Luke 15:20)

The prodigal son of the New Testament and the twenty-first-century rocker both can't believe it. What they're saying is, "I have sinned... I am no longer worthy." But the Father's grip is too tight, and His kisses are real. Everything changed for these two guys because they were willing to humble themselves and return home to the Father who ran out to embrace them.

Nothing like being broke and smelling like the hind end of a pig to wipe out whatever pride you had left.

It's clear that the songwriter titled the song "My Struggle" because this unconditional love is a struggle to receive. But when you really get that God, who is superior to you in every way, loves you just because you're His son, you should be sold. No need to wrestle with God anymore; you're Gumby on steroids! Instead of being a slave to your dark side, you're marching to the beat of a different drum, all because you realize that it's not a mistake. He loves you so much that you can't resist obeying his requests upon your life. Living a godly life is not a burden anymore—it's a privilege.

If you can't see the God gap or Lord love—assuming the number one position is out of order and thinking He does not have your best interests in mind—your heart will stay hard toward God. You will isolate yourself from God's purposes, never obey wholeheartedly, and never experience the joy of listening to your loving Maker.

REFUSAL TO HEED

Young men who know better but refuse to heed God's voice create misery for themselves and for those around them. I have seen my share of guys who think they have it all figured out at eighteen or nineteen, and they frustrate the snot out of me. These guys would never think they're coming out against God, but their choices and even their questions reek of pride. Most of all, these guys isolate themselves from people of truth and plug their ears to voices of truth. It's a frustrating pattern that has been repeated for centuries among God's men. Aaron is one of the most recent examples.

These guys would never think they're coming out against God, but their choices and even their questions reek of pride.

Aaron became a believer with Matt, Ron, and Darren at a Harvest Crusade at Angel Stadium in Anaheim last summer. He and his buddies experienced a great summer of growth and fellowship as they plugged into church and a Monday night Bible study. Everything went well for Aaron until he left to go back East for college. Unconnected and unaccountable for his faith, it was like Aaron forgot to pack along God. Even though Aaron was on the other side of the country, God *was* there, and He wasn't going to let Aaron remain comfortable in his sin.

E-mails from Matt and Ron, which got into spiritual stuff, were answered by Aaron in a way to make it appear like he was a junior Moses. His new crew of friends had no idea this was happening because Aaron never talked about his faith. Every time he partied, though, Aaron felt like someone was watching him, so much so that he couldn't enjoy the scene as much.

This made him feel anxious, unsettled. He knew that deep down the guilt was there—guilt for turning his back on something that felt so right to him. He questioned everything—including whether he could ever live the way he felt God wanted him to live.

During first-quarter midterms, Aaron was by himself on the north side of campus, where he had found a great place to study in the architecture building. A little after one o'clock in the morning, he looked at his watch and decided to walk back to his dorm. Since iPods weren't invented yet, usually he would drop a Coldplay or Creed CD in his Discman and enjoy the walk home. Tonight, however, the only CD in his carrying case was a worship CD that Matt had bought for him almost three months earlier.

During the summer he had loved listening to this CD, but things were different now. A thought popped into his head that labeled him a hypocrite for thinking he could go there, considering the life he was living. He didn't know if he even wanted to go there—but since he had the disk in his hand and nothing else, he popped the worship CD in and pressed play. Sounds of days gone by came through the earphones.

He questioned everything—including whether he could ever live the way he felt God wanted him to live.

As Aaron walked across the founder's quad, what seemed like a long-ago past came flooding back through the strong acoustic melody, flooding his senses *and* now his spirit. Yes, it had been ages since he'd even *thought* about God, but the music sailed past his mind and drilled deep down into his soul. His eyes filled with tears as track four declared God's love and forgiveness—it was still his favorite. He stopped in front of the student union.

He had to sit down and pray and tell God how he felt and how sorry he was for turning his back on such love.

When he got back to his dorm room, he immediately fired up his laptop and composed an e-mail to Matt explaining how God had used the CD to bring him back to his faith. More important, he described his prayer in front of the student union, rededicating himself to God. His odyssey away from the Lord was over, and for the first time since he left home, Aaron felt peaceful inside.

Aaron took thirty minutes composing his e-mail to Matt. He was a little worried what Matt would think about him since he had never let on about his vacation from God, but Aaron didn't care. He was loved by God, and it felt good.

Aaron did one more thing before he called it a night. He put on his Discman headphones and advanced the player to track four. Once more, as he listened and took the lyrics to heart, he could feel his resistance to God's Holy Spirit fading away. What took its place was what he needed to face in the morning.

Some tough decisions lay ahead, but there was no turning back. He could feel an openness flooding his heart to do God's will. He was nodding off when the thought occurred that he should end his day with a verse of Scripture. He got up and fished around the back of the closet in the dark until he felt a soft leather Bible fill his hand. He flipped open to a bookmarked page, which happened to be Matthew 23, where he had once highlighted verse 12 in yellow. He smiled as he read, "But those who exalt themselves will be humbled, and those who humble themselves will be exalted" (NLT).

Aaron said a silent prayer thanking God for His loving patience, and he fell asleep resolved to never get that far away from the Lord of the universe again.

baptizing your brain

In the movie *Big Fat Liar,* Jason Shepherd, the main character, was not unlike a certain author who became very skillful at lying to friends and family to avoid responsibilities at school and at home. The movie's opening scenes make clear that Jason is quite good at this—he's got everyone from his principal to his parents believing his innocent and touching lies.

Meanwhile, he gets away with murder. Jason's always ready with a great reason why he's late, why his paper was not turned in on time, or why he can't be with his family. Jason (played by Frankie Muniz) leverages his baby face, his brains, and his bravado to construct an elaborate network of fabrications. He has an uncanny way of getting people to support his pathological personality.

The first turning point in the film happens when Jason gets caught lying to his parents about a writing assignment. After an uncomfortable closed-door meeting with the principal and his parents, he's given one final chance to redeem himself by completing the original assignment and hand-ing it in the next day. Seeking to earn back his parents' trust, Jason proudly completes his class paper called "Big Fat Liar."

The next morning Jason wakes up, looks at his watch and realizes that he's late for school as usual. Only this time he has to get his paper in on time—a paper that he actually did the work on himself! Scrambling to school on his skateboard, Jason doesn't see a black limousine approach on his left, and he gets nicked. Although he's unhurt, Jason milks the accident to bum a ride to school from unscrupulous and self-centered Hollywood producer Marty Wolf.

While he's getting a lift, Jason tells the producer his story—getting caught for fibbing and the makeup assignment that he's written as part of his assignment. True to his character, Marty tells Jason how he, too, would have lied his way out of trouble. He punctuates their encounter by making the statement, "The truth is overrated, kid."

Jason arrives at school barely on time. After he parts company with the Hollywood producer, Jason discovers that his paper, the one he entitled "Big Fat Liar," is no longer in his notebook. It's missing! His untrusting and suspicious teacher listens as Jason details the truth about getting knocked off his skateboard by a black limousine and then his chance encounter with a Hollywood movie producer. Perhaps his paper got left back in the limousine, he says, which sounds preposterous to the teacher, of course, and to his parents when they hear the latest cockamamie story from their son. Since no adults in Jason's life believe that he lost his paper, Jason is consigned to summer school, a fate worse than death for any teenager.

You'll never guess what happens a few months later. It seems that word gets out that Hollywood powermeister Marty Wolf plans to produce a smash hit movie called *Big Fat Liar.* When Jason gets wind of this, he sets into motion a last-ditch effort to save his credibility and set the record straight. He meets with the big-time producer (only in Hollywood would a school kid get an audience with a moviemaker, right?) and asks the producer to call his dad and tell him that he was telling the truth.

When the Wolfman blows the kid off, however, phase 2 is hatched. The biggest laughs in the movie come from a high-tech campaign of humiliation against the ruthless producer, a process designed to bring the cruel movie mogul to his knees and force him to come clean. Ingeniously, Jason and his sidekick Kaylee (played by Amanda Bynes) steal Wolf's PDA (personal digital assistant), which holds all the information they need to make this producer's life miserable.

Wolfman's schedule, they learn, calls for a swim every day at the same time. Jason comes up with the perfect prank to pull on their unsuspecting victim.

The takedown is launched right on time when Jason and Kaylee sneak into the backyard of the producer's mansion. Jason pulls out two huge bottles out of his backpack—bottles with labels reading "Blue Dye #34." With a smirk on his face, Jason dumps the contents into the producer's pool moments before Marty Wolf, clad in his swimsuit and dancing to Duran Duran's famous song "Hungry Like the Wolf," steps outside and plunges into the water.

The camera frame pans over to the pool's edge, where we see the clueless producer swimming laps, blissfully unaware that his epidermis is becoming beautifully blue. Meanwhile, Jason and Kaylee set traps inside the house.

The next time we see "Bluto" is when he exits the pool. The dye has done its deed—the cold-blooded cutthroat has morphed into one of those blue men from a Las Vegas show. We're talking a barbarous blue bozo. The directors of the film milk this moment by delaying the Wolfman's surprise until the last possible moment—a mirror scene that results in a primal scream heard from Malibu to Monrovia. Aah…the sweet taste of revenge. (Don't be getting any crazy ideas now.)

You Are What You Think

Jason's revenge is a perfect illustration of baptism. Yes, I said baptism. The original meaning of this Greek word is to dip or immerse something. The outcome of baptizing something is that the object being dipped or baptized is changed. For example, white cloth can be "baptized" in red dye, which changes it into red cloth. Thus Marty Wolf was baptized into the blue color because he soaked in the dye long enough for his skin to take on the character of the blue dye. The point of baptism is that you identify with whatever you soak in.

In a similar fashion, your mind takes on the character or colors of whatever you are soaking in. When you place your life in the mirror, what's reflected back tells you what color dye your brain is soaking in. Let me show you how this works from my own life.

I was soaking my mind in the wrong stuff.

You already know about how I worked weekends in a liquor store during my high-school years. That experience whetted, in a bad way, my budding appetite for sexual things. To use my baptism analogy, I dipped my mind right into the pages of those pornographic magazines. Thank God I worked there only one day a week, but the imprints upon my mind were powerful. I remember taking one of those girlie magazines home and hiding it underneath my mattress. Before showering, I would dip my mind into those tantalizing pictures and then act out my mental fantasy in the shower. I am not proud of this, but my story illustrates how looking at pictures of nude women led to wrong actions. I was soaking my mind in the wrong stuff.

My practice of looking at pictures and fantasizing about those images led to the practice of looking at real-live girls and girlfriends and fantasizing about them. I needed more flavor—more chili pepper for my marinade—and that meant mentally undressing nearly every girl I saw. I certainly wasn't looking at them as individuals or as God's precious diamonds, but as sex objects to be woven into my sick and sinful mind reels. The worst part was that I inherited my mom's dark island skin, which attracted unsuspecting girls my way. If you can believe this, my best man at my wedding toasted me and my bride by boasting that "Kenny had all these girls in high school." On my wedding day! (Thanks a lot, Brad.)

When I would go out on dates, let's just say I was a fast mover. I didn't really care about anything else but connecting physically and satisfying my sexual curiosity. Fortunately, a lot of the girls I dated had more character than me and didn't allow me to take advantage of them (how sad is that!). Like I said, in my BC days (before Christ), I was left to fend for myself and was totally unconnected to anything spiritually healthy. Those poor girls had no idea how my fertile mind put them in uncomfortable situations that no girl should *ever* have to endure.

The Bible clearly teaches that you are what you think, that a young man will take on the characteristics and identity of whatever occupies the majority of his thoughts.

Now contrast this with the Kenny who committed himself to Jesus on a summer night before entering UCLA. When I handed over control of my life to Jesus Christ, the old recipe book—along with the sexy magazines under my bed, the Dirty Word Scrabble, and the dark music dedicated to the devil—got thrown out. (Actually, my brother had me torch them in our Weber grill). That commitment turned out to be the main ingredient of my personal marinade: from then on, I immersed my brain in what the Bible taught. My mental pool, which was saturated with the sexy dye of porn and mental fantasy, was slowly drained and replaced with the pure water of Christ's living words. After soaking my mind in the Word of God, I had the necessary ingredients to begin sharing my faith in Christ with others, which would eventually lead to opportunities to help thousands of men every year around the globe.

Two Kennys, two marinades, two very different directions—but one undeniable fact: the content of my mind created my character. This concept isn't hard to grasp when you look at the choices awaiting you in life. The world wants you to mentally focus on making money and buying toys like pickup trucks and powerboats. Guys who do this become materialists. Dudes always thinking about how to impress others or be accepted by them have the distinctive coloring of narcissists—*let's stop talking about you and talk about me.* Guys who constantly conceive new ways of satisfying their physical or sensual appetites are known in the dictionary as hedonists. (And if you're waiting for the Chicago Cubs to play in the World Series, you could be accused of being a masochist.)

Kidding aside, the Bible clearly teaches that *you are what you think,* that a young man will take on the characteristics and identity of whatever occupies the majority of his thoughts. Scripture says it best: "As water reflects your face, so your mind shows what kind of person you are" (Proverbs 27:19, NCV).

So what are you? Really?

Sow a Thought, Reap a Destiny

A killer statement I have never forgotten was when I heard a guy on the radio quote Samuel Smiles, a writer from the 1800s: "Sow a thought, reap an action. Sow an action, reap a habit. Sow a habit, reap a character. Sow a character, reap a destiny." Did you know that the journey of a thought has such power? If the first truth I need to know about my mind is that *I am* what I think, then the second truth I have to understand is that *I do* what I think.

Consider Jim's thoughts and the destiny he forged for himself.

"Kenny, Michelle was too irresistible, and I blew it last night." He made this statement in my office.

"Tell me exactly what you mean by that," I inquired, smiling so Jim would relax.

"I mean that when we were alone, something inside took over. I could not fight it, so I pushed the boundaries. There was no way out, dude."

I thought for a moment. "So let me ask you another question. Before that moment, how much were you thinking about doing what you eventually did with her? Was it just the last few days? Or was it every day for the last few weeks—or even months?"

Looking straight at the ground, Jim whispered, "Since spring break seven months ago."

Hello!

When I speak at colleges to the guys, I tell them flat-out: there is no such thing as an irresistible temptation. The truth is that Jim went down a mental pathway *way in advance* of his sin, building to a bunch of sexual scenarios with Michelle long before he actually did anything. His tempting thoughts broke up the ground of his mind, then they spread fertilizer on it, watered it, and weakened his will to the point where he was cooked no matter what he did. It was just like a dad or mom saying, "Son, you can do anything if you put your mind to it." That old platitude is true for the good *and* for the bad. If you put your mind to work on an issue, stand back and watch what happens—because it will happen. Car salesmen know this.

They can spot anxious customers from the way they walk on to the lot. Their body language is saying, *I've just got to have that hot car!*

The Bible issues a code red for the threat that sinful thoughts pose to us guys. Several warnings can be found in the book of Proverbs, including this one: "Be careful what you think, because your thoughts *run your* life" (Proverbs 4:23, NCV).

The bottom line is this:
your mind is a force that God says
will determine your destiny.

God warns us because He knows how much horsepower he's built into that amazing engine between your ears. When you step on the gas, it goes! Your mind:

- is one hundred billion neurons strong
- can store one hundred *trillion* facts
- can make two hundred separate calculations per second
- can make fifteen thousand separate decisions to coordinate the function of the human body

The bottom line is this: your mind is a force that God says will determine your destiny.

What's Your Personal Marinade?

Perhaps you're thinking, *Okay, Kenny. I get it. How do I get God's mind then?* The Bible has a term for this: it's called *meditation*. Just like when I marinate my world-famous ribs by putting them in a tasty blend of sauces, God says you need to do the same thing by bathing your mind in His Word.

He's very clear on this. Psalm 119:23 says, "Your servant will meditate on your decrees."

God doesn't say His servants *might* meditate on His decrees when it works into their schedules. Instead what He's saying is that He wants us to think deeply and continuously on His Word, its meaning for us, and how to integrate it into our daily lives.

The secret of every successful Christian man whom I have known has been his love affair with God's Word.

Just like Monty Wolf from *Big Fat Liar* takes on the character of blue after soaking in the pool, so the man who immerses himself in God's Word takes on the very character of God; he will be transformed into a new person. That is one of the things I never have to worry about when it comes to leading men, because I know that if they are committed to the study and thoughtful observance of God's Word, they *will* change. This is the single most important discipline that you'll ever develop in your walk with God. In fact, God equates studying His Word to hanging out with Him:

> How well God must like you—
> you don't hang out at Sin Saloon,
> you don't slink along Dead-End Road,
> you don't go to Smart-Mouth College.
> Instead you thrill to GOD's Word,
> you chew on Scripture day and night.
> (Psalm 1:1-2, MSG)

A choice to be in God's Word is a choice to hang out with God. Only a fool would pass on that one! God's young man should be all over that, and you should understand by now the value of marinating your mind in Scripture. The secret of every successful Christian man whom I have known has been his love affair with God's Word. Some of the great men of the Bible had this to say about God's Word:

Job

> I have not departed from the commands
>   of his lips;
> I have treasured the words of his mouth more
>   than my daily bread. (Job 23:12)

David

> The law of the LORD is perfect,
>   reviving the soul.
> The statutes of the LORD are trustworthy,
>   making wise the simple.
> The precepts of the LORD are right,
>   giving joy to the heart.
> The commands of the LORD are radiant,
>   giving light to the eyes....
> They are more precious than gold,
>   than much pure gold;
> they are sweeter than honey,
>   than honey from the comb.

> By them is your servant warned;
>> in keeping them there is great reward.
>>> (Psalm 19:7-8,10-11)

Peter

Simon Peter answered him, "Lord, to whom shall we go? You have the words of eternal life." (John 6:68)

Jesus

Your word is truth. (John 17:17)

TIME PRESSURES

When I talk to younger guys about how much or how little time they spend in God's Word, their universal response is, "I don't have time." They then walk me through a laundry list of everything that they have to get done in a day, from school and sports and part-time work to studying so they can keep their grades up. When I hear stuff like this, I give them the "face." It's an unmistakable look that communicates: Who do you think I am? Shovel that stuff in someone else's lap, but not in mine. When a guy says to me that he doesn't have time for God's Word, he's not stating a fact, he's stating a priority. I'm black and white on this one.

A busy young man named Alan used to say the same thing to me. When I look at all the things he does, I can understand why. He's the starting point guard on his college team, he's involved with the Fellowship of Christian Athletes, he keeps an A average in school, and he works part time at the YMCA in the recreation department. He's up early to take morning classes so he can practice basketball in the afternoon, and he must study for hours after dinner. We're talking full days.

Alan was sitting in an audience full of high-school and college athletes when I asked everybody to give me feedback on two polar-opposite questions:

1. What keeps you *out* of God's Word?
2. What keeps you *in* God's Word?

Alan raised his hand, and I called on him. He dove in and stated that God's Word wasn't always a priority for him, but as he entered his senior year of high school, he was confronted with several big decisions. He wanted God to guide his actions, so he read his Bible for answers. He said he learned this from his father.

When a guy says to me that he doesn't have time for God's Word, he's not stating a fact, he's stating a priority.

"My consistency in reading the Bible was real shaky until I asked my dad what his secret was," Alan said.

"What did he say?" I asked on behalf of everyone in the room.

"He said that about ten years ago, he decided to put God in his Day-Timer and make Him his first appointment of the day. In other words, Dad wanted to treat Christ the same way he treated everybody else on his calendar—like a real person. That hit me hard."

"So what did you *do?*" I followed.

"Simple. I decided Jesus would have my first appointment of my day too. It's from 7:00 to 7:30 a.m. downstairs in the living room. I read my Bible next to the window so I can see the mountains."

"Why there?"

"It's quiet, and I know there will be no interruptions."

Two very cool things about his answers are worth your consideration. First, he took Jesus very personally. I love that. To Alan, Jesus became a real person who deserved his time, not an abstract concept he could blow off. Second, he knew he needed structure and quiet. Setting aside a time and a place made a statement, and to Alan, his time with God was just as important to his walk as practicing free throws was for his basketball game. He mastered the basic disciplines so that he could excel.

To Alan, Jesus became a real person who deserved his time, not an abstract concept he could blow off.

You can't move toward greatness in anything until you master the fundamentals. As God's young man, you can't move on to greater commitment, depth, and service until you have mastered a regular time with God.

THE TENT OF MEETING

A time and a place is all that is required to meet with the living God. When Moses had his hands full while leading one million people out of Egypt, finding a time and a place to meet with God was tough. But God assigned such a high value to their times together that *He* carved out a time and place for Moses to have an uninterrupted conversation and dialogue. God called it the Tent of Meeting. It was in this special place that God said, "There I will meet you and speak to you" (Exodus 29:42).

My tent of meeting is in my office—door closed—from 8:15 to 9:00 a.m. Your tent of meeting can be *anywhere*. You may already have a regular place in your daily flow that lends itself to a good meeting with God, but it really doesn't matter when or where—just establish a place and a time and keep it. Every young man striving to be God's man stores up a rich reward when he soaks in the Scripture. Listen to what God said to Moses's successor Joshua in the midst of the hectic planning and preparation to cross the Jordan River:

> Study this Book of the Law continually. Meditate on it day and night
> so you may be sure to obey all that is written in it. Only then will
> you succeed. (Joshua 1:8, NLT)

God told Joshua to do what was counterintuitive, given the circumstances. There are certainly plenty of demands upon the guy who has to organize, lead, and direct a million bodies across an active river. But God said to him that his success in this undertaking was contingent on his connection with God through His Word. Joshua needed to baptize his brain in the waters of Scripture before he took the plunge with the people. If Joshua thought hard about what God had to say in his Word (meditate), success would follow him.

What's going to be your secret of success? God says both influence and affluence flow from thinking deeply and continuously on his Word. Can you handle that? Then you better be handling His Word daily.

One of the best ways to ensure that you are in God's Word is by having what I call Red Zone Friends. In the next chapter we're going to show you how your friendships will either help you to reach your goals to become God's young man—or sabotage them.

do you need sharpening?

When I was five years old, I found a steak knife lying in the grass of our side yard. According to Luck family legend, my brothers had been peeling oranges the night before and left it sitting in the tall grass.

When I laid my eyes on the six-inch steel blade that morning, I got jacked up. A boring playtime in the yard now got very interesting. The possibilities were endless.

With my coonskin cap on, I regarded the knife for a moment, wondering what to try first. I know—I could throw the knife at our fence and watch it stick in the wood. Back then I didn't know the difference between a steak knife and a buck knife—I just wanted to see that sharp weapon stick in the wood just like on television. After many failed attempts, however, I could not get the knife to stick, so I moved on to a patch of ice plant in the front yard.

It was like Edward Scissorhands meets *Extreme Makeover: Gardening Edition*. I hacked away at the ice plant with my shiny knife—until I saw some bugs crawling around the ground. A wicked thought crossed my mind: *How many legs does a spider need to walk?* Then I spotted a worm wriggling in the dirt. I threw the knife at him but missed. I thought about cutting him in half but shrugged off that idea. As you can see, my imagination was running wild.

So was my little body. I sprinted toward the garage with the knife held high in my right hand—attacking marauders unite! I was about to stab my invisible adversary when I tripped over a crack in the sidewalk. I did a face plant and rolled into a heap—and suddenly I felt this intense pain on the right side of my face. I looked at my empty—and bloody—right hand and screamed. What had happened?

In shock I stood up and staggered toward the front door like the Mummy, screaming my lungs out. My oldest brother Pat (twenty-two years old at the time) heard the commotion and came running out. I'll never forget his look of horror.

"Oh my God!" he yelled. "You've got a knife in your face." Pat scooped me up and rushed me into the house, where he laid me on the kitchen table.

My big brother took stock of the situation. He proceeded to gently pull the knife out of my face very slowly because the tip of the knife was less than a quarter of an inch away from my eyeball. When that operation was successfully completed, he carried me to his car for a frantic ride to the emergency room where, nine stitches later, I learned a hard lesson about playing with sharp knives, the number one lesson being: don't run with a knife in your hand.

In the Luck household, one thing you could always count on was a sharp blade. My dad had an electric sharpening stone (just like the pros), a razor strap for his straight-edge razor, and an electric can opener that had two different kitchen knife sharpeners built into it. He even had a hand-held sharpening stone for his pocket knives. Dull blades, my dad reasoned, had no place in his workbench or in his home. A knife or blade needed to cut sharply and decisively when called upon.

Surgeons, chefs, butchers, hunters, landscapers, gardeners, and even your local hair stylist all know the value of sharp blades. A razor-sharp edge makes all of these blade runners efficient and happy in their work, whether they're cutting out an appendix, chopping an onion, sectioning off flank steaks, gutting a deer, mowing grass, or cutting hair.

Knives and scalpels need to be sharpened regularly, and professionals use sharpening stones. These steel-shaping instruments come in various sizes and shapes for all sorts of jobs and cutlery. While these stones are as diverse as the knives and implements they service, they have one central mission: creating the edge.

Sharpening stones accomplish this task because they are made from aluminum oxide, diamond-bonded steel shafts, and silicon carbide, which are all harder than the metal they actually sharpen. They even have levels of coarseness, like sandpaper, ranging from extra coarse to fine, depending on what level of sharpness or angle of cut is needed. Some of the more sophisticated devices sharpen and realign the cutting edge of a blade at the same time. Why am I telling you all this?

In a word: *function.* When called upon, these instruments and tools have to perform an important task.

The Blade and the Stone

Now that you've heard about my close encounter of the sharp kind, let's talk about how being sharp affects your walk with Christ. My point is that every young man needs another young man in his life to sharpen and realign him in his walk with God. To be God's young man requires placing a high value on male relationships that keep you spiritually strong. One of my favorite Scriptures says it best: "As iron sharpens iron, so one man sharpens another" (Proverbs 27:17).

Most young men I counsel overlook this important biblical principle, which is a shame. Think about when you were younger. Making friends and having relationships was easy. Your entire life was about playing and having fun and letting your imagination run wild.

If you're unsharpened by the presence of another committed friend, your commitment to God won't perform.

Now life has changed as you've grown and matured. You have a natural desire for adult things because you're no longer a kid. At one time, watching Saturday morning cartoons was fun. Now you'd rather read *Playboy* cartoons. At one time, yanking on Sally's hair was the height of hilarity. Now you'd rather pull her top off. Truth or Consequences isn't as fun as Truth or Dare, since the latter game involves what you will or won't do sexually.

If you're unsharpened by the presence of another committed friend, your commitment to God won't perform. It will be duller than a steak knife that's been played with in the dirt all morning long. But a young man who's got a spiritual sharpening stone in his life—another brother headed down the same path toward God—can make the transition to the bigger issues of manhood with support, confidence, and encouragement to do the right thing.

Take Jordan for example. He had no sooner lugged all his stuff into the dorm during freshman orientation week when this guy knocked on the door. He said he was with a campus group that sponsored a guys' Bible study on Tuesday nights. Jordan accepted the flyer and remarked that he was a Christian too. "See you there," Jordan said, remembering what his parents had told him during their teary departure earlier that day. His dad said that one of the first things he needed to do was get involved with a ministry on campus. Now was his chance—an opportunity handed to him on a silver platter.

That yellow flyer found a spot on Jordan's desk, but a couple of days later, as the excitement of new classes, making new friends on his floor, and the rush of independence took front and center position in Jordan's life, he ignored it. Then one evening he tossed the flyer into his trash can. *There isn't time*, he thought. *I'm meeting a lot of new people, especially those girls on the floor above and the floor below. They sure are friendly.*

Let's step back and be objective for a moment. At this crucial juncture in his life, Jordan is not:

- reporting his raging temptations to anyone
- connecting with any guys headed the same way
- giving any significant time to God's Word
- accountable for his eyes and mind on the Net with anyone
- realizing any spiritual growth

As Jordan experiences go-for-the-gusto total freedom, he is:

- isolated and vulnerable to spiritual attack
- connecting with non-Christians who do not share his faith or his values
- giving a lot of thought to what it would be like to sleep with that hottie from Sacramento
- going backward in his faith
- well on his way toward becoming toast

I know we've talked about the fairer sex a lot in *Every Young Man, God's Man*, but the number one dilemma facing God's young men today is not sexual temptation. It's isolation. It's a pattern passed down to you by your culture and by a generation of dads for whom independence was the highest virtue. Growing up, they were told to blaze their own trail, and it's been that way for generations. It's still headed in that direction. From my seat in the bleachers, I don't think that a majority of young men are connected to other guys for any meaningful or deep purpose. Guys who wouldn't think twice about risking it all to get a date with a girl won't risk getting honest with another guy to stay true in their commitment to Christ. Make no mistake: isolation is not God's plan.

PUBLIC VERSUS PRIVATE

If you're like most young men, you live a double life between your public image and private reality. This is not unusual; you wouldn't be normal if you didn't pay attention to how others perceive you. The public guy is the cool dude you trot out there for others to see. He is synthetic, planned, and created to make an impression of having it all together, someone who is cool and strong at the same time.

The private guy is hidden away. He's the one with conflicts and problems that create personal stress for him and, eventually, for others. The private guy has secrets he hides from people—habits, sins, attitudes, feelings, and worries. He keeps the public at arm's length by making sure that conversations stay in the shallow waters of school, sports, girls, or weekend happenings. Others can talk to him about the Bible as long as they don't get too serious about it.

If you're like most young men, you live a double life between your public image and private reality.

You never let the public self discuss private matters, because then the whole image that you've worked so hard to build up would be obliterated.

People would know who you *really* are versus what you have them *thinking* you are. That's why the private guy desperately needs people who he can talk to because this is the way he can make progress with God.

I have found that young men who aren't making the transition to spiritual manhood have reached their sad state because they're connected to other guys who dull their edge to their goals as God's men. In this group of friends, they don't:

- risk getting honest about the tough stuff burning a hole in the pit of their stomachs
- watch one another's backs spiritually
- pray for one another regularly
- push one another to be in God's Word
- ask how a guy's walk with the Lord is going
- encourage one another to take bold risks for Christ
- care enough to confront behavior that doesn't square with Scripture

God's standard and plan are different for you and your group of friends. They should help you become the man God created you to be:

My brothers, if one of you should wander from the truth and someone should bring him back, remember this: Whoever turns a sinner away from his error will save him from death and cover over a multitude of sins. (James 5:19-20)

When you are connected to other guys for the purposes of spiritual growth, you won't need to trot out the public guy anymore. You can be you—warts and all. Listen, the guys you think have it all together are just as whacked out as you! The discovery that is helping today's young men win their big spiritual battles is that they are learning they need better relationships with their *God-focused* peers. When I encourage young men to pursue relationships with their guy friends, I see many change their thinking about their guy connections and use them in ways that God intended.

THE CASE FOR CONNECTION

I remember when I was in college and I flew to see my brother Lance in Alabama. Lance had led me to the Lord, so I was naturally looking forward to connecting on a spiritual level with a brother I rarely got to see. I looked forward to three things happening during my visit: eating massive amounts of greasy food, playing his guitar late into the night, and talking about Jesus until our eyelids wore out.

The script played out exactly as I thought it would on the first night: mounds of fried chicken and rounds of laughs combined with picking the "gee-tar." But then I saw what looked like a cigarette sticking out of Lance's vest pocket.

"What's up with that?" I asked with a "You idiot" frown on my face.

Lance pushed back. "Uh, what's it look like, Ken? A cigarette."

"Why?"

"It's just a few a day—tops."

At that moment, I whipped out the Bible that *he* had bought me and plopped it open. I fanned over to 1 Corinthians 6:19-20, pointed my finger at the verse, and then slid the Bible across the table for Marlboro Mouth to read. "Doesn't it say right there that your body is a temple where God lives and to glorify God with your body?" I asked.

A long pause followed. Then Lance did the unthinkable: without saying a word, he snapped the cigarette in half and threw it in the trash. "That's enough of that," he declared.

Awesome.

It wasn't about me so much as his respect for God's Word: *If God says it,*

I'll stop doing it. (If you are reading this, and you're a smoker, I realize that the Bible doesn't specifically prohibit smoking. But it's a no-brainer that your body was designed to breathe air, not smoke, so do your lungs a favor and quit.)

**It wasn't about me so much as his respect
for God's Word: If God says it, I'll stop doing it.**

Lance never looked back. He made his decision, and that was it. No patch, no scaling back. He quit cold turkey in front of my eyes and has not touched a cigarette in twenty-one years. I'm confident that his decision will buy him many more years to enjoy his wife, Gina, their children, and his children's children. But as I look back to that day, I can assure you that I felt totally *connected* to my brother when we got real about his smoking.

The reason God wants His men connected to one another is because when you come together under his banner, He shows up too. "How good and pleasant it is when brothers live together in unity!... For there the LORD bestows his blessing, even life forevermore" (Psalm 133:1,3). The bottom line is that you can experience *more* of God when you team up with other young men. You will stretch one another spiritually. You will be there for one another. But just in case you are tempted to abandon your God-given sharpening stones, here's what God has to say about the science of being sharp:

- Jonathan said to David, "The LORD is witness between you and me" (1 Samuel 20:42).
- "An open rebuke is better than hidden love! Wounds from a friend are better than many kisses from an enemy" (Proverbs 27:5-6, NLT).
- Paul advised Timothy, "Pursue righteousness, faith, love and peace, along *with those* who call on the Lord out of a pure heart" (2 Timothy 2:22).

- King David commented, "My eyes will be on the faithful in the land, that they may dwell with me; he whose walk is blameless will minister to me" (Psalm 101:6).
- "And let us not neglect our meeting together, as some people do, but encourage and warn each other, especially now that the day of his coming back again is drawing near" (Hebrews 10:25, NLT).
- "Let the godly strike me! It will be a kindness! If they reprove me, it is soothing medicine. Don't let me refuse it" (Psalm 141:5, NLT).
- "I will fulfill my vows to the LORD in the presence of all his people" (Psalm 116:14).

What's God saying to every young man? You're a better man when you're connected and accountable. So the question now is, are you?

Get Connected Now

Marcus Junius Brutus and Gaius Julius Caesar had been through a lot of ups and downs in their relationship. In fact, historians would record that Julius had developed a brotherly trust and healthy love for Brutus. Then on March 15, 44 BC, with Brutus standing by, sixty plotters attacked and began stabbing his friend, the Roman military leader. One of Caesar's final images was Brutus rushing at him with a dagger and plunging the blade deep into his chest.

The shock of seeing a trusted friend among the assassins moved Caesar to utter, "Et tu, Brute?"—"You, too, Brutus?" Caesar didn't know who his friends really were as he drew his final breath.

Your journey to become God's young man has to include real friends who provide real accountability. You need to have guys in your life whom you can have fun with *and* share your failures with. So often I see that the margin of victory for a young man is simply another guy battling with him.

Like Caesar, you could be swimming with "friends" who don't have your best interests at heart. You and your friends have to adopt a foxhole mentality—a band of brothers outlook on your campaign to end the stranglehold of sin in your life and for years to come.

Brian made a really hard decision last semester. He decided he needed a different set of friends. They might not be as cool or as accepted as his old friends, but he needed a new set to hang out with to become God's young man. It was easy for the old group to pull him down to their level—"Dude, everyone's going to be at the kegger." For sure, Brian knew if he fell in with that crowd that his actions wouldn't cut it with God because of the compromises. He would be traveling backward.

**You need to have guys in your life whom you can
have fun with and share your failures with.**

The big step was meeting Shaun at a chapel event during a lifestyles week on campus. He fell in with a break-out group of guys, and the leader laid it out there. "We're going to talk about sexual purity, masturbation, and stuff on the Internet." It just so happened that these were issues that Brian was dealing with.

Shaun was the first to open up. "I have been no saint," he began, "which is why I need you guys to help me get past this stuff." Brian found himself nodding approval. The campus chaplain said he would host a group for Bible study for the rest of the semester, and if everyone jelled, they could keep going in the new year.

Five months later, this cell group of guys was like a band of brothers. It's been a simple deal: they meet weekly, talk honestly, pray for one another, and watch one another's back. They see the progress that young men who make a strong decision for God experience. Instead of being shipwrecked and becoming spiritual castaways, they have a supporting cast behind them.

Brian, the last time I checked, had his edge back. But it took courage to subject himself to the sharpening stone. As we'll see in the next chapter, when you're trying to get razor sharp as God's young man, you're gonna see some sparks fly.

breaking the silence

At a Christian college in Ohio, I spoke about friendship and sexual purity—how the guys could help the gals remain sexually pure and how the gals could help the guys do the same. When I looked into the audience, I could tell by their rapt attention that this topic was *very* interesting to these college students. I know just as well as you do that sex is a mysterious and exciting prospect for young adults, and while it can be embarrassing to discuss in mixed company, it does need to be addressed.

Since I'm older and have spoken on sexual integrity issues for years, I felt at ease talking about sex to this group of students. I described how I struggled to be victorious, fought "the fever" as a younger man, and experienced the huge blessings of sexual integrity. I want younger audiences to connect with me as someone who knows *exactly* what they're going through.

That morning in Ohio, I made the following points:

- True friends help others succeed in the area of their greatest struggle.
- Our characters cannot become more immoral and more like Christ's at the same time.

- Sex outside of God's plan is like spiritual anthrax—deadly.
- Every young man and woman is called and commanded to exercise sexual self-control.
- Taking liberties with or advantage of a brother or sister in Christ does not help anyone become more like Christ.
- Set down some rules in advance so that the goal of completing your sister in Christ—which is your job—will be accomplished.

After presenting this advice, I pulled back the covers on my struggles with sexual purity back in my college days, which helped me reach into this student body's secret sins and pull back *their* covers without embarrassing them. Afterward, when I was done, groups of girls thanked me for taking some of the pressure off them, and lots of guys asked if they could speak confidentially with me later. I responded by posting some office hours during the afternoon to counsel guys only. I made myself available for eight thirty-minute slots, which filled up in a matter of minutes.

All eight guys felt the monkey come off their backs as they talked truthfully about their situations, looked at God's Word, made a plan, and prayed with me

---

My sessions that afternoon reminded me that there was still plenty of sexual temptation out there, even at a Christian college, but I was proud of the guys who made courageous decisions to break their silence. For any God's young man, confiding in me about a secret, a temptation, or a problem is a strong indicator that he's serious about his relationship with Christ. It shows he's willing to pay the price, face potential rejection, and trust God with the results.

Let me hit some highlights from that afternoon of counseling. All eight guys:

- wanted to talk about sexual temptation
- needed someone to listen to them and encourage them
- felt their lack of sexual self-control was sin
- were torn up on the inside because they had never discussed this stuff with anyone
- were nervous at first but glad they faced their fears and risked opening their hearts to another guy
- were swimming in friends but only felt safe with a total stranger they would never see again
- felt the monkey come off their backs as they talked truthfully about their situations, looked at God's Word, made a plan, and prayed with me
- were glad they faced their fears and risked opening their hearts to another guy

Have you noticed how girls seem to have more friends and seem to do more talking? In fact, behavioral scientists say that women speak an average of thirty thousand words a day compared to men, who utter a mere ten thousand words a day. Women are built by God to process everything, and they seem predisposed to talk about their feelings. I mean, why do women seem to head off to the powder room in packs while guys just do their business in the bathroom and go?

One day I was at a nearby park with my kids, and I noticed two ladies in deep conversation. I couldn't help but eavesdrop a little—after all, I have ears! They were talking about their families, their marriages, their kids, and just about everything a guy would *never* discuss with another guy. They must have jabbered for a good hour when I saw one of them look at her watch.

"Oh, my goodness, where does the time go?" she said. "I'm sorry, but I have to run along."

What happened next blew my mind. The lady who had to leave stood up, stuck out her hand, and said, "It was *so* nice to meet you."

What? I thought to myself. *They just met?* I hope they didn't notice the look of surprise on my face.

**We prefer to stuff our emotions, maintain
a stiff upper lip, and carry on with harboring
what's really going on inside.**

Women must process—everything. Ever notice in the movies how a young woman will call her best friend whenever she's anxious or stressed out by something? The fairer sex is far more relational, nurturing, and friendly than us guys. Those qualities are part of their DNA programming—their strength, to be sure, but also their weakness—especially when they have a need to make a quick decision and there's no time to talk it through with a friend.

Guys don't even *think* about discussing their feelings or what's churning inside with another friend. We prefer to stuff our emotions, maintain a stiff upper lip, and carry on with harboring what's really going on inside. I know as well as you do that it's not natural for a guy to come right out and talk about a problem, a weakness, or a temptation in his life with another guy. In fact, most young men don't have a clue on how to connect with another guy at a deeper level, because they never saw that openness modeled in their fathers or by a prevailing culture where "strong" men keep their emotions under close wraps. "Never let them see you sweat," is the motto we heard growing up. Guys are this way because God hardwired us to be emotionally compartmentalized and task-oriented to fulfill our roles of protector and provider when we get to the age of marriage and form families.

The result is that we're pretty bad at dealing with our emotions. Here's a quick list, and ask yourself if any of these hit your bull's-eye:

- You mask anger with sarcasm.
- You avoid serious conversations by making fun of the subject.
- You "gotta go."
- You change the scenery.
- You keep secrets.
- You avoid guilt through rationalization.
- You deflect mistakes.
- You blame others.
- You hang out with shallow people who don't go there.
- You change the subject.

ROPE-A-DOPE

Muhammad Ali always said he was The Greatest of All Time, and on most judges' scorecards, he probably was the greatest boxer to ever roam the square circle. His "float-like-a-butterfly-and-sting-like-a-bee" footwork and powerful jabbing style were brutally beautiful. After beating Smokin' Joe Frazier in 1973, Ali earned the right to contend for his second heavyweight title against the reigning champion George Foreman. This fight, held in the heart of the African Congo in Kinshasa, Zaire, was labeled the Rumble in the Jungle and attracted an unprecedented worldwide audience. Although Ali talked his usual smack in the months preceding the fight, nearly every boxing expert felt like the younger, stronger Foreman would outlast and outpunch Ali, who was thirty-two years old and considered over the hill. Some even feared that Ali would exit the ring on a stretcher.

In the early stages of the fight, most observers scratched their heads in disbelief over Ali's boxing tactics. Instead of dancing, jabbing, and outboxing Foreman—the float-like-a-butterfly-and-sting-like-a-bee strategy seen in every Ali fight up to that time—Muhammad leaned against the ropes while Foreman unleashed combination after combination to his midsection and torso. Then thirty seconds before the bell, Ali would bounce off the ropes and tag Foreman with a flurry of stinging jabs, just to remind him who was boss.

When it comes to getting honest with others about what's really going on in their lives, many young men pull the old rope-a-dope.

The eighth round started just like previous ones—with Ali retreating to the ropes and holding his gloves up while Foreman threw haymaker hooks. As Ali absorbed the blows, Foreman's punches were becoming more laborious when, suddenly, Ali sprang off the ropes midway through the round and took the offensive against the bigger, heavier opponent.

The momentum was all Ali's as he made Foreman look like a bobble head with blow after blow. A roundhouse right to the jaw, and another, and Foreman began to fall, almost in slow motion, to the canvas. He got up on one knee and tried to shake the cobwebs out of his head, but he couldn't stand up before the ten count had been given. Muhammad Ali was declared the undisputed heavyweight champion of the world before a delirious stadium full of African fans screaming, *Ali bomaye!*—"Ali, kill him!"

Ali's boxing strategy became known as rope-a-dope—tiring out your opponent in order to destroy him. Today some people use the term to describe a scam or shady tactic that disguises what someone is *really* up to, just like Ali disguised his tactics by cowering against the ropes.

When it comes to getting honest with others about what's really going on in their lives, many young men pull the old rope-a-dope. They use spin, employ shady tactics, or just flat-out lie to deliberately lead people to think all is well when the reality is they need help, advice, or even rescue. Consider the following situations and see if you can identify with any of them:

Tom's dad called his cell phone to say hello. When he asked how school was going, Tom replied, "Awesome." He failed to tell his dad that he'd been on academic probation since the beginning of the semester and would get kicked out if he didn't pass two of his four classes.

Rope-a-dope.

Brandon finished a midterm early and walked in on Mike and Kelly while they tongue-wrestled on the couch and Kelly's blouse was unbuttoned. After Kelly excused herself to freshen up in the bathroom, Brandon confronted his accountability partner. Mike admitted he might have been crossing the line, but he denied that it went further than first base.

Rope-a-dope.

Warren's pastor at the Christian Life Center asked each guy in their cell group to share their number one struggle. When all eyes looked toward Warren, he talked about having a hard time trusting God. With graduation from college and an important interview with a local tech company coming up, he said he was too worried to pray and really wondered if God had a plan for his life. What Warren did not share was how his brain had been hijacked by an adult entertainment Web site and how he masturbated nightly to the images he saw on his computer screen.

Rope-a-dope.

Each of these young men has not discovered that confession—not cover-ups—move you into the Man Zone with God.

CONFESSION IS NOT FOR COWARDS

Most young men do not have the stomach for confession because it forces them to confront themselves or their actions. (Newsflash: *no one likes to do that!*) Revealing your dirty laundry is like showing the world your dirty underwear. No one wants to do that, so it's better to resort to rope-a-dope. The problem is that the only one getting roped is you! Satan loves it when a young man believes his smoke screens are working, because the longer he stays unconfessed and self-deceived, the longer he can keep inflicting losses on someone who could be living for God.

Which reminds me of a little list I came up with:

The Top Ten Reasons Satan Wants You to Keep Secrets

10. You lose out on the support God provides in the body of Christ.
9. You lose confidence spiritually.
8. You lose the ability to develop self-control, and you repeat the cycle of sin.
7. You lose fellowship with the Holy Spirit.
6. You lose your connection to the truth.
5. You lose credibility with others.
4. You lose intimacy with your family.
3. You lose intimacy with others (it's not the real you).
2. You lose days, weeks, months, even years of joy and peace.
1. You lose intimacy with God.

Confession is all about breaking the silence and risking being found out. If this sounds scary and difficult, it is for two reasons:

1. Satan will bombard you with fearful thoughts of rejection or shame to get you to stay in the lie and keep everything

unconfessed. Secrets are a foothold for him and give the devil power in your life.

2. Secrets are often the last hot gate of personal control in a young man's life. Satan loves to give you the illusion of power and control over your life by holding back certain parts from accountability. It's scary and feels uncomfortable because there's so much to lose if this spiritual foothold is won back for God. That's why confession is so courageous.

Bringing the *real* problems and temptations you face into the open means you can receive *real* help from God and His people to defeat sin in your life. Your closely held secret (or secrets) can be the source of continuing misery or the key to the most significant spiritual victory of your young life. I look at confession as giving Satan a bloody nose, and that's what happens when you punch back with God's truth.

**Confession is all about breaking
the silence and risking being found out.**

If you think I'm off base on this, just listen to how strongly God encourages His people to practice the discipline of confession with Him and others, then make a note of the consequences. My italics are in the places where you need to slow your eyes down:

People who *cover over* their sins will *not prosper.* But if they *confess* and forsake them, they will *receive mercy.* (Proverbs 28:13, NLT)

If we say we have no sin, we are only fooling ourselves and refusing to accept the truth. But *if we confess* our sins to him, he is faithful and just to forgive us and cleanse us from every wrong. (1 John 1:8-9, NLT)

Make this your common practice: Confess your sins to each other and pray for each other so that you can live together whole and healed. (James 5:16, MSG)

But *you desire honesty* from the heart, *so you can teach me* to be wise in my inmost being. (Psalm 51:6, NLT)

God requires confession. The reason why is that you cannot get close to Him or to His people when you are withholding a huge part of yourself from them. He wants maximum closeness with you, and confession brings you to that place.

Another truth to consider is that confession is not for God's benefit (He knows all your secrets anyway), but confession will definitely benefit *you.* He knows that the longer you hold on to a secret, the sicker your character becomes, and the sicker your character becomes, the sicker your conduct will become. When your actions reflect the sickness of your secrets, it not only breaks your relationship with God, but it also ruins your relationships with others.

Lastly, confession must involve other believers. In your case, that means other guys. The passage from James does not leave any wiggle room on this when it says to confess your sins "to each other and pray for each other." Why does God put us in this uncomfortable place?

First, it requires faith. Confession is a huge step of faith that will cause you to stick your neck out there for God and trust Him like never before. Second, your problems become more concrete and real when they're put out in the open versus some issue you debate only in your own mind.

Third, confession takes you off your convenient and comfortable timetable for dealing with sin and puts you on track for resolving the issue more quickly since it's out in the open. Fourth, confession to another guy or group of guys generates healthy accountability, which affects how you think about and act toward whatever's causing you to sin.

Confession is not for God's benefit
(He knows all your secrets anyway), but
confession will definitely benefit you.

Fifth, confession brings encouragement and good advice from other brothers. (I experience this regularly with college guys at my conferences.) Lastly, honest confession provides courage to come out of hiding for others struggling with the same problem.

SECRET POWER

Rich approached me and asked to speak in private. When we got out of earshot of the other guys, he put it straight to me: "I really wonder what's in it for me if I come clean about masturbation and surfing adult Web sites with my college group. Won't people be angry with me since I've got this junk in my life and I'm supposed to be a leader? Can't I just come clean with you and that's it?"

"Do you want victory?" I replied.

"Absolutely," he said.

"Then here's what you say to your group: 'This is the first time I have shared this with anyone, but I have something important to tell you…' and then share what you need to share. Don't stop until everything is all on the table. I guarantee you that you'll feel your heart racing a mile a minute, and every fiber in your being will want you to run, but I think you should just go for it."

"That's it?" he questioned.

"That's it. Then I want you to call me and tell me what happened."

I knew that confession would be a step of faith for Rich, but I also knew that God would invade that moment. All of the things God loves are present in an honest confession: truth, faith, humility, courage, risk, and love for God's way versus man's way.

It doesn't take any faith to keep a secret.

It doesn't take any courage to hide a problem.

Any coward can rope-a-dope;

only the courageous can confess.

About a week later Rich called me. "I was fighting it on the inside, just like you said. But then another guy opened the door by talking about how he got spammed by a porn site and he took the bait. That's when I jumped into the water."

"So what happened?"

"This big guy named Jerry said, 'Finally, I've been waiting for you to say something I believe. Welcome to the club.'"

"What else?"

"Oh, we finished our study and prayed for everybody's stuff. One of the guys offered to come to my dorm room and help me download this software that we can use to check on one another. I feel like a big load just fell off my back. No more secrets, dude."

Rich discovered the power of confession the same way the apostle Paul did when God said to him, "My power works best in your weakness." When Paul realized the power that comes with confession, he shared his discovery with others when he wrote, "So *now* I am glad to boast about my weaknesses, *so that the power of Christ may work through me*" (2 Corinthians 12:9, NLT). He was saying that when God's young man is at his most vulnerable place—when he's out there risking it all—that's the moment when God's power flows into his life in the most real way. Confession unlocks this power.

It doesn't take any faith to keep a secret. It doesn't take any courage to hide a problem. Any coward can rope-a-dope; only the courageous can confess. But where do you find the boldness, the courage to do that? Jesus told His guys the power to be bold comes from one source: the Holy Spirit. We'll unpack that statement in our next chapter.

never lost

It was 11:30 p.m. when I stepped off the plane and into an empty airport terminal in Charlotte, North Carolina. Towing my carry-on and laptop down a long corridor, I was beginning to feel the jet lag from a transcontinental flight. I looked up and saw the signs for baggage claim and rental cars, pointed myself in the right direction, and kept pumping my legs.

As I walked my mind replayed my journey to this point. It had begun at 4:30 that morning when I woke up from a dead sleep to get to the airport early. The terror level had been recently elevated by Homeland Security, so I knew the lines to pass through security would be a bear. I couldn't cut it close by arriving just one hour before my early flight, so it had been a *long* day.

I walked outside the arrival terminal and spotted the rental car shuttle stop. A Hertz bus was waiting for me. During the ride to the rental car agency, my mind recounted the day's events: eating two Egg McMuffins at the John Wayne Airport in Orange County, working on my computer during the flight to Dallas, eating Dickey's barbecue at the DFW Airport, and sitting scrunched in the middle seat from Dallas to Charlotte while unsuccessfully trying to sleep. Now I had just one more leg of the journey to go—the drive from the airport to the hotel.

Getting the rental car turned out to be the easiest part of the trip—no lines at midnight! I loaded my bags in the back, jumped into the Ford Taurus, turned the ignition, and then it hit me—I had no clue how to get to the hotel from the airport. Argh! Hungry, angry, lonely, tired, and lost is a bad combination for any coast-to-coast traveler. Then an idea popped into my frazzled head—I could call the hotel on my cell phone. Oops. My cell phone battery was dead, and I had left my car charger back in Southern California. What next? Then I saw just what I needed: a little black box protruding out of the floorboard.

It was a Global Positioning System (GPS), waiting to save me from a total meltdown. "Thank You, Jesus!" I yelled at the top of my lungs. If you're wondering why I wet my pants with excitement, then you probably aren't aware of the beauty of this wonderful technology—especially when you're a lost man who hates to ask for directions.

For me, the lyric from that old-time hymn, "Amazing Grace"—"I once was lost but now am found"—is the essence of GPS satellite technology, which was designed by the U.S. military for tracking enemy movements. What happens is that a transponder signals its position to various satellites circling the earth, and through complex triangulation, pinpoints anything in the world to within a few feet or so.

Talk about an answer to prayer. With this onboard GPS system, all I had to do was enter the name of my hotel and type in Charlotte, NC, on a digital keypad, and my GPS system—named NeverLost—calculated the shortest route in nanoseconds. As I left the airport that evening, it was like having a personal assistant sitting next to me, letting me know what exit to take, what my next turn would be, and when I would arrive at my destination. All I had to do was listen to it and glance at the visual display on the screen every now and then.

During my drive, I heard the woman's recorded voice say, "Proceed to the next stop light and turn left in point five miles." When I arrived at that stoplight, a little bell announced the next direction: "Left turn approaching." The friendly voice—I named her Caroline—knew exactly where I was and where I needed to go.

Can you imagine what would happen if, during my trek to the hotel, I switched off the GPS? Do you think I would have been able to navigate the streets of Charlotte without a map or directions that night? Of course not. I needed to hear Caroline's voice.

You Need a Friendly Voice

That night I would have been an idiot *not* to depend on this global positioning system to take me to my ultimate destination. In a similar fashion I see huge mistakes being made out there by young men attempting to move forward in their faith without using the spiritual GPS that God implanted in them at salvation. They leave their driveways and burn rubber for God, ready to make their mark, but they forget they could get there quicker and with less frustration if they simply remembered to engage the friendly voice of the Holy Spirit.

Most of the young men I know possess a foggy understanding of the person, presence, and purpose of the Holy Spirit in their lives. If you are part of this crowd, don't worry about it. Most guys I counsel have not engaged the ministry of the Holy Spirit, the third person of the Trinity, and all He can do for them. Perhaps you're unaware that Jesus described His character and ministry with such words as *counselor, comforter, helper, spirit of truth,* and *guide.* The Holy Spirit is ready and willing to speak the right direction in your mind. All you have to do is let Him do this, and when that happens, He will guide you through every temptation and help you avoid many of the traps others fall into.

It was like the first time I tried snowboarding. For several years, ever since I saw the X Games on ESPN, I wanted to try snowboarding. I couldn't wait to experience the speed and freedom of carving turns in fresh powder. So I took Cara and Ryan with me to Snow Summit, a ski area a couple of hours from Los Angeles, to give this sport a try. I figured that after taking a beginner class, we would be shredding the slopes in no time.

The Holy Spirit is ready and willing to speak the right direction in your mind. All you have to do is let Him do this.

When we arrived at Snow Summit, we joined hundreds of other folks duded up in brand-new snow gear and waiting in line to rent equipment. Then we trudged out to the bunny hill for our first day of snowboarding, which, as I recall, was run after run of falling, getting up, and falling again—all in about a hundred yards of hill. I remember thinking, *Whatever happened to carving freely in the powder?* That dream was shattered as the falls and frustration mounted.

We took a break for lunch, followed by a couple of more runs before our afternoon lesson. When I found Ryan struggling to get up after yet another tumble, he wasn't so sure a clean run would ever happen. "This isn't very fun, Dad," he said.

"I told you guys it wouldn't be easy the first day out."

Cara added her two cents. "My arms are all bruised, Daddy, from falling," she whined.

"This is part of learning something new," I chirped. "You just gotta keep at it. Remember what I say about training in soccer. Practice—"

My kids finished the sentence. "—under pressure over time creates confidence," they chimed in by rote.

"Right. Remember that. I know it's hard getting the hang of this snow-boarding thing, but we'll get it."

Ryan sought more assurance. "How long will it take?" he wondered.

"I don't think it will be that long, because I'm actually starting to get this."

**When you risk changing for Him,
the change always takes
you to the next level.**

That was a statement of optimism, not fact. The reality was that I had no clue when we would turn a corner, but sure enough, after a few more runs, all of us were staying up on our boards and making clean runs down the bunny slope. We even felt confident enough to take the main lift and try an intermediate run later that afternoon. Today we're solid snowboarders who love getting into the half-pipe, and that day on the bunny slope is a distant memory. What happened is that we tried something we didn't know how to do and improved ourselves.

For God's young man, trusting that the Holy Spirit will be there to guide you and counsel you is kind of like taking that first run down the bunny slope. It's a risk because you're practically guaranteed to fall. But one thing I've learned about being God's young man is that when you risk changing for Him, the change always takes you to the next level. Spiritually speaking, you'll go from the bunny slopes to carving some serious powder in the back bowls.

HE LIVES IN YOU TO LEAD YOU

Sure, learning about the Holy Spirit may be new to you, but my advice is to risk getting to know Him and keep at it.

The whole issue of getting to know the Holy Spirit is about leadership. Jesus's men experienced the Master's leadership for three full years, a time when they came to rely on His physical presence, voice, and example. Yet the Gospels tell us that when Jesus talked about leaving to go back to the Father, the disciples felt like they would be left floating in a boat without oars or a rudder. They had been so used to seeing, feeling, and talking to Jesus that the thought of all that going away inspired a fear of being spiritually abandoned. Knowing this, Jesus reassured the disciples by telling them how there would be a transfer of leadership from outside of them (through His physical presence) to an internal presence that would be directly connected to Him and the Father. This is how Christ said it:

> If you love me, you will obey what I command. And I will ask the Father, and he will give you another Counselor to be with you forever—the Spirit of truth. The world cannot accept him, because it neither sees him nor knows him. *But you know him, for he lives with you and will be in you. I will not leave you as orphans; I will come to you.* (John 14:15-18)

This concept of Jesus's taking a new form in the person of the Holy Spirit and living inside them was new—extremely new. So later, in the same conversation with the disciples, He tried a new angle to consider. He added more specifics about the continuing connection that He would have through the indwelling GPS system of the Holy Spirit:

But when he, the Spirit of truth, comes, *he will guide you* into all truth. He will not speak on his own; he will speak only what he hears, and *he will tell you what is yet to come.* He will bring glory to me by taking from what is mine and making it known to you. All that belongs to the Father is mine. That is why I said *the Spirit will take from what is mine and make it known to you.* (John 16:13-15)

Jesus must have thought, "All righty, then. That ought to do it." The disciples, on the other hand, responded by saying to one another, "We don't understand what he is saying" (John 16:18). Jesus did not expect them to fully understand the implications of this transition, but He laid the groundwork for what Peter and the rest of the disciples would later need as leaders of the early church.

Most young men, whether they've been attending church their whole life or are new in the faith, comprehend the importance of reading and applying God's Word, the importance of serving others, and the importance of connecting with other believers. Very few, however, pursue a relationship with the Holy Spirit on a day-by-day and moment-by-moment basis the way Jesus described.

If you leave the Holy Spirit untapped and unused, however, God is deeply disappointed, because He knows that disowning the Holy Spirit can lead to disobedience.

How would you characterize your relationship with the Holy Spirit? Are you letting His voice guide and direct you on the issues you face daily? God has spelled out exactly how He wants to use the Holy Spirit in your life and how you, as God's young man, need to start working with Him. Like any relationship, the first step is to learn more about Him so that you can partner more closely. And what a great partner He is! The Holy Spirit can:

- change the way you feel about doing God's will (see Ezekiel 36:26-27)
- remind you of exactly what Jesus wants you to do (see John 14:26)
- help you discern truth from lies so you can make better choices (see John 16:13)
- give you boldness in talking to others about God (see Acts 1:8)
- free you from guilt (see Romans 8:1)
- make your thinking more consistent with God's (see Romans 8:5-8)
- turn you away from evil behaviors (see Romans 8:13)
- remind you of your identity as a son of God (see Romans 8:16)
- give you some spiritual gifts to use for God right now (see 1 Corinthians 12:11)
- provide you with more victories over the dark side (see Galatians 5:16)

Like the NeverLost GPS system in my rental car, the Holy Spirit has an awesome capacity to help you get where you want to go, but you have to take a step to embrace Him and listen to Him. When you were saved, God installed the Holy Spirit in you for a purpose—to eliminate the need for you to navigate your way through life by listening to the unfriendly voices of the dark side—the devil and the world.

When you reach out to the Holy Spirit and give total control of your body and mind to His control, you will experience a new awareness of God's power. If you leave the Holy Spirit untapped and unused, however, God is deeply disappointed, because He knows that disowning the Holy Spirit can lead to disobedience. Check out this Scripture:

Do not bring sorrow to God's Holy Spirit by the way you live. Remember, he is the one who has identified *you* as his own, guaranteeing that you will be saved on the day of redemption. (Ephesians 4:30, NLT)

In other words, make God smile by working together with the Holy Spirit.

GET TANKED!

I roomed with Corey, a great guy, during my freshman year at UCLA. We met at freshmen orientation during the summer, and since we were both from the San Francisco Bay Area and had some acquaintances in common (we attended rival high schools), we thought that rooming with each other would be better than rooming with a total stranger. So there we were, sharing a tiny room in Hedrick Hall.

Corey did everything with gusto—at school and *after* school. But the Corey I knew sober and the Corey I knew under the influence were two totally different people. For instance:

- The sober Corey didn't talk much. The sauced—or well-tanked— Corey talked a ton.
- The sober Corey didn't share his feelings very often. The sauced Corey would hug me and say, "I love you, Kenny."
- The sober Corey was reserved and serious. The sauced Corey was engaging and outgoing.
- The sober Corey got up at the crack of dawn and was off to class. The sauced Corey slept all day the next day.
- The sober Corey never sang in public. The sauced Corey was the life of any karaoke party.

When you are under the influence of alcohol, or any other substance, you surrender control of your actions to the influence of whatever you swallowed, smoked, or injected. Consequently, your physical and cognitive abilities become impaired, and your actions take on a new, self-destructive character.

**When God's young man yields total control
to the influence of the Holy Spirit, his life will
produce actions consistent with God's ways.**

In the following scripture, the apostle Paul took the negative picture of going under the influence and turned it into a positive spiritual metaphor for our relationship with the Holy Spirit. He advised us to take a good, long swallow of the good stuff:

Don't drink too much wine. That cheapens your life. *Drink the Spirit of God,* huge draughts of him. Sing hymns instead of drinking songs! Sing songs from your heart to Christ. Sing praises over everything, any excuse for a song to God the Father in the name of our Master, Jesus Christ. (Ephesians 5:18-20, MSG)

When God's young man yields total control to the influence of the Holy Spirit, his life will produce actions consistent with God's ways. Notice the passage above is not a suggestion; it's a command, an imperative, an order. Drink the Spirit of God! Drink and watch your actions change. Go for it. Be different. Be a new man for God:

So *I advise you to live according to your new life in the Holy Spirit.* Then you won't be doing what your sinful nature craves. The old sinful nature loves to do evil, which is just the opposite from what the Holy Spirit wants.... These two forces are constantly fighting each other, and your choices are never free from this conflict....

But when the Holy Spirit controls our lives, he will produce this kind of fruit in us: love, joy, peace, patience, kindness, goodness, faithfulness, gentleness, and self-control. (Galatians 5:16-17, 22-23, NLT)

So many young men ask me, how can I know when I'm living under the control of the Holy Spirit? The answer is simple: when you're consistently saying no to the wrong desires and saying yes to God's desires for your life. That's how God's Word says you'll know. That's why when I speak to young men, I tell them to practice saying no to themselves in ways that honor God and to practice saying yes to everything that pleases Him.

In real life, this means saying:

- no to masturbation
- yes to prayer over your temptation
- no to porn
- yes to accountability
- no to skipping Bible study
- yes to fellowship
- no to impressing people
- yes to pleasing God alone
- no to indulging your mind in fantasy
- yes to memorizing God's Word
- no to keeping secrets
- yes to confession
- no to your own agenda
- yes to ministry in others' lives

Say yes to the Holy Spirit right now and every day. You do that by simply talking to God and asking him to fill you with the Holy Spirit. Activate the GPS (God's Powerful Spirit) that's in you right now by praying a simple prayer like this one:

> Holy Spirit, thank You for living in me so that *You* can be my guide. I need to rely on You more. I want You to control my life, not me. I want You to show me the choices I need to make, not me. I am sorry for taking over control when I shouldn't. Take control of me right now. Lead me, guide me, speak to me, and fill me with Your presence. Open my eyes to God's plan and give me the power to choose it quickly. Thank You for Your continued presence in my life. Thank You for taking control. I ask this in the name of Jesus. Amen.

You will recognize the Holy Spirit's clear voice the next time you have to make a choice that matters to God. Some decisions don't require His leading, like what toppings to order on your next deep-dish pizza. Others, like deciding to make time to read God's Word or not being a sexual slave in body or mind, definitely matters to God.

Just remember that listening to the Holy Spirit under life's pressure builds confidence over time. One direction the Holy Spirit will often lead you toward is prayer, which is the subject of the next chapter.

enthusiasm versus power

Three months of training.

Eight thousand feet of vertical elevation.

Forty-four miles.

Five and a half continuous hours on the bike.

When my friend Paul told me about a race sponsored by the Warrior's Society out here in California, my ears perked up. I'm no superjock, but I love physically challenging stuff. Still, the prospect of participating in this annual mountain bike powwow in the nearby Santa Ana Mountains sounded daunting. I knew I wasn't in top shape, and my mountain bike skills were novice at best. Meanwhile, Paul was a stud marine F-18 pilot who ignored physical pain like I ignored the weeds filling my flower beds in the backyard. When he shared this mountain bike challenge with me, my first thought was, *This might be for you, but not for me.*

Paul assured me that he would help me prepare for the challenging powwow. With his encouragement ringing in my ears, I reluctantly signed up. For the next three months, we rode together twice a week, steadily increasing the length of our training sessions until I was up to the full ride one week before the race. In addition, we met two mornings a week in the gym to ride stationary bikes and lift weights. I pointed all my efforts toward finishing the ride without keeling over at the finish line.

On the day of the powwow, I started well. I arrived at the first qualifying station at the two-hour mark, which was a good sign. Riders who did not arrive there within two and a half hours were not allowed to continue, because they would not have enough daylight to finish the race.

**The difference between desire and "done"
is the power to do it.**

I kept pedaling and pedaling, and five and a half hours later I crossed the finish line, crying for my mama. I finished a respectable sixty-first, which was in the middle of the pack. But more important, I learned a huge lesson. All I had to do was get on the bike, strengthen my legs, and let them carry me to the end.

Mountain biking is all about power and performance, and if you've got no power, you've got no performance. Seems simple, but it's a bummer when you call upon your legs to push and nothing's there. Around our homes, work, and school, we also require various sorts of power to make things happen. Things such as you:

- flick the switch, and the light comes on
- turn the ignition, and your engine starts up
- need to sprint, and your legs respond
- press a pad on top of your cell phone, and the phone comes alive
- use a cordless drill to drive a screw into a post
- feel the power of a jet plane lifting off the runway and carrying you into the sky

- watch your school's football team run a student-body-right running play, which opens the field for a big gain
- speak into the microphone, and your voice is amplified
- summon all your strength to bench-press a heavy set of weights to full-arm extension

Aaaaaah! Isn't it great when things work right and you achieve what you set out to accomplish? In all these instances, the difference between desire and "done" is *the power to do it.*

Batteries and biceps.

Engines and electrical boxes.

Hoover Dam and combustion power plants.

Fuel cells and solar cells.

Power is a good thing, and prayer is the outlet that God has chosen to connect you to His vast reservoir of power.

Not Just Any Search Engine

When Larry Page met Sergey Brin in 1996, they loved to argue about the best way to retrieve information from this growing phenomenon called the World Wide Web. The pair were graduate students in computer science at Stanford University, and despite their differences of opinion, they began working together toward a common goal: developing a Web site that would link users to certain specific information available on the Internet. They developed this newfangled thing called a search engine and named it Google. Although this start-up didn't attract much attention in the burgeoning dotcom world, the two partners managed to land a million dollars in seed money.

The name Google was a play on the mathematical term *googol,* which refers to the numeral one followed by a hundred zeros. Page and Brin said

Google reflected their goal of organizing the nearly infinite amount of data on the Internet and bringing the power of the information to as many people as possible. Today Google is the world's largest search engine, sporting a four-billion page index of information that allows hundreds of millions of people a month to find information on just about anything. Larry Page and Sergey Brin harnessed the amazing power of the Internet, which has made them very wealthy men.

There is a living spiritual engine within you that can search the mind of God.

Google and other search engines have had dramatic impacts in ordinary people's lives. Consider these stories that I came across:

After thirty-four years of not knowing who my father was, I typed his name into Google.com and found a link that I thought might help me. I sent an e-mail to the link's Web site, who then forwarded the information. Two days later I received a lengthy e-mail from the man who I thought was my father. It was indeed him. He had also been looking for me for years but to no avail. I just wanted to say thank you, as now I have the opportunity to meet my father, introduce him to his new grandson, and meet my two half brothers and half sister.

Our miniature dachshund got a treat stuck in his throat, was choking, and couldn't breathe. My husband told me to do a Google search on "choking dog." The first selection was "How to Do a Heimlich Maneuver on a Dog." I clicked on the site and read it quickly to my husband. He performed the maneuver, and the treat shot across the room. Thanks to Google, our dog was saved.

Google helped me discover that my daughter's strange medical problems were part of a rare genetic syndrome that most of her doctors had never heard of. My discovery helped her cardiologist diagnose another patient with the same syndrome.

The numbers of Web pages, searches, hits, and stories like these are so titanic we cannot fathom how many lives are affected every day by Google. Yet all of that astonishing power cannot come close to the storehouse of personal spiritual power available to you as God's young servant, which is made possible through the power of prayer. Start your search here:

God can do anything, you know—far more than you could ever imagine or guess or request in your wildest dreams! He does it not by pushing us around but by *working within us,* his Spirit deeply and gently within us. (Ephesians 3:20, MSG)

Most young men don't get it that God's tool bar is loaded right onto the home page of their lives. There is a living spiritual engine within you that can search the mind of God for:

- hope and direction for your future (see Jeremiah 29:11)
- answers to your most perplexing questions (see Jeremiah 33:3)
- relief from pressure (see Matthew 11:28-30)
- peace to replace your anxiety (see Philippians 4:6-7)
- freedom from guilt (see Psalm 32:1-5)
- rescue from a troubling situation (see Psalm 40:1-2)
- new spiritual energy after blowing it (see Psalm 51:10-12)

- the Holy Spirit (see Luke 11:9-13)
- a new heart to live for Him (see Psalm 86:11)
- His kingdom, will, forgiveness, and power over temptation
  (see Matthew 6:8-13)

Just as the power of the Internet was waiting to be harnessed by the Google inventors, God is waiting for you to access His awesome strength. Everything is just a prayer away. If you're clueless to the personal benefits of prayer, or in too much of a hurry to slow down and get into the practice of prayer, here's what you need to know: your network card was installed in you at salvation, and talking to God is done wirelessly. So what are you waiting for?

> This is GOD'S Message, the God who made earth, made it livable and lasting, known everywhere as GOD: "*Call to me* and I will answer you. I'll tell you marvelous and wondrous things that you could never figure out on your own." (Jeremiah 33:2-3, MSG)

To Get Versus to Get to Know

Josh's alarm went off at 6:45. He got out of bed, scratched himself, and then hit the bathroom. Fifteen minutes later, eyes wide open and dressed, he scampered downstairs to eat a bowl of Cheerios before Barry would pick him up. They had plans to meet Luke down at the coffeehouse to go over the review questions for their comparative government final. As he put his breakfast bowl in the dishwasher, Josh whispered, "Lord, please help me today with this final exam."

The review with the guys was tedious. So many things to go over, and they had only an hour before their final at Campbell Hall. As Josh quizzed

Barry on the differences between socialism and communism, he remembered that his parents were arriving at three o'clock to drive him back home for winter break. He wasn't packed or anything. When this thought came to mind, he asked God for mercy.

**It took a crisis situation before it even
dawned on him to talk to God in prayer.**

The final was brutal. He noticed several people finishing early, which made him nervous because he was only halfway through his third essay question, and the clock was ticking. He needed an A, or at least a high B, to keep his dream of law school alive. *Oh, God, I need this grade,* he prayed in his head. *I know I didn't prepare as well as I should have, but can You help me on this?*

When the test was over, he headed back home to check his e-mail and call his mom's cell phone, but she beat him to the punch. She said they would pull in around 4:30, later than planned, and they had to get back on the road because Aunt Eleanor was flying in and would arrive at 9:00 p.m. "Mom, we'll make it," he said. "Listen, I gotta get some Christmas presents from the student bookstore. See you when you get here." Holy cow. He closed his eyes. *Lord Jesus, help me.*

His cell rang. "Hi! How'd your test go?" Cindy was on the line.

"Good." Short answers were best with Cindy. He knew that the last thing he needed was a relationship with her right now—she wasn't that attractive—but then again he shouldn't have kissed her good night a few evenings ago. Or let his hands roam. Now she was calling him twice a day, clinging. Brother!

"I have a little present for you before you go home for Christmas. Can

I meet you at your apartment before you go?" The apartment was where he let the fingers do the walking last time. *You idiot. Sorry about that, Lord. I knew I was crossing the line with her.*

"Sure. Can you come around four o'clock? My parents are picking me up a little later, so I only have fifteen minutes, okay?"

"I'll seeeee ya then."

"Uh, bye."

Josh reviewed how his day was going so far. *Let's see. First the test—no better than a B-minus or C for sure. Then my parents—I'll have to fake like I'm doing good in school. I'll have to work to pay for those Christmas presents—and that Cindy—oh, mama. Not good. What next? How did I get here?* He pocketed his cell phone, took a huge breath, and cupped his face in his hands. *Lord, what do I do?*

Josh's scenario is typical of most young men when it comes to prayer: it took a crisis situation before it even dawned on him to talk to God in prayer. Let's put it this way: Josh was certainly mindful of God when he needed something or when he was in a setting that called for prayer, like during chapel or when his Bible study was finishing up. He realizes that his dialogue with God is shallow and selfish most of the time (like today), but he can't seem to work in more conversations with God.

Prayer, for you, is a secret power, an adventure in trusting the living God.

Do you ever wonder what the Creator thinks when He views this kind of prayer life? Isaiah heard it loud and clear: "And so the Lord says, 'These people say they are mine. They honor me with their lips, but their hearts are far away'" (Isaiah 29:13, NLT).

Can you imagine a friend who only called up when he needed a ride?

Or he only e-mailed you when he needed to pick your brain? I don't think you would naturally pick that person out of a lineup to be a close friend.

What drives you to pray and share what's going on in your life with Jesus? Is it to get—or is it to get to know? If you claim to be God's young man, and you name Jesus as your forgiver and leader, then your impulse to talk to Him should not be driven by a present need, a sudden crisis, or past sins. No, you have to consider the experience that bonds you together and makes the relationship possible in the first place—a bloodstained cross.

Even if you don't feel like it, He's earned a daily thank-you for His sacrifice that made it possible for you to spend eternity with Him and share His inheritance. But God's young man goes beyond a thank-you to a consistent dialogue between a King and a servant who is always seeking, ever trusting, and fervently devoted. Prayer, for you, is a secret power, an adventure in trusting the living God. When a young man recognizes this privilege, he moves beyond the task of prayer to the treasure of being present with God. As Scripture says, "A single day in your courts is better than a thousand anywhere else!" (Psalm 84:10, NLT)

Quick and Quality Is an Oxymoron

While God receives and responds to all kinds of prayers (by that I mean anything from signal flares to caring worship), His earnest desire is that you recognize that your communication with Him should be more than just a presentation of your personal problems. He wants to *be with you.* Jesus wants you to slow down long enough to connect: "Look at me. I stand at the door. I knock. If you hear me call and open the door, I'll come right in and sit down to supper with you" (Revelation 3:20, MSG).

If you follow Jesus in the Gospels, one of the first things you'll notice is that He loved to sit down, visit with friends, share meals, and talk for hours.

In fact, if you were a busybody and couldn't slow down, you just might get cautioned for not being wise enough to slow down and be with Jesus. One of Jesus's close friends found out the hard way!

> As Jesus and the disciples continued on their way to Jerusalem, they came to a village where a woman named Martha welcomed them into her home. Her sister, Mary, sat at the Lord's feet, listening to what he taught. But Martha was worrying over the big dinner she was preparing. She came to Jesus and said, "Lord, doesn't it seem unfair to you that my sister just sits here while I do all the work? Tell her to come and help me."
>
> But the Lord said to her, "My dear Martha, you are so upset over all these details! *There is really only one thing worth being concerned about.* Mary has discovered it—and I won't take it away from her." (Luke 10:38-42, NLT)

For Jesus, quick connection and quality relationship was an oxymoron—two totally contradictory ideas that don't go together. The message to Martha was simple: *You can't connect with Me on the fly!* He wouldn't cheat Martha's sister, Mary, out of their time together by cutting it short. But I know plenty of young men who have cut Jesus short on prayer because they simply don't know how to slow down, relax, and talk with their Savior about stuff.

This doesn't mean that you have to be in church, in your room alone, or even at a Bible study. The Bible teaches that wherever you choose to connect with Jesus is holy ground. In fact, there are no boundaries to where or when you should pray—only the encouragement to do it as much as possible, whenever and wherever possible. Search the Bible, and you will find no starting or stopping points, appropriate or inappropriate settings, or set or loose times. Prayer belongs to you everywhere and anytime. Here are some examples of how prayer is described in God's Word:

- Jesus illustrates the need for constant prayer by telling His followers a story (see Luke 18:1).
- Prayer is for all times and for every occasion (see Ephesians 6:18).
- We should always pray for others (see Colossians 1:3).
- We should live a lifestyle of prayer (see Colossians 4:2).
- We should pray continually, thanking God in everything (see 1 Thessalonians 5:17-18).
- God's men, specifically, should be unashamed in prayer (see 1 Timothy 2:8).

What's the distinguishing feature of your spiritual life as a young man? What marks your approach to the things that really matter in your life? What attitude do you adopt toward the situations you face and the relationships in which you find yourself? If you care about the answers to these questions, you should invest more and more of your time in prayer and dialogue with God over anything that might have an eternal, spiritual, or practical impact on your life or someone else's.

Trying to manage your life without praying is like trying to ride a bike with flat tires. It can be done, but life is sure going to be tiring, laborious, and no fun.

Trying to manage your life without praying is like trying to ride a bike with flat tires. It can be done, but life is sure going to be tiring, laborious, and no fun. You certainly can't enjoy the ride or feel the wind in your face. Only a total dork would choose to do that, but that is exactly what you are choosing to do if you neglect the power of prayer.

I'm sure you've gotten the point of this chapter, but let me sum things up in this way: *Prayer is the power that fuels the performance of your faith.* Put it to work today, hit Send in Jesus's name, and you'll be tapping into a wealth of joy, peace, patience, confidence, faith, and godly character. Do these things, and God will help you finish the great work He's started in you.

In the next chapter you'll see that the pressures you face aren't put in your life to hinder you but to drive you to prayer *and* call out your faith and courage.

pressure means progress

Every Monday night at my fraternity house, one block away from the UCLA campus, we would hold something we called Chapter. All 120 of us would cram into the basement—which we called the Chapter Room—and conduct the business and rituals necessary to run our fraternity. The most notable thing about Chapter nights was how formal they were.

Everyone came dressed in coat and tie—or you didn't eat. The house chaplain would pray over the food, which was served in three courses. House officers—the president, vice president, and so on—were seated at the head table, and dinner was served by pin number, or seniority, in the fraternity.

Whenever we had guests, such as parents or friends, they were grandly introduced to the assembly, and any female visitors were serenaded by 120 voices. Fraternity members were only allowed to pin their girlfriends on Monday nights. Pledge training, along with Formal Chapter, as we called it, were mandatory, and we held initiation ceremonies on Chapter nights.

As a navy brat, I loved all the formality. As a Christian, it was one of the few nights the guys would act civilized and well-mannered. I was often asked to pray before meals, which allowed me to be a light. But I'll never forget a Chapter night during my junior year that was different from all the rest.

We were politely polishing off our last bites of steak and au gratin potatoes when a gorgeous young blonde dressed suspiciously in a trench coat came waltzing into the dining hall. On her right arm was a bulky guy in sunglasses holding a boom box. As she stood seductively before us, one of the brothers stood up and announced that as a birthday gift to his little brother, we would be treated to a special performance by Miss Trench Coat in the living room after pledge training. Talk about a carrot and a stick.

This red-meat announcement was greeted with a wild outburst, high-fives, whistling, and applause. Meanwhile, I steamed from my seat at the head table. One thing was for sure: in less than an hour, the boom box would be turned on and the trench coat would come off. Va va voom!

God taught me a powerful lesson that day: pressure is a good thing, because it never leaves you where it finds you.

The little brother in this case was a pledge, and I was his pledge trainer. This meant that the main audience for Miss Trench Coat would be a group of young men I met with every Chapter night to impress upon them the more "noble" principles of our fraternity. During those sessions I quizzed them on fraternity history in preparation for initiation at the end of the quarter.

After Miss Trench Coat's unexpected appearance, however, I felt like Daniel in a pagan palace asked to swallow food offered to idols. I could not stomach this, nor could I participate in it. But what else could I do? It was just me against a tidal wave of testosterone.

One hour later, my pledge class was over. Lo and behold, in walked Miss Trench Coat and her personal security officer. *Here we go.*

I stood up and informed the pledges that they did not have to stay for the performance. Then I exited, stage right. Wanna guess how many came with me? Right—zero out of twenty-five—and other fraternity brothers filed into the room. When I realized that I led a parade of none, I stomped up to my room on the second floor, my blood boiling and my mind spinning. Part of me wished that I was still on the other side so I wouldn't have this intense battle raging inside. The other part of me said, *Fight!*

From my room, I heard the fast-paced music with a heavy beat come on. *Lord, what do I do?* I paced about my room and actually thought about going downstairs and ripping out the plug. That would go over real well. I figured that one of my fraternity brothers had paid good money to see some live flesh, and he'd rip me a new one if I interfered. So I prayed: *Lord, what do I do? What am I going to do about this?*

Suddenly, a searing thought landed like a grenade in a foxhole: *Pray Miss Trench Coat out of there.* I bowed my head and prayed: *Jesus, greater are You who is in me than He who is in the world. In the name of Jesus Christ, I come against every evil in this house and command it to be gone.*

I listened for the music, which was still blaring. I could hear the bass beat and the roars of the guys. Five minutes passed by, so I prayed again: *Lord Jesus Christ, make this evil go. Make her leave, and You will receive the glory. Make her go. Get her out of this house in Your name.*

The music was still going strong as another five minutes passed—five minutes of live nude action that would be imprinted on their minds for a *long* time. *Lord Jesus, make the boom box break. Make it break. Do something to stop this in Your name.*

Suddenly, the music stopped. I listened closely and could make out some kind of commotion downstairs. I bolted down the staircase and uncomfortably walked into an unhappy mob of eighteen- to twenty-two-year-old men who looked like they just got their chocolate cake taken away after one bite. I watched Miss Trench Coat, who was still *wearing* her trench coat, stride purposely for the front door with the big goombah bodyguard fast on her heels.

"What happened?" I exclaimed.

"The boom box broke," said one of the plebes, "and she didn't want to continue."

I don't know who was more in shock—me or them! Miss Trench Coat's short-circuited performance was over. Done. Bye-bye!

God taught me a powerful lesson that day: pressure is a good thing, because it never leaves you where it finds you. What I mean is that there were only two directions I could have taken. I could have joined in the fun and compromised. Or I could make the best stand under the circumstances and fight with the tools God gave me. In the end, I faced ninety minutes of pressure—from the announcement during dinner to the striptease act, but I received a clear view of God's awesome power.

When similar situations come your way, think of how God wants to use this pressure to make you a new man. Most young men have a one-sided view of pressure, temptation, and trials—a negative one. But that's how the world, the dark side, and Satan want you to see it. God wants you to see it His way:

> So do not throw away your confidence; it will be richly rewarded.
> You need to persevere so that when you have done the will of God,
> you will receive what he has promised.... "But my righteous one will
> live by faith. And if he shrinks back, I will not be pleased with him."
>
> But we are not of those who shrink back and are destroyed, but
> of those who believe and are saved. (Hebrews 10:35-36,38-39)

God's plan to make you a man doesn't include a provision to remove you from pressure. In fact, He's most likely to *throw* you into pressure-packed situations, because He knows that will increase your faith and grow your character in Christ. More often than not, you'll have to choose God and trust Him with the results. God tests you because you're still growing up.

Rising Makes the Man

Ask guys a few years older than you, and they will agree when I say that young men experience a *lot* of growth from the time they leave high school to the time they finish college or start a job. Up to this point, your faith has probably been insulated from any real pressure because of the protective forces of family, friends, or church. But when you land in a secular school or join the ranks of salaried men, your faith will be tested. You'll see things you never saw before—or be asked if you *want* to see things you never saw before. You'll likely experience ups and downs and the occasional face plant, but that's okay because you aren't perfect (nor am I). Only one man scored a perfect ten on earth, and He's not you! So just chill out and cut yourself some slack, because God certainly does. Listen to His encouraging voice speak to your journey:

- "For though a righteous man *falls seven times,* he *rises again*" (Proverbs 24:16).
- "*Continue to work out* your salvation with fear and trembling, for it is God who works in you to will and to act *according to his good purpose*" (Philippians 2:12-13).
- "Being confident of this, that he who *began a good work in you will carry it on to completion* until the day of Christ Jesus" (Philippians 1:6).

- "The path of the righteous is like the light of the dawn, that *shines brighter and brighter* until the full day" (Proverbs 4:18, NASB).

God sees you like a boxer who keeps getting knocked down but rises again to continue fighting, just like Rocky Balboa. Hear what He's saying: *Stumbling is expected, but rising makes the man.*

God sees you like a miner, covered in black, who continues to work in the mines, chipping away until he comes out with the gold. Hear what He's saying: *Go back down in there in the pit and come out of the darkness with My purpose in your hands.*

When you see pressure the right way, you become very dangerous for God's purposes.

God sees you like a running back, straining to get outside so you can turn the corner and turn on the jets à la Priest Holmes or Marshall Faulk. Hear what He's saying: *Keep running hard for the goal, and I will keep throwing some key blocks to get you out of the red zone and into the end zone.*

God sees your spiritual journey like sunrise coming over the mountains that gets progressively stronger until you hit your goal of becoming God's young man. Hear what He's saying: *The sun doesn't start out at the top of the sky. It's a progression of brightness.*

God wants you to be both realistic and optimistic. He wants you to fight and push hard every time He hands you the ball. Sure, you may get gang-tackled every now and then, but ready yourself for another run at it. Take the long view and remember:

- When you see pressure the right way, you become very dangerous for God's purposes.
- When you see pressure the wrong way, you set yourself up for failure.

- When you accept pressure as a steppingstone to growth, you will be encouraged and empowered toward victory.
- When you perceive pressure as a stumbling block, you will get deflated and depressed over your mistakes.
- When you feel pressure and choose God's way, you will experience relief.
- When you allow pressure to build up, it will either crush your faith or explode your witness.

EQUALIZE THE PRESSURE IN YOUR LIFE

Scuba divers know all about pressure because their lives depend on it. Author Scott Larson wrote about this phenomenon in an article in the magazine *Men of Integrity.* He explained exactly why these deep-sea daredevils must get the pressure equation right:

> If you were to breathe air at the surface, hold it, and then submerge twenty feet or so, your lungs could collapse. That's because pressure at the surface is much less than the pressure in water twenty feet deep. In the same way, if you breathe in air at twenty feet below the water's surface and hold your breath until you come to the surface, your lungs could explode because the pressure around you becomes less and less and the air in your lungs expands to equalize. A scuba regulator equalizes the pressure of the air you breathe from your tank to match the pressure in the water around you, but it doesn't help if you don't keep breathing.[1]

---

1. Scott Larson, "Pressure," *Men of Integrity,* August 10, 2004.

206 | EVERY YOUNG MAN, GOD'S MAN

You need God's overpowering strength within you to equalize the pressure being put on you by the culture, the dark side, and the devil. Lots of young men I meet are under huge spiritual pressure, grappling with their faith to make sense of their temptations, their choices, and various issues in their lives, such as:

- divorcing parents
- family problems
- isolation
- loneliness
- masturbation
- grades
- sexual discontent
- spiritual responsibility
- parents who can't be pleased
- breakups with girlfriends
- sexual boundaries with girlfriends
- friendships that pull them down
- guilt from living a double life
- failing in school
- identity crises

God might have you at the crossroads, and if He does, He wants you to look up and read this sign before you make one more choice: "Blessed is the man who perseveres under trial, because when he has stood the test, he will receive the crown of life that God has promised to those who love him" (James 1:12). This signpost of Scripture clearly shows: *Perseverance under pressure pleases God.* The way you persevere is by choosing to match the pressure on you with pressure going back out. For you this may mean:

- staying with God's way in spite of your feelings
- trusting God with things outside your control
- continuing to turn the pressure over to God and asking Him to relieve it one way or another
- letting go of a relationship and putting it in God's hands
- not missing your accountability group
- continuing to work hard in school
- confessing a sin to another brother
- forgiving first
- keeping your word

Charles H. Spurgeon, an English evangelist from the late 1800s, once said: "I owe more to the fire and hammer and file than anything else in my Lord's workshop." His point: success and growth as God's servant can only come through looking into the fires of life and allowing God to put you into them, knowing you will come out stronger for His purposes and more prepared for His plan.

Perseverance under pressure pleases God.

This is why God never wants you to run from pressures or problems. Perseverance is a core discipline of a young man, so don't cheat yourself out of becoming a strong God's man by bailing. Instead, work it till it hurts. View the pains of growth in your character not as things that cramp your style or steal your fun but as signs that you're growing stronger every day. See your growth pain as spiritual gain. See pressure as the road to progress:

> Consider it a sheer gift, friends, when tests and challenges come at you from all sides. You know that under pressure, your faith-life is

forced into the open and shows its true colors. So *don't try to get out of anything prematurely.* Let it do its work so you become mature and well-developed, not deficient in any way. (James 1:2-4, MSG)

It's been said that those who fail to plan, plan to fail. We'll take a look at how God's young man plans to win in the next chapter.

planning victory

Growing up in the last part of the nineteenth century, George S. Patton wanted to be a hero. The stories of his ancestors in the American Revolution, the Mexican War, and the Civil War created an insatiable desire to learn and execute the so-called art of war. He rose quickly through the military ranks and developed a reputation as a master tactician. His study of how to prosecute war caused him to comment one time that he could smell a battlefield.

Patton's military leadership abilities caught the attention of Supreme Allied Commander Dwight D. Eisenhower, who appointed Patton as the commander of the Third Army during World War II. This decision helped define the outcome of the war: Patton's army liberated Belgium, Luxembourg, and France and raced toward Berlin. His speedy tanks and combat-hardened troops broke through the German lines at a breakneck pace, which created great respect, fear, and admiration among the Nazi military establishment. Field Marshal Erwin Rommel, known as the "Desert Fox" and Germany's most decorated field commander, called Patton's wartime actions "the most astonishing achievements in mobile warfare." So what was his secret?

Planning. Patton considered the battlefield before he engaged the enemy. He was a master at picking the right spots, studying terrain, outlining a battle plan, and strategically using his forces to achieve surprise, overwhelm, and surround. His philosophy for making war is captured in some of these famous lines:

- "Never let the enemy pick the battlefield."
- "I always believe in being prepared, even when I am dressed in a white tie and tails."
- "A pint of sweat [in planning and preparation] is worth a gallon of blood."
- "Good tactics can save even the worst strategy. Bad tactics will destroy even the best strategy."
- "In war the only sure defense is a good offense."
- "I fight where I am told, and I win where I fight."

One of Patton's famous victories happened on German soil—the Hunsruck Mountains, where ten German divisions had assembled to stop him. After thinking through various scenarios, Patton deployed an encircle-and-cut-off-the-enemy strategy. To do this, however, he had to divide his army so that his armored divisions could break through the rear line from the south as well as from the north. After encircling the Germans, he could cut their supply lines and force a surrender.

"Never let the enemy pick the battlefield."

The result at Hunsruck: ten German divisions captured.

Some of Patton's greatest victories cost the Third Army the fewest lives because of his commitment to planning. Such planning protected Patton's forces from high numbers of casualties and provided him freedom to pursue his responsibilities with energy. Planning gave him unparalleled confidence in battle, which tipped the scales on the battlefield. We can learn something from Patton's planning abilities in our war against the dark side.

CUTTING OFF AND STARVING SIN

As God's young man, you, too, must have a plan for the key battles in your future. In these circumstances, it helps to think like General Patton for a second. The following questions are designed to help facilitate your planning process:

- What footholds in my life do I need to liberate from the Enemy and win back for Christ?
- What are my patterns of temptation?
- What can I do to be better prepared?
- What situations make me vulnerable to attack by the dark side or the devil?
- Who am I with when I am tempted?
- Where am I when I am tempted?
- What are high-risk environments for me?
- What are the strengths and strategies of the Enemy?
- What are my weaknesses?
- What boundaries have I set up that demonstrate how I know my weaknesses?
- What limits to my freedom will help me win?
- What does my lack of discipline cost me in my relationship with Jesus?
- Who is in my band of brothers?
- Am I dictating the way my battles are fought?

Thinking about your answers will help you develop a code to live by—one you won't want to stray from. One of the reasons so many young men suffer defeat regularly in spiritual warfare is that they fail to engage the Enemy or take a proactive approach to battle. They just show up and expect that's enough to conquer direct attacks against their faith. If Patton thought like that, we might all be speaking German today.

What situations make me vulnerable to attack by the dark side or the devil?

This code of conduct, laid out in advance, dictates the battle. I also like to call this code of conduct by another term—*boundaries*—those fluorescent lines in the sand that show us where we will and will not go as God's young men. Living up to these boundaries requires humility and diligence, as Scripture reminds us: "Keep the rules and keep your life; careless living kills" (Proverbs 19:16, MSG).

To get the men of His day thinking ahead like this, Jesus used some dramatic language to drive home the importance of showing no mercy to sin when it comes to defeating it:

> If your hand causes you to sin, cut it off. It is better to enter heaven with only one hand than to go into the unquenchable fires of hell with two hands. If your foot causes you to sin, cut it off. It is better to enter heaven with only one foot than to be thrown into hell with two feet. And if your eye causes you to sin, gouge it out. It is better to enter the Kingdom of God half blind than to have two eyes and be thrown into hell, "where the worm never dies and the fire never goes out." (Mark 9:43-48, NLT)

Jesus knew how to get a man's attention—and I'm just glad He didn't mention other parts of the male anatomy! What He was saying in blunt language was this:

- Sin is the enemy.
- Cut sin off at the source.
- Keep God and eternity in mind as you make choices.
- Know your weaknesses so that you can cut them out effectively.

When I was a chaplain in a cancer unit during my seminary training, I became very aware of a world where surgeries, chemotherapy, and radiation were employed to save the lives of my patients. Cancer in the brain, breasts, or prostate usually called for skilled surgeons to cut away the malignant cells before they metastasized (spread). The picture of cutting out sin in your life is similar in three ways:

1. *Surgeries are painful.* Even though surgeries and treatments are extremely painful, nearly all patients tell their doctors to go for it because they want to live. You want to live a full life with Christ, right? Then cut out the sin.

2. *Surgeries are thorough.* Oncologists never say to a cancer patient, "Your surgery went well, Mr. Jones. We took out half of your tumor and left the other half inside of you." No, they go after *every* malignant cell, otherwise the cancer could come back. You want to be just as thorough in attacking the sin in your life.

3. *Surgeries are worthwhile.* The words that cancer patients couldn't wait to hear after the operation was, "We got it all." The feeling you want to have at the end of the day is, *I dealt with it all.*

For a lot of young guys, cutting out a sexual habit or behavior that they know is inconsistent with God's plan is painful. They rather *liked* doing that activity because it was fun or felt really good. But the mind-set that every young man must switch over to is this: knowing and serving Christ is worth any sacrifice or perceived loss. To do this you have to decide *now* to cut off sin at its source.

No Cherry-Picking

Carlos Ruiz is a soccer legend in his native Guatemala, but he also has a growing fan club in Southern California where he plays for the Los Angeles Galaxy. Carlos led his team to the 2002 Major League Soccer (MLS) championship and is always vying for the league's top goal scorer award. I've taken in several of the Galaxy's games, and what I find exciting is watching Carlos. He plays the striker position and athletically times his runs (or sprints) to get to the ball and score.

> I've run into lots of young guys
> who play the game of life thinking
> they can cherry-pick and still win.

In soccer there's a very strict rule that prevents players from cherry-picking easy balls from behind the defense. (The rule is called offside.) So a striker like Carlos must time his connection with balls kicked to him, or a penalty will be called and the other team will get the ball. If he manages to get to a leading pass without being offside, Carlos can break through the team's defenses and often beat the goalie by kicking the ball into the back of the net.

As with all world-class athletes, Carlos trains and trains at the fundamental aspects of the game. He works on his collections of the ball, his footwork, his passing, his heading, and his shooting nearly every day so that when his opportunity comes, he is ready. But what if Carlos decided the offside rule didn't apply to him? For starters, none of his goals would officially count. Second, the other team would get the ball. Third, he'd be out of a job. His individual success requires him to observe the rules carefully. The heart and the will to get that ball into the net *require that he respect the rules* to find success.

In what ways can you rearrange your life so that sin no longer looks good?

I've run into lots of young guys who play the game of life thinking they can cherry-pick and still win. They may possess good spiritual skills, be trained in good spiritual habits, and be connected to other guys, but when it comes to putting their dedication, training, and relationships together to win their spiritual battles, they get called for a foul because they thought it wouldn't matter if they crossed God's offside line. That's when they lose their chance to score big for God.

What keeps a lot of guys from scoring for God is their inability to follow the necessary rules that would help them take advantage of their efforts, abilities, and relationships for Christ. Just as Carlos can't score goals without respecting the game's rules, God's young man cannot win his key battles without boundaries. Trying to cherry-pick—thinking there is a shortcut to the Man Zone—is never gonna cut it; a specific plan needs to be drawn up and pursued. This will mean planning out, in advance, the specific actions that will help you practice your faith, preserve your commitment, and allow you to get the results you are chasing as God's young man.

Best-selling author and pastor John Ortberg put it this way: "The key task of spiritual vitality is that we must arrange life so that sin no longer looks good." In what ways can you rearrange your life so that sin no longer looks good? Consider:

- the places you will go
- the places you will not go
- the images you will put before your eyes
- the images you will not put before your eyes
- friends you will keep
- friends that you will avoid
- habits you will pursue
- habits you will not pursue
- phrases and words you will speak
- phrases and words you will not speak
- relationships with the opposite sex you will participate in
- relationships with the opposite sex you will not participate in
- thoughts you will allow your mind to dwell on
- thoughts you will not allow your mind to dwell on

More specifically, predetermined boundaries may involve cutting off and starving sin in the following ways:

- carving sexy R-rated films out of your cinematic repertoire
- deciding that the bar scene or drinking parties will not be the place where you connect with friends
- refusing to keep sexual secrets that put distance between you and God
- accepting sexual accountability
- inviting people you spiritually respect to ask you the tough questions
- committing to not mentally undressing any woman
- getting software that allows someone to see where you have been on the Net
- committing in writing with a girl you're dating the dos and don'ts of the physical relationship

If you're really serious about your relationship to God, then you'll agree that wise planning reduces temptation. When you deal with issues *before* you're tempted, you enter the battle with a plan versus just showing up clueless about what happens next. When you execute a plan like this, you're counting the cost of what it takes to build a solid spiritual life. Counting the cost is a smart thing to do, as Jesus Christ says in this passage of Scripture:

> For which one of you, when he wants to build a tower, does not first
> sit down and calculate the cost to see if he has enough to complete it?
> Otherwise, when he has laid a foundation and is not able to finish, all
> who observe it begin to ridicule him, saying, "This man began to
> build and was not able to finish." (Luke 14:28-30, NASB)

The biggest issue for you to decide is this: *How am I going to play the game of life?* Maybe you haven't performed too well up to this point, but that doesn't matter, because it's how you play the game from here on that counts. That's why I've spent a great deal of time talking about the importance of friends, guarding your eyes, staying away from situations that place sexual temptation in your path, and having a plan so that you know where you're going.

**If you're really serious about your
relationship to God, then you'll agree that
wise planning reduces temptation.**

Before, when you were a kid, your decisions weren't that important. Think about it—what was so important to decide at age ten? What flavor your Baskin-Robbins ice-cream cone would be? But these days your day-to-day decisions have long-term consequences. Those who start drinking in their teens are far more likely to become alcoholics than those who don't drink before they're twenty-one. Those who get hooked on porn today will have that affect their marriage in the future. Those who fool around sexually now are 100 percent more likely to become fathers out of wedlock than guys who remain sexually pure. Good boundaries now, especially sexual ones, will help you finish this phase of your race as a young man in a good position. More important, staying inside His boundaries will prepare you for promotion in God's army to leadership and ministry, because the church needs a few good men.

Good boundaries bring you clarity, focus, and moral direction by giving you a predetermined path to follow. But make no mistake—setting and keeping them is a discipline. The good news is that your training will pay off, and like General Patton, you, too, will be able to smell a battlefield.

Oswald Chambers, author of *My Utmost for His Highest,* observed the making of this transition to spiritual manhood. "Impulse is all right in a child, but it is disastrous in a man," he said. "Impulse must be trained into intuition through discipline." The apostle Paul also wrote of this concept in his letter to the Corinthians: "When I was a child, I talked like a child, I thought like a child, I reasoned like a child. When I became a man, I put childish ways behind me" (1 Corinthians 13:11). Strong boundaries in a young man's life are a sign to me that he is making this transition.

It's paradoxical but true:

true freedom requires restraint.

The things that a guy tends to resist—limits, godly boundaries, and rules—are the very things you need to become the man God wants you to be. The dark side, the popular culture, and the devil will attempt to convince you that these commitments are old school and take away your independence. In my experience, most young guys who believe this become slaves to the very attitudes and actions they were told represented freedom. Ask the teenagers of the sixties, who are now your moms and dads. It's paradoxical but true: true freedom requires restraint.

When you get this, you see the Scriptures in a whole new light. God encourages good planning and good boundaries because it makes you more honest about your struggle and your need for Him. He gives us boundaries so that wrong desires can be starved and good desires can be fed. And lastly, good boundaries produce strong men who keep commitments, become good marriage material, and fight for their Savior and win.

These boundaries will give you confidence in your battles against sin and help you honor Christ above all. We'll discuss what honoring Him looks like for God's young man in our final chapter.

honoring the sacrifice

One million black soldiers served in the U.S. military during World War II. Not one received a medal for his valor or bravery during the conflict. Fifty years later the Department of Defense made amends by presenting medals to seven African Americans denied awards because of their race.

Only one was alive to receive his country's honor for his heroism, so I can't imagine what was going through his mind. According to the commission that researched black American participation in the conflict, black soldiers put up with what the report called a "wave of racism." It began after Pearl Harbor, when blacks were thought to be unfit to serve by the U.S. military establishment. But as pressure mounted from the black community in the first few years of World War II, the Army formed two black divisions—"separate but equal"—in 1943. The Ninety-second Division was shipped off to Italy, and the Ninety-third Division was sent to the Pacific theater.

One of the men in the Ninety-second was Lt. John Fox from Boston. He had been assigned to the 366th Infantry as a forward observer in Sommocolonia, Italy. He was the eyes and ears for a battalion of one thousand men assigned to guard a thirty-mile battlefront in the Italian countryside. On December 26, 1944, Fox spotted large numbers of Germans moving in quickly to overrun his position. He immediately called his fire-control officer and directed an artillery assault near his position. But as Lieutenant Fox scanned the horizon further, the number of German soldiers coming his way was more than he initially thought.

This is where Fox did something so heroic, I find it nearly impossible to believe. He placed a second call to the fire controller and asked for an artillery barrage *directly* on his position.

The fire-control officer refused Fox's request, but the black lieutenant protested and asked again. Hearing the urgency in Fox's voice, the officer summoned the colonel commanding the battlefield to talk to Fox. Once again, Fox called for fire directly on his position. The colonel refused as well, because he understood the implication: he would be signing Fox's death warrant. Fox pleaded with the colonel. "There are hundreds of them coming—put everything you have on my OP!" he said, referring to his observation post. Hesitantly, the colonel rang division headquarters for approval. After explaining Fox's request, he got the green light. Almost immediately a thunderstorm of high-explosive shells rained down on Fox's position, sealing his fate. His unit later retrieved his body from the shattered wreckage of his post, surrounded by one hundred dead German soldiers.

Sixty years after John Fox called his fire controller, his command—"Put everything you have on me!"—still resonates for anyone hearing about this incredible story today. John Fox overcame fear and lived strong as a man long before Lance Armstrong came on the scene. He was selfless in his duty, and he did not let racism deter him from doing what he felt that moment demanded—which required him to take the hit for his battalion. He didn't take no as an escape clause, because he wanted a yes for a thousand guys behind him. For that incredibly selfless act, I salute you, 1st Lt. John R. Fox, 366th Infantry, Ninety-second Division. May your memory live on.

IGNORANCE IS A SIN

As a military kid I was raised to revere our armed forces, so I'm quite pleased that the U.S. military made it right by honoring John Fox and his brave black compatriots, although it took more than a half century. As we come to the close of this book, you will have to make it right by Jesus Christ as well. Just like the U.S. Army failed to remember, failed to recognize, and failed to honor these brave African American soldiers, most young men have not taken to heart the gravity of what Jesus has done for them. My goal is to help you understand the sacrifice that God's Son made for you so that when you battle sin in your life, you'll remember that sacrifice and act accordingly. You will live differently acting on that knowledge. As Charles H. Spurgeon so aptly said, "A dying Savior is the death of sin."

Most guys experience the sacrifice of Christ in an abstract sense, which doesn't leave room for an emotional connection. That is why I recommend that every young man journeying toward Jesus see Mel Gibson's *The Passion of the Christ* to discover the hero of your faith and the captain of your salvation. Why? Because to move you from the have-to-do Christian experience to the want-to-please-You life of God's young man, you must feel the personal nature of what took place.

Your energy and commitment to become God's young man hinges on what motivates you. Just to be clear, meditate on what the Scriptures say about what should be driving your life.

He died for everyone so that those who receive his new life will no longer live to please themselves. Instead, they will live to please Christ, who died and was raised for them. (2 Corinthians 5:15, NLT)

Do not offer the parts of your body to sin, as instruments of wickedness, but rather *offer yourselves to God, as those who have been brought from death to life;* and offer the parts of your body to him as instruments of righteousness. (Romans 6:13)

He himself bore our sins in his body on the tree, *so that we might die to sins and live for righteousness;* by his wounds you have been healed. (1 Peter 2:24)

Or have you forgotten that when we became Christians and were baptized to become one with Christ Jesus, we died with him? For we died and were buried with Christ by baptism. And just as Christ was raised from the dead by the glorious power of the Father, *now we also may live new lives.* (Romans 6:3-4, NLT)

For every excuse young men may give, there is a bloodstained cross staring back at them. Although many young men like to explain away their lack of commitment because their parents have been hypocrites, their church is filled with whacky people, or they've been shunned by fellow Christians, those things don't matter in the end. It's between you and God; that's what it's about. The Bible says it is only a matter of remembering, recognizing, and responding. No more, no less.

For every excuse young men may give, there is a bloodstained cross staring back at them.

Jesus stood in the observation post at one time. He was our forward observer who saw the potential of sin to overwhelm and destroy your life.

Then He called for fire directly on His position, saying, in a sense, "Put it all on Me!" And that's when hell and death and sin fell upon Him. Friends protested. "Never, Lord!" said Peter, but Jesus refused to back off. He turned toward His Father and said, "I want your will, not mine" (Luke 22:42, NLT).

How do you honor that kind of sacrifice? By making it part of your life.

Is Your Life a Thank-You?

My daughter Cara was twelve when we attended a communion service at our church one Sunday night. I had been asked to lead the Communion part by our pastor. Everything went well, and nothing out of the ordinary happened, but when I got home, I felt particularly burdened to talk with Cara. So at bedtime I sat down at the edge of her bed and asked her about our experience that night. Before she could answer, this ball in the pit of my stomach left the middle of my body and exploded in my eyes as tears. I wasn't saying a word, but tears were streaming down my cheeks.

"What's wrong, Daddy?"

No sense pretending. "Your dad is always emotional when he does communion."

"Why?"

"Because it hits me. You know, what Jesus did up there on the cross."

I reached into my pocket and retrieved a replica of a Roman crucifixion nail given to me by another pastor. The crude nail was nine inches long, and I showed her the blunt tip, which was made for staying in the wood. I placed the nail on top of my left wrist and then on my crossed feet to show her where the nails were placed. Then I briefly described how someone physically dies on a cross. Cara and I talked about how Jesus was pierced by a Roman centurion and how a mixture of blood and water came out of Jesus's side, indicating that His heart had ruptured.

"So, Cara, Jesus died of a broken heart up there on the cross."

"I have never thought of it like that before."

Time seemed to stand still. "Cara. Look at me."

"Yes, Dad."

"Do you know why Daddy does what he does? Goes places and talks to people?"

"To tell people about Jesus," she answered brightly.

"That's part of it, but the main reason Daddy does what he does is because I want my life to be a thank-you for this," I said, holding up the nail.

I don't believe I am supposed to get over the Cross.

I don't care what Cara thought of seeing her father cry so openly, but I didn't try to hold back on that tender night. It's always been hard for me to stem the flow of tears when it comes to Communion, a song, or a message that brings me to the foot of the cross.

Why is recalling Christ's sacrifice so powerful to me? Like no other force in my life, His sacrifice:

- reaches my heart
- renews my determination
- reshapes my relationships
- redirects my passions
- redefines my purpose
- rescues my perspective
- reveals my motives
- redeems my failures
- restores my hope
- requires change

I don't believe that the Cross was ever supposed to become anything less to me. I don't believe I am supposed to get over it. I don't believe any man can live out the truths discussed in these pages and become God's young man without recognizing his rescuer:

> I waited patiently for the LORD;
>> he turned to me and heard my cry.
> He lifted me out of the slimy pit,
>> out of the mud and mire;
> he set my feet on a rock
>> and gave me a firm place to stand. (Psalm 40:1-2)

HOW YOU CAN HONOR THE SACRIFICE

Your life will reflect the value you assign to your relationship with Christ. To be completely in His will requires courage in the face of rejection, discipline in the face of temptation, and motivation to fight hard. Here are three things you can do to get there:

1. Recognize the Sacrifice

It took fifty years, but the army finally recognized its African American heroes from World War II by taking a thoughtful look at what these men did, evaluating the significance of their contributions, and making a public effort to recall, remember, and reward their heroic efforts. The act of recognizing means acknowledging something that happened and to give attention to it. In your situation, this means:

- acknowledging the personal sacrifice of Christ *for you*
- accepting His gift of salvation and forgiveness

- admitting your need for His forgiveness and leadership in your life on a daily basis

If this expresses the desire of your heart, you may want to pray this prayer of recognition:

Jesus, I want to personally recognize what You did for me. I want to thank You for dying for my sins. Thank You for forgiving me of all my sins. Take control of my life and help me to always remember what You did. Help me to continually honor your sacrifice. Amen.

2. Respond with Your Life

A person who is saved by another person's heroism reacts to the rescuer with words of gratitude, with the offering of gifts, and if possible, a desire to repay the debt. Since Jesus took everything the Enemy had when He hung from the cross, you have been rescued from eternal damnation. This means giving to Jesus:

- all that you are—inwardly in the form of your devotion and loyalty
- all that you have—outwardly in the form of your time and your talents
- all that you hope to be—your dreams, aspirations, hopes, and desires

3. Release Yourself to God's Purposes

Your feelings about what Jesus did for you and your desire to live your life for Him means that your life will reflect His purposes, not your own. God's young man focuses himself on these five things to bring God the most glory:

1. Bringing God pleasure with your life. This is the purpose of worship.
2. Connecting with God's people. This is the purpose of fellowship.
3. Becoming like Christ. This is God's purpose of discipleship.
4. Serving the body of Christ. This is God's purpose of ministry.
5. Telling others about Christ's love for them. This is God's purpose of evangelism.

———

Right now you are building the foundation of the rest of your life. The next few years are the window of time God is using to shape you for the future. That's why I have strongly encouraged you to take spiritual responsibility for your life and not make excuses.

With God's help, and with the encouragement and accountability of other brothers in Christ, you can weather the storms of temptation and tests that are bound to come—especially the sexual ones. How you live your life matters to God—and should matter to you.

So go for it. Become God's young man. And while you're at it, never, ever, ever forget the price that He paid.

workbook

questions you may have about this workbook

What will the *Every Young Man, God's Man Workbook* do for me?

Are you making progress where it counts? Are you dealing with the same character issues or fighting the same battles you fought a year ago? Are your relationships improving? Are you closing the gap between what you believe and how you really live? Many young Christian men are discouraged by their honest answers to these questions. But there is hope: God has a plan to help His young men complete the personal drive toward spiritual maturity and genuine manhood.

Part of the acclaimed Every Man series by popular counselor and speaker Stephen Arterburn, this workbook is specially designed to help you personalize and apply the groundbreaking principles revealed in the best-selling book, *Every Young Man, God's Man*. Participants will be encouraged to evaluate where they are in their spiritual journeys; to become more intimate with God and truly give Him every area of their lives; and to live lives of lasting quality, purpose, and integrity.

Is this workbook enough or do I also need to read *Every Young Man, God's Man*?

Included in each weekly study you'll find a number of excerpts from *Every Young Man, God's Man,* each one marked at the beginning and end by this symbol: 📖. Nevertheless, your best approach is to also read *Every Young Man, God's Man* as you go through this companion workbook. You'll find the appropriate chapters listed at the beginning of each weekly study.

The lessons look long. Do I need to work through each one?

This workbook is designed to promote your thorough exploration of all the material, but you may find it best to focus your time and discussion on some sections and questions more than others.

To help your pacing, we've designed the workbook so it can most easily be used in either an eight-week or twelve-week approach.

• For the eight-week track, simply follow along with the basic organization already set up with the eight different weekly lessons.

• For the twelve-week track, the lessons marked for Weeks 2, 5, 6, and 7 as shown can be divided into two parts (you'll see the dividing place marked in the text).

(In addition, of course, you may decide to follow at an even slower pace, whether you're going through the workbook individually or in a group.)

Above all, keep in mind that the purpose of the workbook is to help guide you in specific life application of the biblical truths taught in *Every Young Man, God's Man.* The wide range of questions included in each weekly study is meant to help you approach this practical application from different angles and with personal reflection and self-examination. Allowing adequate time to prayerfully reflect on each question will be much more valuable to you than rushing through this workbook.

in the man zone
or just a poser?

This week's reading assignment:

chapters 1–2 in *Every Young Man, God's Man*

At one time, I was stupid enough to believe that I could play Christian and also play cool with the party and girl scene at school. I'll never forget one hottie telling me, "You are like the perfect blend of religious and cool."…

[But] you're in the Man Zone now. The game has changed. Old ways don't cut it anymore.

—from chapter 1 in *Every Young Man, God's Man*

EVERY YOUNG MAN'S TRUTH
(Your Personal Journey into God's Word)

As you begin this first study, take some time to check out the Bible passages below. They'll tell you about integrity, loyalty, and being the real you, no matter what people think. In fact, the three men in these scriptures are great mentors for you as you strive to become God's young man. King David learned to accept testing from God as a way to grow stronger. General Joshua drew a line in the sand and declared, "I'm for God. Period." And Jesus, even in His human nature, refused to let peoples' opinions get Him off track. He had a mission to accomplish, and He stuck to it. These men lead the way into the Man Zone. Are you willing to follow?

David praised the LORD in the presence of the whole assembly, saying, "Praise be to you, O LORD, God of our father Israel, from everlasting to everlasting....

"I know, my God, that you test the heart and are pleased with integrity. All these things have I given willingly and with honest intent. And now I have seen with joy how willingly your people who are here have given to you." (1 Chronicles 29:10,17)

Joshua said to all the people: "This is what the LORD, the God of Israel, says: 'Long ago your forefathers, including Terah the father of Abraham and Nahor, lived beyond the River and worshiped other gods. But I took your father Abraham from the land beyond the River and led him throughout Canaan and gave him many descendants. I gave him Isaac, and to Isaac I gave Jacob and Esau. I assigned the hill country of Seir to Esau, but Jacob and his sons went down to Egypt.

"'Then I sent Moses and Aaron, and I afflicted the Egyptians by what I did there, and I brought you out. When I brought your fathers out of Egypt, you came to the sea, and the Egyptians pursued them with chariots and horsemen as far as the Red Sea....'

"Now fear the LORD and serve him with all faithfulness. Throw away the gods your forefathers worshiped beyond the River and in

Egypt, and serve the LORD. But if serving the LORD seems undesirable to you, then choose for yourselves this day whom you will serve…. But as for me and my household, we will serve the LORD." (Joshua 24:2-6,14-15)

They came to him and said, "Teacher, we know you are a man of integrity. You aren't swayed by men, because you pay no attention to who they are; but you teach the way of God in accordance with the truth. Is it right to pay taxes to Caesar or not?" (Mark 12:14)

1. King David knew that God tests our hearts. What good—or joy—can come from this? How have you seen this work in your own life?
2. Joshua was an army general who had to keep his loyalties straight amid constant battles. Remembering God's great works of the past helped him do it. So list some of the ways God has worked in your own life so far. How does this make you feel?
3. Even Jesus' enemies considered Him a man of integrity. According to them, how did Jesus show this integrity? When is it toughest for you to "pay no attention" to what others think of you?
4. Think about the most recent situation when this question was a big deal for you: Where is your loyalty going to lie? What did you do?

☑ EVERY YOUNG MAN'S CHOICE
(Questions for Personal Reflection and Examination)

📖 You're becoming a man, and that means you have to start thinking like one. Similarly, to become God's man, you have to think like one of His sons. To help you think like God's man, you need to think through the following statements that I've come up with. I call them "Kenny's Code." Read each one slowly. 📖

📖 Before you get into tough situations as a man, you have to get your identity settled and strong. Then you can focus on being who you are versus someone who oscillates between God Guy and Poser Guy, between Sunday Guy and Tequila Shooter Guy, or between Bible Study Man and Porn Studies Man. 📖

5. Go back and review the statements in Kenny's Code. Think: Which of these do I already believe? Which of them do I need to believe?

6. Think about someone who knows of you just by seeing you around. If this person were asked *what defines your identity,* what do you think he or she would say? Why? (What about a guy you hang out with all the time?)

7. Recall the story of Jim, the guy who was a poser during his high-school years. Which of his faces do you tend to wear during a routine day? What would it take for you to start wearing your real face more often?

👟 EVERY YOUNG MAN'S WALK
(Your Guide to Personal Application)

📖 One night I would hang out with my Christian friends at a Bible study, and the next night I would be laughing my head off at a huge beer bash with the "stoners." It's a good thing that I had friends praying that God would rattle my world and get me back on track. I needed my cage rattled, because there were parts of me that really liked the feelings of acceptance and the danger of dancing with sin.

What I didn't like was the war raging within me, which made me miserable. But I never discussed those feelings with anyone. 📖

📖 So many men, young and old, are caught between competing identities that divide their loyalty, just like Brandon. Maybe you've worn a mask or rationalized your faith away when it's been uncomfortable. If your inner loyalty and commitment to Christ is divided, how can you expect to overcome the fear of what other people think about your being a Christian? Moving into the Man Zone means... having a clear and personal picture of Jesus Christ's passion for you on the cross and then letting your heart match His with love and loyalty. 📖

8. Kenny talks about nights with the Bible and nights with the stoners. Can you see any splits like this in your own actions? What kind of world rattling could help you?

9. Suppose you feel your loyalty is divided. Do you agree with Kenny that "having a clear and personal picture of Jesus Christ's passion for you" will meet your need? Why?

10. When could you spend some quiet time prayerfully remembering how much Jesus loves you? Jot down your weekly schedule and make your plans.

11. Kenny says: "I am in your space to remind you that your loyalty will be tested so that your spiritual backbone can develop." On a scale of 1 to 5, how strong is your backbone at the moment? What prayer would you like to lift to God about this right now?

12. In quietness, review what you have written and learned in this week's study. If further thoughts or prayer requests come to your mind and heart, you may want to write them down.

13. What for you was the most meaningful concept or truth in this week's study? How would you talk this over with God? Write down your response as a prayer to Him. What do you believe God wants you to do in response to this week's study?

Every Young Man's Talk

(Constructive Topics and Questions for Group Discussion)

Key Highlights from the Book for Reading Aloud and Discussing

📖 For the first time in my life, I expressed to God what I really wanted more than anything—a real encounter with Him.... He knew I had been deliberately fooling myself, but He also saw someone who was experiencing turmoil regarding who Christ was. When I expressed a longing from deep within my heart—as simple as it was—He seized that measly effort to invade my room and bring me closer to Him as never before. 📖

📖 God had told Hezekiah that he was going to die, which would certainly get my attention. In response, Hezekiah dialed 911, and amazingly, he was granted a fifteen-year extension on earth! While Hezekiah knew God was all-powerful, he also knew that God was also a *rewarder* of those loyal to him, and that a "loyal heart" produced "what was good in Your sight." 📖

📖 I was enrolling at UCLA, that bastion of babes, beer, and beach time.... We're talking Babeville with the hottest-looking girls on your left, on your right, and dead ahead, but I was committed to honoring

God and remaining loyal to Him. I made that commitment public; I let other people in on the fact that I was a Christian. 📖

Discussion Questions

An opening question: Which parts of these chapters were most helpful or encouraging to you? Why?

A. What do you *really* want more than anything? How can you tell?
B. Review the story of Hezekiah in 2 Kings 20:1-6. What does this story tell you about a loyal heart? If you were to do a quick heart check right now, what would be your L.Q. (Loyalty Quotient)?
C. Have you ever lived in—or visited—Babeville? Was that cool for you? How hard or easy is it for you to go public with your Christian identity in that town? Talk it over!
D. Together, review the closing paragraphs of chapter 1 in the book, which tell what you'll be learning in the coming chapters. Share about which one or two topics you most want to explore.
E. Kenny talks about admiring guys who work hard on their sport or craft in order to be successful. But we don't get it when it comes to training to become God's young men. What kinds of practical training brings this kind of success? (Tell about what has helped you the most.)
F. To close out this first session, ask one of the guys to read aloud Proverbs 10:9 and 11:3. Discuss what's so great about walking in integrity—and then pray for one another's walk during the coming week.

hard to do:
no mind games!

This week's reading assignment:

chapters 3–4 in *Every Young Man, God's Man*

"When I am alone with my temptations, I choose pleasure. Feeling like I'm all alone in it makes the situation worse and causes me to be spiritually lazy. On the other hand, when I am with friends or can interrupt the temptation with a phone call, prayer, exercise, or something else, then that interruption keeps me out of the situation."…

Here's my point: you are not alone when you admit your battle with sexual temptation, and you are not alone if you fail.

—from chapter 3 in *Every Young Man, God's Man*

📖 EVERY YOUNG MAN'S TRUTH
(Your Personal Journey into God's Word)

What's your most treasured reward for good work, a nice performance, a fine sports season? You've probably got those trophies and ribbons sitting on a shelf somewhere, right? But what about rewards in your life with God? Here, too, you can win awesome payoffs. Because *God rewards obedience.* The scriptures below will help you understand the reward for embracing and acting upon the truth. And they'll encourage you to stay disciplined in your efforts against temptation.

It's true that you're saved only by God's grace and could never earn His favor. But that doesn't mean you can't please Him by following His will. When you choose His ways, He loves to give you the high-five.

> Do not store up for yourselves treasures on earth, where moth and
> rust destroy, and where thieves break in and steal. But store up for
> yourselves treasures in heaven. (Matthew 6:19-20)

> So we make it our goal to please him, whether we are at home in
> the body or away from it. For we must all appear before the judg-
> ment seat of Christ, that each one may receive what is due him
> for the things done while in the body, whether good or bad.
> (2 Corinthians 5:9-10)

> Consider him who endured such opposition from sinful men, so that
> you will not grow weary and lose heart.
>> In your struggle against sin, you have not yet resisted to the point
> of shedding your blood. And you have forgotten that word of
> encouragement that addresses you as sons:
>
>> "My son, do not make light of the Lord's discipline,
>> and do not lose heart when he rebukes you,

> because the Lord disciplines those he loves,
> and he punishes everyone he accepts as a son."

Endure hardship as discipline; God is treating you as sons. For what son is not disciplined by his father? If you are not disciplined (and everyone undergoes discipline), then you are illegitimate children and not true sons. Moreover, we have all had human fathers who disciplined us and we respected them for it. How much more should we submit to the Father of our spirits and live! Our fathers disciplined us for a little while as they thought best; but God disciplines us for our good, that we may share in his holiness. No discipline seems pleasant at the time, but painful. Later on, however, it produces a harvest of righteousness and peace for those who have been trained by it. (Hebrews 12:3-11)

1. What is the difference between storing up treasures on earth and in heaven? Where is your biggest bank account located at the moment?
2. On the cross Jesus suffered the full penalty and judgment for our sins. While we won't be judged, the quality of our works on earth will be judged some day. How does this make you feel?
3. How is Jesus a great example of sticking with obedience, no matter what?
4. What are some of the rewards of accepting God's discipline, according to the author of Hebrews?

Section I: focus on chapter 3. Note: for an eight-week study, include Section II starting on page 247.

☑ Every Young Man's Choice

*(Questions for Personal Reflection
and Examination)*

📖 I recently asked a room of young men, ages seventeen to twenty-one, to take an anonymous survey that contained the following question: what are the top three battles you face as a younger man?

One hundred percent of them—every guy in the room—wrote that sexual temptation, lust, masturbation, or porn topped his list. 📖

📖 I believe that being a Christian and having character are not the same thing. When God entered your life, you instantly inherited many things. You were forgiven of all your sins, you became a child of God, and you were placed spiritually in heaven with Christ.… [But] a fundamental change in your character traits (who you are and how you react under pressure) was *not* on the list. God has chosen to bring us character only when we decide to do hard things that require faith in His way. 📖

5. Why is sexual temptation so high on the list of battles for most guys? Of the listed reasons why guys *lose* this battle, which most closely relates to your own struggles?

6. God made character development a growth process. In your opinion, why didn't He just give you a good character when He made you His child?

EVERY YOUNG MAN'S WALK
(Your Guide to Personal Application)

Mark, for example, knew exactly what God's plan for sex was, but he rationalized and debated with himself about the whole idea of remaining pure. Once the debate began in his mind, he worked through various scenarios regarding his girlfriend, Kelly. Like a kitchen faucet with a slow leak under the cabinet, Mark began allowing certain things to happen. For instance, their good-bye kiss went from a peck to a full-on session of deep kissing. He figured that was okay because everyone still had their clothes on.

When you resist change, however, God has other ways to get our character in order, and those usually involve His calling a time-out on your plans. God can forge character by allowing difficulties, delays, or even the consequences of your choices to act as His agents of change. The Bible is filled with examples of His making men uncomfortable so He could teach them something about character. Just ask these guys: Joseph…Moses… David…Jonah…Job…Paul.

7. Recall the story of Mark and Kelly. If you were Mark's best friend, what advice would you have given him at the beginning of his relationship with Kelly?

8. When has God made you uncomfortable in order to get you to change? Of the six biblical characters listed, which has the most to teach you, personally, about this? Why?

9. Kenny says that "God's young man risks letting God be in control and managing him freely." But what's the big risk? What is the scariest part for you?

10. What for you was the most meaningful concept or truth in chapter 3 of *Every Young Man, God's Man*? How would you talk this over with God? Write down your response as a prayer to Him. What do you believe God wants you to do in response to this week's study?

👤👤 EVERY YOUNG MAN'S TALK
(Constructive Topics and Questions for Group Discussion)

Key Highlights from the Book for Reading Aloud and Discussing

📖 God's men have a long-range plan. God's men think through questions—tough questions. Have you ever asked yourself:

• Why can't I grow past sexual temptations and thoughts?

• Why am I not getting closer to the standard I know is right?

• Why do I keep repeating the same mistakes over and over?

If you are asking yourself these questions, then you are searching for the one thing that separates the men from the boys—character. 📖

📖 God's man Hosea was speaking to a group of spiritually immature men in Israel. He used their knowledge of farming to explain God's work in their lives and how they could be productive for him. The picture he painted was the all-too-familiar one about hard work and sweat paying off at harvest time. Any good Israelite knew that a fruitful yield started with the condition of the soil. Hard soil was bad, and soft soil was good. Hard soil offered little chance of taking the seed, while tilled land yielded a crop—perhaps a bountiful one. The farmer had to do the hard work (breaking up the unplowed ground) to get the results.

Hosea's metaphor works today as well. If you want to be God's man on the outside, you've got to pull out the jackhammer and get to work on the inside. 📖

📖 One of the most difficult things I have ever done was to talk about this [masturbation] habit with the men in my Bible study. It was also one of the best things I ever did. When I confessed my situation to my brothers, God gave me the strength to say no to the flesh and say yes to His Spirit in the moments of testing. He knew it took guts for me to give up my "dirty little secret." He knew it required faith and humility because I risked rejection for a stronger walk with God. 📖

Discussion Questions

An opening question: Which parts of this chapter were most helpful or encouraging to you? Why?

A. Are you a boy or a man (based on the questions you ask yourself)?
B. What would it mean for you to pull out the jackhammer and work on your inside? Be as specific as possible.
C. Why is it so hard to talk about our dirty little secrets with other guys who care about us? What helps you gain the courage to do it?
D. Kenny says: "You can't necessarily expect immediate results when

you choose to do the right thing." In your experience, what can you expect?

E. How do you react when you hear God saying no to you?

F. Kenny makes this statement: "Sometimes God's will *feels* like a cruel joke—even sucks, if you're honest." Tell about a time when this was true for you. How did you deal with it?

Section II: focus on chapter 4.

Note: if you're following a twelve-week track,
save the rest of this lesson for the following week.
If you're on the eight-week track…then keep going.

☑ EVERY YOUNG MAN'S CHOICE
(Questions for Personal Reflection and Examination)

📖 My appetite for pleasure and fun controlled my life. Why should I say no to what I wanted to do? I was young enough, insecure enough, and lonely enough *not* to listen to the voice in my head questioning some of my decisions. While I am ashamed to reveal everything about my BC (before Christ) days, they reveal a fundamental truth about me: when it was in my interest, I was a pro at playing mind games to get what I wanted when I wanted it. 📖

📖 Our actions reveal our true heart and our maturity in Christ. When Jesus shows up on your porch with some truth about your present direction, an attitude that needs adjustment, or an action that needs to be addressed, how do you react? 📖

11. What are some of your favorite mind games for getting what you want?

12. In the second quotation above, how do you answer Kenny's question about your reaction to Jesus?

EVERY YOUNG MAN'S WALK
(Your Guide to Personal Application)

📖 Danny used these same mind games when he complained to Ashley that she didn't really love him. When they started dating four months earlier, he respected her virginity. He bought into the "true love waits" motto. But as he daily fantasized about her, the whole virginity thing became less attractive to him. He resented the firewall she had installed regarding physical intimacy.

Danny's mind became one track—and it was no longer on God. 📖

📖 His parents were right, but Tom could not admit that. He fought them tooth and nail about getting a summer job to pay for *his* car insurance, *his* gas, and *his* car repairs. His mom and dad told him that since he was not taking summer school classes, the next three months would be a great time to find a part-time job to cover his car-related expenses....

He had other things on his mind—like sleeping in and hanging out with his friends. 📖

13. How could Danny change so much in just four months? If you were Danny, what could you have done to help yourself stick with "true love waits"?

14. Have you ever been like Tom? What did he learn about a man's responsibility—and what have *you* learned so far?

15. Carefully read John 4:4-30, focusing on verse 23. Think: how would you answer Kenny's five questions about self-honesty?

   a. Am I being honest with myself about my spiritual commitment to Christ?

   b. Am I being totally honest with God about my life?

   c. Have I been honest with others about my spiritual life and struggles?

   d. Am I willing to hear the truth from God and other brothers about my spiritual direction?

   e. Will I do what they say?

16. What for you was the most meaningful concept or truth in chapter 4 of *Every Young Man, God's Man*? How would you talk this over with God? Write down your response as a prayer to Him. What do you believe God wants you to do in response to this week's study?

EVERY YOUNG MAN'S TALK
(Constructive Topics and Questions for Group Discussion)

Key Highlights from the Book for Reading Aloud and Discussing

   📖 I bet you've rationalized a few things. You wouldn't be normal if you haven't. It's easy to do. All you have to do is repeat one of the following excuses… 📖

   📖 All of us will stand before God one day and have to account for our actions today. You want that day to be a great one. He won't accept your bogus excuses for why you traded in your commitment to Him for cheap physical thrills or moments of gratification. What will you say to the Lord—the same Lord who reads all your thoughts and exposes your mind games? That's why, when facing a moral dilemma, you have one of two ways to go: either face up to the truth or run from God. 📖

📖 The best habit you can get into is seeing how God's purposes for bringing truth to your life are all about *you!* He's doing this because he loves you. He may be telling you things you may not *want* to hear, but they are things that you *need* to hear to become God's young man. The fact is that He can't help Himself—He *is* the truth. So how do you know when God's speaking His truth to you? It's God talking when… 📖

Discussion Questions

An opening question: Which parts of this chapter were most helpful or encouraging to you? Why?

G. Read the first quotation above, then check out the excuses that Kenny lists in the book on pages 45-46. Talk about which of these you've used at one time or another. What were the results?

H. Do you agree that facing a moral dilemma offers you only two choices? Can you share a personal example about this?

I. In the past, what things has God told you that you didn't want to hear? (What is He telling you right now?)

J. Kenny says: "Sometimes accepting the truth is hard because *change requires action,* which can produce tension." Where do you feel the tension when you face a tough truth about yourself?

K. God sometimes acts like a surgeon with us, cutting in order to heal us. Are you down with going under the knife? Talk it over.

L. Kenny states that God will eventually out us to get our attention. What does he mean?

M. How would you like to pray for one another before closing your group time?

knowing better than to blend

This week's reading assignment:

chapters 5–6 in *Every Young Man, God's Man*

Our whole mission was to let loose, have fun, and play around. That's why all of us bought into every experience the world had to offer. But when we became high-school seniors, we were getting tired of the party and girl scene. It was just stale. In fact, I remember tape-recording a late-night conversation at my kitchen table with some of the guys. Out of the blue I asked my friend Pat, "What would you do if Jesus Christ were here right now?"

—from chapter 6 in *Every Young Man, God's Man*

📖 EVERY YOUNG MAN'S TRUTH
(Your Personal Journey into God's Word)

You live in the world. But how much of the world lives in you? Can you be God's young man and blend perfectly with the culture too? According to the scriptures below, it's impossible. Check them out. As you do, ask yourself what it means, in practical terms, that Christ has called you *out* of the world to be His servant *in* the world: What do you watch? What do you listen to? Who do you hang out with?

Yes, you need to have non-Christian friends if you are to be a witness. You need to understand the values and priorities of others if you are to influence them for Christ. But be wise in the way you go about it. Don't let the world form you into it's mold. Know better than to blend.

> If the world hates you, keep in mind that it hated me first. If you
> belonged to the world, it would love you as its own. As it is, you do
> not belong to the world, but I have chosen you out of the world.
> That is why the world hates you. (John 15:18-19)

> You adulterous people, don't you know that friendship with the
> world is hatred toward God? Anyone who chooses to be a friend of
> the world becomes an enemy of God. Or do you think Scripture says
> without reason that the spirit he caused to live in us tends toward
> envy, but he gives us more grace? That is why Scripture says:

> "God opposes the proud
> but gives grace to the humble."

> Submit yourselves, then, to God. Resist the devil, and he will flee
> from you. Come near to God and he will come near to you. Wash
> your hands, you sinners, and purify your hearts, you double-minded.
> Grieve, mourn and wail. Change your laughter to mourning and
> your joy to gloom. Humble yourselves before the Lord, and he will
> lift you up. (James 4:4-10)

Do not love the world or anything in the world. If anyone loves the world, the love of the Father is not in him. For everything in the world—the cravings of sinful man, the lust of his eyes and the boasting of what he has and does—comes not from the Father but from the world. The world and its desires pass away, but the man who does the will of God lives forever. (1 John 2:15-17)

1. What evidence of the world's values do you see around you? How tempting are these values for you?
2. According to James, what is the cure for being double-minded?
3. How can you tell when you are loving the world? What do you do about it?
4. What encouraging truth comes through to you in 1 John 2:15-17?

☑ EVERY YOUNG MAN'S CHOICE
(Questions for Personal Reflection and Examination)

📖 Then it happened. My car—actually, my mom's—kissed a railroad tie. While it was just a "touch," I ended up denting the driver's side door. Now I was in deep linguine.

My first impulse was practical—save my own skin! 📖

📖 A true God's young man must abandon the middle ground and determine, in his own mind, that he cannot peacefully coexist with his enemies. This pattern of taking a strong stance is well illustrated in the Bible for us to clearly see. Think about: Moses…David… King Hezekiah…Elijah…Daniel…Jesus…Peter and John…and the believers in Revelation who were not afraid to die. 📖

5. When was the last time you were in deep linguine? What was your first impulse? your second impulse? Jot down some notes about how you would *like* to respond the next time you land in a sticky mess.

6. Think through the challenges faced by the men Kenny lists in the second quotation above. Which of these guys do you most respect for their stance against the world? Why?

7. Kenny says that when you wreck your life, either pride will drive you, your fear will deter you, or your faith will direct you. As you look back over your life, assign percentages to each of these three motivators—pride, fear, faith. How often have you let each take control of your responses to serious hassles?

EVERY YOUNG MAN'S WALK
(Your Guide to Personal Application)

📖 [Some young men] are light-years apart from God when it comes to wisdom, yet they fling their "wisdom" around like *they* spoke and created the heavens and the earth. In fact, their ignorance makes them dangerous to themselves and to others. Their mind-set and actions seem to say: "Thanks for coming along for the ride, God, but I'll take the wheel from here." They would never utter those words, of course, but their *actions* say otherwise. I can just imagine God scratching His head in amazement when people shine Him on. 📖

📖 The world wants to define what's normal for you—and it will if you let it happen. Just flip on MTV, study the newest Abercrombie & Fitch catalog, or check out the latest run of *Bachelor*. What the world values isn't hard to pick up. The world will always emphasize feelings over commitment, a free spirit over character. 📖

8. Make a two-column list of the things you are (1) wise about and (2) ignorant about. Then think: *Where in my life do I need more of God's wisdom?*

9. In the second quotation above, check out the sources Kenny names as places where the world's values come through. Can you come up with some specific examples of how they emphasize feelings and a free spirit? Jot down your thoughts about it.

10. Go back to the stories of Jeremy and Nate. They both figured they were missing out on something. When you feel that way, where do you go to hang out? Have you told anybody about that yet?

11. In the middle of chapter 6, Kenny talks about three specific ways you might become more a friend of the world than a follower of Christ. Look at the three ways below and, on a separate piece of paper, jot an example from your own life of an action that demonstrates your kind of friendship.

a. You look at God's forgiveness like a credit card advance:
   How I do this...
   or, how I avoid this...
b. You compartmentalize your behaviors:
   How I do this...
   or, how I avoid this...
c. You allow your feelings to dominate decision making.
   How I do this...
   or, how I avoid this...

12. In quietness, review what you have written and learned in this week's study. If further thoughts or prayer requests come to your mind and heart, you may want to write them down.

13. What for you was the most meaningful concept or truth in this week's study? How would you talk this over with God? Write down your response as a prayer to Him. What do you believe God wants you to do in response to this week's study?

EVERY YOUNG MAN'S TALK
(Constructive Topics and Questions for Group Discussion)

Key Highlights from the Book for Reading Aloud and Discussing

    📖 Pride says [to God]: *I know better....* Fear says: *I'll miss out....* Faith says: *You know better.* 📖

    📖 If you continue to resist God, He has ways of showing you that you don't know better. That's what happened to a guy named Naaman in the Bible. He was a hotshot Syrian general who was powerful, commanding, and successful. Underneath his armor, however, his body was racked by a skin disease called leprosy. On the outside—shining armor and victory. Underneath and on the inside—sores and shame. 📖

    📖 Changing into God's young man requires a change in your perspective about spiritual warfare. You can no longer dismiss it, deny it, or deflect your responsibility to engage it. Instead, you must forget the notion that you can play both sides without taking it in the shorts every now and then. In other words, you cannot *blend* God's purposes with opposing purposes and practices. Specifically, you are warned not to blend with what the Bible describes as the "world." 📖

Discussion Questions

An opening question: Which parts of these chapters were most helpful or encouraging to you? Why?

A. Which of the three voices did you listen to for most of your day yesterday—pride, fear, or faith? How could you tell?

B. Together, go back over the story of General Naaman (see 2 Kings 5:1-14). How did God teach this tough guy humility?

C. How do you define spiritual warfare? In light of Kenny's comments about it, what is your win-loss record over the past month?

D. Kenny talks about the moment in a game when a team surrenders to its fate. Have you ever reached that point with God? What could you share with the other guys about this?

E. Kenny entered UCLA "trying real hard to be cool so people would like me." How cool are you at the moment, dude? Who seems to be impressed?

F. A dead squirrel taught the author: don't delay the instinct to obey. If you agree, tell why.

G. What are your prayer requests to share with the other guys?

out of the dark into defense

This week's reading assignment:

chapters 7–8 in *Every Young Man, God's Man*

The "dark side" was made famous by the Star Wars *trilogies and epitomized by the infamous character Darth Vader. While he and the other* Star Wars *characters are thoroughly the stuff of Hollywood, the saga's core theme reflects a biblical reality, which is this: every man has a dark side, something pulling him to do the wrong thing. This force inside him wages war against his noblest intentions.*

—from chapter 7 in *Every Young Man, God's Man*

📖 EVERY YOUNG MAN'S TRUTH
(Your Personal Journey into God's Word)

The dark side keeps pulling at you, and it's tough to say no. Even the great apostle Paul felt it as a brutal inner battle. You've been there, right? Feeling the power of temptation, wanting to do right but doing wrong instead? Then the guilt. Then the tendency to despair.

But don't give up! Scripture tells you your Lord has already won the war with sin. He calls you to live in the power of His ultimate victory. It's true that willpower can only carry you so far. At some point in your battles you must give up and let Christ carry you through. Call upon Him; as Paul knew, He is ready for the rescue.

I realize that I don't have what it takes. I can will it, but I can't do it. I decide to do good, but I don't really do it; I decide not to do bad, but then I do it anyway. My decisions, such as they are, don't result in actions. Something has gone wrong deep within me and gets the better of me every time.

It happens so regularly that it's predictable. The moment I decide to do good, sin is there to trip me up. I truly delight in God's commands, but it's pretty obvious that not all of me joins in that delight. Parts of me covertly rebel, and just when I least expect it, they take charge.

I've tried everything and nothing helps. I'm at the end of my rope. Is there no one who can do anything for me? Isn't that the real question?

The answer, thank God, is that Jesus Christ can and does. He acted to set things right in this life of contradictions where I want to serve God with all my heart and mind, but am pulled by the influence of sin to do something totally different. (Romans 7:18-25, MSG)

No temptation has seized you except what is common to man. And God is faithful; he will not let you be tempted beyond what you can bear. But when you are tempted, he will also provide a way out so that you can stand up under it. (1 Corinthians 10:13)

God's solid foundation stands firm, sealed with this inscription: "The Lord knows those who are his," and, "Everyone who confesses the name of the Lord must turn away from wickedness."

In a large house there are articles not only of gold and silver, but also of wood and clay; some are for noble purposes and some for ignoble. If a man cleanses himself from the latter, he will be an instrument for noble purposes, made holy, useful to the Master and prepared to do any good work.

Flee the evil desires of youth, and pursue righteousness, faith, love and peace, along with those who call on the Lord out of a pure heart. (2 Timothy 2:20-22)

1. The apostle Paul sometimes felt like a prisoner of the law of sin. When do you feel that way?
2. According to 1 Corinthians 10:13, what is your hope when you feel seized by temptation?
3. What does it mean for you, personally, to "flee the evil desires of youth"?
4. What is your defense plan for the next time serious temptation hits? How have you prepared your heart in advance?

☑ EVERY YOUNG MAN'S CHOICE
(Questions for Personal Reflection and Examination)

📖 This dark side phenomenon makes every man a potential double agent—capable of doing the very worst even when he desires the very best. That's why the Bible makes it clear that the enemy you *really* need to be watching out for is *you*. 📖

📖 As I work with younger men, I've seen how important it is to bottle up the Enemy at various hot gates—or what I call spiritual strongholds—so that larger battles don't have to be fought. How you defend those hot gates determines how the next ten to fifteen years will play out. The Bible warns you to position your forces "so that when the day of evil comes, you may be able to stand your ground, and after you have done everything, to stand" (Ephesians 6:13). 📖

5. Review the five "have you ever" examples of ways the dark side can make you a double agent. What is your own best example?

6. How are you positioning your forces to defend the spiritual hot gates in your life? Rate your battle position: strong or weak?

7. Take a moment to read Ephesians 6:10-18. List the armor and weapons you'll need to defend yourself against dark side attacks. Which pieces do you need to rely on more when temptation hits?

👟 EVERY YOUNG MAN'S WALK
(Your Guide to Personal Application)

📖 You may know my friend. His name is Paul—the apostle. Nearly two thousand years ago, he put into words how everyone feels when the dark side takes over our lives and our actions. Paul labeled this our "sin nature," and the previous description is found in Romans 7:18-20 (MSG). It's good to know we are in good company when it comes to this battle because we all are at war with our dark side. 📖

📖 The dark side doesn't have to influence your actions, though. You can beat him at his own game by committing to a campaign of exposing him constantly. You do that by figuring you have two types of people living in one body, and your Spirit-filled nature has to suppress the dark side—or else. 📖

8. Do you ever feel like the apostle Paul did when facing temptation? Check out Romans 7:25–8:14. How can this passage point you to the way out?

9. Kenny says that suppressing the dark side involves verbally confronting it. What verbal-confrontation phrase would work best for you. Write it down.

10. Why is the hot gate of sexual fantasizing such an important one to defend? What usually happens after your thoughts give in?

11. In quietness, review what you have written and learned in this week's study. If further thoughts or prayer requests come to your mind and heart, you may want to write them down.

12. What for you was the most meaningful concept or truth in this week's study? How would you talk this over with God? Write down your response as a prayer to Him. What do you believe God wants you to do in response to this week's study?

😊😊 EVERY YOUNG MAN'S TALK
(Constructive Topics and Questions for Group Discussion)

Key Highlights from the Book for Reading Aloud and Discussing

📖 In your journey with God, I know you feel the dark side lurking like a shark beneath the surface of your life. The dark side inconspicuously swims in the waters of your character, hiding in your thoughts and dropping ideas into your mind that run counter to God's plan. The dark side contradicts what constitutes sin by muddying the waters so you cannot make out the clear instruction of God's Word. Your dark side is patient until it's time to strike. 📖

📖 Josh just smiled and shook his head—letting Austin feel the stupidity of his little outburst.

"You're right," Josh replied after a long pause. "You are not me, and I am not your dad. But I am your brother—in Christ. I know you don't want to hear that right now because you can't be doing what you're doing with Jessica and still be tight with me or God. I don't care if you push me away, avoid me, or never see me again. But God can't go from being a big part of your life to a small part unless you're making space for the wrong things." 📖

📖 Each mental assault takes it toll and invests Satan with more power so that after a while temptation will *feel* irresistible. To take a cue from Kevin's story: each mental happy meal he indulged in brought the Enemy's victory closer and closer.

Hot gates must be places where you resist and make your stand—not yield. 📖

Discussion Questions

An opening question: Which parts of these chapters were most helpful or encouraging to you? Why?

A. Talk about some of the shark bites you've suffered in the past. What have you learned so far about avoiding shark-infested waters?
B. What are some of the ways Josh was being a good brother to

Austin? Do you see any of these brotherly ways happening in your group? Talk it over.

C. Look at the eleven guys who yield at the hot gates (starting with Dave, Chris, and so on). For them, temptation feels irresistible. What specific brotherly advice would you give to each of these guys in their particular struggles?

D. Kenny basically says to talk to yourself when tempted. What kinds of things are you supposed to say?

E. According to Kenny: "What rocks a young guy's world is not knowing what to do when the shot clock on his temptation ticker is winding down." So what are you supposed to do as you watch that clock—and panic sets in?

F. We can't defend a hot gate without the Holy Spirit's power and direction. Review the four ways of cooperating with the Spirit (under the subhead "Defending a Hot Gate"). Then pray for one another about your areas of noncooperation!

hey Gumby:
baptize that brain!

You follow the beach master's directions to a T and meet up with your new buddies. Your new platoon leader gathers you all together to give you instructions. That's when you notice that he's holding a helmet filled with some guy's brains! His steely eyes glare at every man standing around him in a semicircle. "This is what happens to guys who don't listen to the beach master," he growls. "This whole area is mined. Go where you are told."

He didn't need to say anything more.

—from chapter 9 in *Every Young Man, God's Man*

📖 EVERY YOUNG MAN'S TRUTH
(Your Personal Journey into God's Word)

What comes to mind when you think of meditating? Do you see an orange-robed monk sitting alone on a desolate hillside with closed eyes? Do you picture a new age guru lighting incense and chanting? Or do you see *yourself*—opening up the Bible and letting God's Word soak into your soul?

Stick with that third image! It is exactly what you're called to do as often as you can. Stay in the Bible; let its truths marinate your mind. Don't rush. Think it through and apply it to your everyday concerns. Really, it's pretty simple: simply delight in God's Word. You'll be blessed.

> Be strong and very courageous. Be careful to obey all the law my servant Moses gave you; do not turn from it to the right or to the left, that you may be successful wherever you go. Do not let this Book of the Law depart from your mouth; meditate on it day and night, so that you may be careful to do everything written in it. Then you will be prosperous and successful. (Joshua 1:7-8)

> Blessed is the man
>   who does not walk in the counsel of the wicked
> or stand in the way of sinners
>   or sit in the seat of mockers.
> But his delight is in the law of the LORD,
>   and on his law he meditates day and night.
> He is like a tree planted by streams of water,
>   which yields its fruit in season
> and whose leaf does not wither.
>   Whatever he does prospers.
>   (Psalm 1:1-3)

> How can a young man keep his way pure?
>   By living according to your word.

> I seek you with all my heart;
>> do not let me stray from your commands.
> I have hidden your word in my heart
>> that I might not sin against you.
> Praise be to you, O LORD;
>> teach me your decrees.
> With my lips I recount
>> all the laws that come from your mouth.
> I rejoice in following your statutes
>> as one rejoices in great riches.
> I meditate on your precepts
>> and consider your ways.
> I delight in your decrees;
>> I will not neglect your word.
>> (Psalm 119:9-16)

1. What does being "strong and very courageous" have to do with Bible reading?
2. Do you *delight* in God's law? What other words would you use to describe your relationship to the Bible?
3. How much of God's Word have you put to memory? How does this help you stay pure?
4. Do you agree that you are what you think? If so, what does this say about the importance of meditating on Scripture?

Section I: focus on chapters 9 and 10a
(ending before the subhead "The Great Divide").
Note: for an eight-week study,
include Section II starting on page 273.

☑ EVERY YOUNG MAN'S CHOICE
(Questions for Personal Reflection and Examination)

📖 What does selective obedience look like?
- You hear what *you* want to hear.
- You reject or discount what's not in sync with *your* personal desires.
- You replace God's clear instructions with *your* own plan.
- You act out *your* plan.

Sometimes God's commands don't fit in with your "flow," your image, your friendships, or the lifestyles that go with them. So you set aside His directions because you want to be free to do what you want rather than what God wants. But just like the soldier who didn't listen to the beach master, your freedom will be short-lived. 📖

📖 I see the characters of [Superman and Gumby] reflected in the attitudes of young men everywhere. The hearts of supermen, as I call them, are spiritually made of steel.... These guys...are inflexible in their attitude toward God....

At the other end of the spectrum are the Gumbies—guys flexible and bendable to the will of God. They might get twisted around or bent out of shape from life, but they trust the hands shaping them and their characters. They are willing to be handled like clay in the Master's hands. 📖

5. Name some of the freedom-killing results of selective obedience that you've noticed in yourself. How is selective obedience life-destroying?

6. Are you mostly a Superman or a Gumby with God? What recent behavior gives you the best clue?

📖 EVERY YOUNG MAN'S WALK
(Your Guide to Personal Application)

📖 All men I know have felt the punishing blows that selective obedience brings. It doesn't matter who you are or what you want to become. The Bible is full of stories about great kings who could not bring themselves to complete obedience. On several occasions, good kings could not resist the impulse to fudge on God's clear instructions regarding the worship of pagan gods among His people. Allowing their subjects to build pagan shrines or "high places" among the people of God was the equivalent of erecting a statue of Osama Bin Laden in downtown Manhattan. 📖

📖 The bottom line about 80/20 guys is that their love for God is an act. They consistently put the 20 percent over their love for God. They are like the 80/20 kings of the Old Testament who allowed the high places to exist under their watch when God had said they had to go. Add it all up, and it's easy to make the argument that your 20 percent is an idol as well. 📖

7. Look at the biblical statements about three selectively obedient kings: Jehu, Joash, and Azariah. What do these scriptures tell you about God's attitude toward an "almost" complete commitment?

8. Think about your daily attitudes, words, actions, and relationships. Then categorize them on a separate piece of paper under

(a) the 80 percent of your life that is obedient and (b) the 20 percent of your life that is "free." Write down your insights about your 80/20 ratio.

9. Kenny says that a humble attitude toward God is essential for the relationship to work. Study the ten benefits of a humble attitude toward God (they're printed in the book just before the subhead "The Great Divide"). Name at least three of these benefits that make you think: *It's worth it for me to humbly bow to God's will each day.*

10. What for you was the most meaningful concept or truth in chapters 9 and 10a (before the subhead "The Great Divide") of *Every Young Man, God's Man*? How would you talk this over with God? Write down your response as a prayer to Him. What do you believe God wants you to do in response to this week's study?

EVERY YOUNG MAN'S TALK
(Constructive Topics and Questions for Group Discussion)

Key Highlights from the Book for Reading Aloud and Discussing

The Picking and Choosing Syndrome: Let's look at the case histories of three guys your age who are following in the footsteps of those kings from yesteryear. Brad…Jamal…Mike…

Nelson is a soccer guy—a very successful player and now the coach of female high-school players. Nelson tells me that his biggest struggle as a single young man is masturbation and lusting after being around good-looking babes on the soccer field. It's quite okay to struggle. It's not a sin to be tempted. But it is a sin to RSVP to the temptation and mentally taste the delectable hors d'oeuvres. Nelson knows this, which is why he's seeking ways to tip the scales in his favor by loving God with all his mind and strength. 📖

📖 I identified with Superman and Gumby for different reasons. I think part of me wanted to be a superhero while another part of me definitely had my head in the clouds. Pretty weird combination, if you think about it. One guy was indestructible. The other was soft and bendable. The Man of Steel tried to never get bent out of shape. The green figure made of clay *always* was being handled and changed to become real to me (the viewer). Superman always prevailed over the bad guys in the end. Gumby, on the other hand, always had his heart changed by the end of an episode—in victory or defeat. 📖

Discussion Questions

An opening question: Which parts of these chapters were most helpful or encouraging to you? Why?

A. Kenny talks about the picking and choosing syndrome. Go back and look at how Brad, Jamal, and Mike do it. Can you see yourself in any of their attitudes and actions? Tell about it.
B. What specific plan did Nelson come up with to keep himself from RSVPing to temptation? Evaluate together the strengths and weaknesses of his plan.
C. What is good about being a Gumby in your walk with God?

Section II: focus on chapters 10b
(beginning with the subhead "The Great Divide") and 11.

Note: if you're following a twelve-week track,
save the rest of this lesson for the following week.
If you're on the eight-week track…then keep going.

☑ **EVERY YOUNG MAN'S CHOICE**
(Questions for Personal Reflection and Examination)

📖 Then there was the time I mountain-biked down the summit of 11,053-foot-high Mammoth Mountain and felt like I was riding through someone else's yard (namely, God's). Those are the moments when I see how big and powerful He must be and how small and insignificant I am. I see David's point in real time: who am I that that He should even think of me?

When a man recognizes this God gap, there is only one way he should respond: silence. 📖

📖 Jason's revenge is a perfect illustration of baptism…. Thus Marty Wolf was baptized into the blue color because he soaked in the dye long enough for his skin to take on the character of the blue dye. The point of baptism is that you identify with whatever you soak in.

In a similar fashion, your mind takes on the character or colors of whatever you are soaking in. When you place your life in the mirror, what's reflected back tells you what color dye your brain is soaking in. 📖

11. Read and meditate on Psalm 8, focusing on verse 4. For Kenny, God's majesty in nature brought on humility. When have you, too, felt humbled by God's total awesomeness?

12. How did the story of Jason's revenge (in the movie *Big Fat Liar*) affect you? What have you been soaking your brain in this week? during the past month?

👟 EVERY YOUNG MAN'S WALK
(Your Guide to Personal Application)

📖 God is always one up, and we're always one down. That should be enough, but we're human, so we often keep forgetting stuff like this. It helps to remember the depth of the love behind His power and His position. This makes every God's man *want* to be flexible in His hands. 📖

📖 My mental pool, which was saturated with the sexy dye of porn and mental fantasy, was slowly drained and replaced with the pure water of Christ's living words. After soaking my mind in the Word of God, I had the necessary ingredients to begin sharing my faith in Christ with others, which would eventually lead to opportunities to help thousands of men every year around the globe.

Two Kennys, two marinades, two very different directions— but one undeniable fact: the content of my mind created my character. 📖

13. Prayerfully read Isaiah 45:6-7. How is God one up on you? What is your gut-level response?

14. Check the waters in your mental swimming pool for a moment. How would you rate the purity levels?

    ___ A welcome sight: crystal clear and sparkling waters

    ___ A filter problem: dirt clinging to the bottom

    ___ A scrubbing challenge: ugly stains, lots of debris

    ___ A death trap: one stinking mess of scum and sludge

15. If you're wondering, *How do I get God's mind?* Kenny's answer is *meditation.* So choose one of the scriptures mentioned in chapter 11 of the book. Right now, spend ten minutes meditating on it. Then think: *What did I notice?*

16. Alan took his relationship with Jesus very personally. How is that different from having a disciplined devotional life?

17. What for you was the most meaningful concept or truth in chapters 10b (beginning with the subhead "The Great Divide") and 11 of *Every Young Man, God's Man*? How would you talk this over with God? Write down your response as a prayer to Him. What do you believe God wants you to do in response to this week's study?

👨‍👦 EVERY YOUNG MAN'S TALK

(Constructive Topics and Questions for Group Discussion)

Key Highlights from the Book for Reading Aloud and Discussing

📖 Young men who know better but refuse to heed God's voice create misery for themselves and for those around them. I have seen my share of guys who think they have it all figured out at eighteen or nineteen, and they frustrate the snot out of me. These guys would never think they're coming out against God, but their choices and even their questions reek of pride. Most of all, these guys isolate themselves from people of truth and plug their ears to voices of truth. It's a frustrating pattern that has been repeated for centuries among God's men. Aaron is one of the most recent examples. 📖

📖 In the movie *Big Fat Liar,* Jason Shepherd, the main character, was not unlike a certain author who became very skillful at lying to friends and family to avoid responsibilities at school and at home. The movie's opening scenes make clear that Jason is quite good at this—he's got everyone from his principal to his parents believing his innocent and touching lies. 📖

📖 A killer statement I have never forgotten was when I heard a guy on the radio quote Samuel Smiles, a writer from the 1800s: "Sow a thought, reap an action. Sow an action, reap a habit. Sow a habit, reap a character. Sow a character, reap a destiny." Did you know that the journey of a thought has such power? If the first thing I need to know about my mind is that *I am* what I think, then the second truth I have to understand is that *I do* what I think. 📖

Discussion Questions

An opening question: Which parts of this chapter were most helpful or encouraging to you? Why?

D. Aaron thought he had it all figured out. Go back and think through his story. How did God break through Aaron's pride?

E. Have you ever been a big, fat liar? What are some of the short-term benefits of this approach to life? What are some long-term drawbacks?

F. According to Kenny, what is the first truth to know about your mind? What is the second? How well do you really know these two principles—based on your lifestyle?

G. Kenny says: "God equates studying His Word to hanging out with Him." Do you agree? What is hanging out with God like for you?

H. Together, list as many reasons you can think of for *not having enough time* to marinate yourself in God's Word. Then discuss Kenny's statement: "When a guy says to me that he doesn't have time for God's Word, he's not stating a fact, he's stating a priority."

I. Before ending your session, share your prayer requests for the coming week.

stay sharp and speak up

This week's reading assignment:

chapters 12–14 in *Every Young Man, God's Man*

Every young man needs another young man *in his life to sharpen and realign him in his walk with God. To be God's young man requires placing a high value on male relationships that keep you spiritually strong. One of my favorite Scriptures says it best: "As iron sharpens iron, so one man sharpens another" (Proverbs 27:17).*

Most young men I counsel overlook this important biblical principle, which is a shame.

—from chapter 12 in *Every Young Man, God's Man*

📖 EVERY YOUNG MAN'S TRUTH

(Your Personal Journey into God's Word)

An old 1970s song says: "He ain't heavy, he's my brother." It speaks of caring for the other guy, because "his welfare is my concern," so "the load doesn't weigh me down at all."

Is it really possible to feel that way about other human beings? In the church, it's absolutely essential. As Christ's band of brothers, we are called to shoulder one another's burdens. We are to risk realness in our words. Speak the truth of our hearts. And just plain love one another. That way, we keep one another sharp for kingdom battles.

It starts by looking at Jesus, our mentor. Though He was Lord of all, He knelt to wash the feet of His brothers, declaring Himself to be their servant. Can you do it—serve the guy next to you in your small group? Really care about his problems and needs? The scriptures below will help you decide.

Carry each other's burdens, and in this way you will fulfill the law of Christ. (Galatians 6:2)

Speaking the truth in love, we will in all things grow up into him who is the Head, that is, Christ. From him the whole body, joined and held together by every supporting ligament, grows and builds itself up in love, as each part does its work....

Therefore each of you must put off falsehood and speak truthfully to his neighbor, for we are all members of one body. (Ephesians 4:15-16,25)

Above all, love each other deeply, because love covers over a multitude of sins. Offer hospitality to one another without grumbling. Each one should use whatever gift he has received to serve others, faithfully administering God's grace in its various forms. If anyone speaks, he should do it as one speaking the very words of God. If anyone serves, he should do it with the strength God provides, so that in all things God may be praised through Jesus Christ. To him be the glory and the power for ever and ever. Amen. (1 Peter 4:8-11)

1. Can you think of a time when a Christian brother really needed your help? What did you do?
2. According to Ephesians 4, why is speaking the truth an important part of our life in the body?
3. What does it mean to you that love covers a multitude of sins?
4. How would you define *hospitality* in your own words? What would it look like if the guys in your small group were offering "hospitality to one another without grumbling"?

Section I: focus on chapters 12 and 13a
(ending before the subhead "Confession Is Not for Cowards").

Note: for an eight-week study,
include Section II starting on page 284.

☑ EVERY YOUNG MAN'S CHOICE
(Questions for Personal Reflection and Examination)

📖 If you're unsharpened by the presence of another committed friend, your commitment to God won't perform. It will be duller than a steak knife that's been played with in the dirt all morning long. But a young man who's got a spiritual sharpening stone in his life—another brother headed down the same path toward God—can make the transition to the bigger issues of manhood with support, confidence, and encouragement to do the right thing.

Take Jordan for example… 📖

📖 Since I'm older and have spoken on sexual integrity issues for years, I felt at ease talking about sex to this group of students. I described how I struggled to be victorious, fought "the fever" as a younger man, and experienced the huge blessings of sexual integrity. I want younger audiences to connect with me as someone who knows *exactly* what they're going through.

That morning in Ohio, I made the following points… 📖

5. Who is your spiritual sharpening stone? How does he help you the most? Who might be a good candidate to become your sharpening stone in the future?
6. Review the points Kenny made during his talk in Ohio. Choose the one that sparks the most interest for you—and jot down the reason.

👟 EVERY YOUNG MAN'S WALK
(Your Guide to Personal Application)

📖 Listen, the guys you think have it all together are just as whacked out as you! The discovery that is helping today's young men win their big spiritual battles is that they are learning they need better relationships with their *God-focused* peers. When I encourage young men to pursue relationships with their guy friends, I see many change their thinking about their guy connections and use them in ways that God intended. 📖

📖 Guys don't even *think* about discussing their feelings or what's churning inside with another friend. We prefer to stuff our emotions, maintain a stiff upper lip, and carry on with harboring what's really going on inside.…

The result is that we're pretty bad at dealing with our emotions. Here's a quick list, and ask yourself if any of these hit your bull's-eye:

- You mask anger with sarcasm.
- You avoid serious conversations by making fun of the subject.
- You "gotta go."
- You change the scenery.
- You keep secrets.
- You avoid guilt through rationalization.
- You deflect mistakes.
- You blame others.
- You hang out with shallow people who don't "go there."
- You change the subject. 📖

7. What's the difference between a peer and a God-focused peer? How many friends of each do you have? Which relationships do you actively pursue?

8. Take up Kenny's challenge in the second quotation above and mark which two or three emotion-avoiding tactics hit your bull's-eye.

9. What for you was the most meaningful concept or truth in these chapters of *Every Young Man, God's Man*? How would you talk this over with God? Write down your response as a prayer to Him. What do you believe God wants you to do in response to this week's study?

😊🗨 EVERY YOUNG MAN'S TALK

(Constructive Topics and Questions for Group Discussion)

Key Highlights from the Book for Reading Aloud and Discussing

📖 I know we've talked about the fairer sex a lot in *Every Young Man, God's Man,* but the number one dilemma facing God's young men today is not sexual temptation. It's isolation. 📖

📖 I have found that young men who aren't making the transition to spiritual manhood have reached their sad state because they're connected to other guys who dull their edge to their goals as God's men. In this group of friends, they don't:

- risk getting honest about the tough stuff burning a hole in the pit of their stomachs
- watch one another's backs spiritually
- pray for one another regularly
- push one another to be in God's Word
- ask how a guy's walk with the Lord is going
- encourage one another to take bold risks for Christ
- care enough to confront behavior that doesn't square with Scripture 📖

📖 When it comes to getting honest with others about what's really going on in their lives, many young men pull the old rope-a-dope. They use spin, employ shady tactics, or just flat-out lie to deliberately lead people to thinking all is well when the reality is that they need help, advice, or even rescue. 📖

Discussion Questions

An opening question: Which parts of these chapters were most helpful or encouraging to you? Why?

A. If you agree with Kenny that isolation—not sexual temptation—is a young man's number one dilemma, how do you explain it?

B. How can another guy dull your spiritual edge? (See the seven listed don'ts.) How can he sharpen you?

C. When have you seen the old rope-a-dope in action among a group of guys? How effective was it?

D. Look again at the seven scriptures that Kenny lists to show "what God has to say about the science of being sharp." Discuss how each of these passages could apply to a twenty-first-century guy.

Section II: focus on chapters 13b
(beginning with the subhead "Confession Is Not for Cowards") and 14.

Note: if you're following a twelve-week track,
save the rest of this lesson for the following week.
If you're on the eight-week track…then keep going.

☑ EVERY YOUNG MAN'S CHOICE
(Questions for Personal Reflection and Examination)

📖 Most young men do not have the stomach for confession because it forces them to confront themselves or their actions. (Newsflash: *no one likes to do that!*) Revealing your dirty laundry is like showing the world your dirty underwear. No one wants to do that, so it's better to resort to rope-a-dope. The problem is that the only one getting roped is you! Satan loves it when a young man believes his smoke screens are working, because the longer he stays unconfessed and self-deceived, the longer he can keep inflicting losses on someone who could be living for God. 📖

📖 Most guys I counsel have not engaged the ministry of the Holy Spirit, the third person of the Trinity, and all He can do for them. Perhaps you're unaware that Jesus described His character and ministry with such words as *counselor, comforter, helper, spirit of truth,* and *guide.* The Holy Spirit is ready and willing to speak the right direction in your mind. All you have to do is let Him do this, and when that happens, He will guide you through every temptation and help you avoid many of the traps others fall into. 📖

10. In silence, with a heart open to God, reflect: *Do I have a stomach for confession? Have I been rope-a-doping lately? How unconfessed am I at the moment?*

11. Would you like to engage the ministry of the Holy Spirit today? Well, just let Him. Jot down your request to the Holy Spirit.

👟 EVERY YOUNG MAN'S WALK
(Your Guide to Personal Application)

📖 I look at confession as giving Satan a bloody nose, and that's what happens when you punch back with God's truth.

If you think I'm off base on this, just listen to how strongly God encourages His people to practice the discipline of confession with Him and others, then make a note of the consequences. 📖

📖 For God's young man, trusting that the Holy Spirit will be there to guide you and counsel you is kind of like taking that first run down the bunny slope. It's a risk because you're practically guaranteed to fall. But one thing I've learned about being God's young man is that when you risk changing for Him, the change always takes you to the next level. Spiritually speaking, you'll go from the bunny slopes to carving some serious powder in the back bowls. 📖

12. You can rely on God's Word and give Satan a bloody nose! Meditate on Psalm 51:6, Proverbs 28:13, James 5:16, and 1 John 1:8-9. Then jot down the consequences of practicing—or *not* practicing—the discipline of confession.

13. When you face temptation or tough times, does it feel risky to switch from willpower to relying on the Holy Spirit? Why? What can make this kind of reliance more of a habit in a guy's life?

14. Go to the prayer that appears toward the end of chapter 14. Consider whether you'd like to make those words your own. If so, spend a few moments offering them to the Holy Spirit with a sincere heart.

15. What for you was the most meaningful concept or truth in these chapter readings from *Every Young Man, God's Man*? How would you talk this over with God? Write down your response as a prayer to Him. What do you believe God wants you to do in response to this week's study?

🙂🙂 EVERY YOUNG MAN'S TALK
(Constructive Topics and Questions for Group Discussion)

Key Highlights from the Book for Reading Aloud and Discussing

📖 Rich approached me and asked to speak in private. When we got out of earshot of the other guys, he put it straight to me: "I really wonder what's in it for me if I come clean about masturbation and surfing adult Web sites with my college group. Won't people be angry with me since I've got this junk in my life and I'm supposed to be a leader? Can't I just come clean with you and that's it?"

"Do you want victory?" I replied.

"Absolutely," he said.

"Then here's what you say to your group…" 📖

📖 Practice under pressure over time creates confidence. 📖

📖 God has spelled out exactly how He wants to use the Holy Spirit in your life and how you, as God's young man, need to start working with Him. Like any relationship, the first step is to learn more about Him so that you can partner more closely. And what a great partner He is! The Holy Spirit can… 📖

Discussion Questions

An opening question: Which parts of this chapter were most helpful or encouraging to you? Why?

E. Do you agree that Rich needed to bring things out into the open with his guys' small group? If you were him, how nervous would you be at the moment of truth?

F. Kenny lists ten things the Holy Spirit can do. Go through them, one by one, in your group. Comment on how these truths can be encouraging to guys like you. Be as specific and practical as possible.

G. One of Kenny's favorite sayings is: "Practice under pressure over time creates confidence." What's your opinion about it? How does it apply to the challenge of learning to depend on the Holy Spirit?

H. Have everyone look at the prayer to the Holy Sprit found at the end of chapter 14. Ask one another: "Who prayed this prayer when you were filling in your workbook before the group time?" Spend some time sharing about who has prayed—and who would *like* to pray— these words for themselves.

power, pressure, and progress

This week's reading assignment:

chapters 15–16 in *Every Young Man, God's Man*

I kept pedaling and pedaling, and five and a half hours later I crossed the finish line, crying for my mama. I finished a respectable sixty-first, which was in the middle of the pack. But more important, I learned a huge lesson. All I had to do was get on the bike, strengthen my legs, and let them carry me to the end.

Mountain biking is all about power and performance, and if you've got no power, you've got no performance....

Power is a good thing, and prayer is the outlet that God has chosen to connect you to His vast reservoir of power.

—from chapter 15 in *Every Young Man, God's Man*

EVERY YOUNG MAN'S TRUTH
(Your Personal Journey into God's Word)

Pressure and prayer. They really are related, as you'll see in this session. Logically, it makes sense: when trouble hits, you go to God.

Sadly, many of us make a pit stop first. We first try to engineer our way out. We throw all our own power at the problem. Then, if things don't work out, we come before God with hat in hand.

Is it just a sign of laziness? "Why are you sleeping?" Jesus asked His friends when they should have been praying. Is He asking you the same tough question?

Be still, and know that I am God. (Psalm 46:10)

Jesus went out as usual to the Mount of Olives, and his disciples followed him. On reaching the place, he said to them, "Pray that you will not fall into temptation." He withdrew about a stone's throw beyond them, knelt down and prayed, "Father, if you are willing, take this cup from me; yet not my will, but yours be done." An angel from heaven appeared to him and strengthened him. And being in anguish, he prayed more earnestly, and his sweat was like drops of blood falling to the ground.

When he rose from prayer and went back to the disciples, he found them asleep, exhausted from sorrow. "Why are you sleeping?" he asked them. "Get up and pray so that you will not fall into temptation." (Luke 22:39-46)

Do not throw away your confidence; it will be richly rewarded. You need to persevere so that when you have done the will of God, you will receive what he has promised. For in just a very little while,

"He who is coming will come and will not delay.
But my righteous one will live by faith.

> And if he shrinks back,
>> I will not be pleased with him."

But we are not of those who shrink back and are destroyed, but of those who believe and are saved. (Hebrews 10:35-39)

1. In a typical day, when are you still before God?
2. According to Jesus, how does prayer relate to our temptation battles?
3. How does God view your willingness to persevere in tough times? Why?
4. How would you like to improve your prayer life? What first step could you take today?

Section I: focus on chapter 15. Note: for an eight-week study, include Section II starting on page 295.

☑ EVERY YOUNG MAN'S CHOICE
(Questions for Personal Reflection and Examination)

📖 We cannot fathom how many lives are affected every day by Google. Yet all of that astonishing power cannot come close to the storehouse of personal spiritual power available to you as God's young servant, which is made possible through the power of prayer.... There is a living spiritual engine within you that can search the mind of God for... 📖

📖 Josh's scenario is typical of most young men when it comes to prayer: it took a crisis situation before it even dawned on him to talk to God in prayer. Let's put it this way: Josh was certainly mindful of God when he needed something or when he was in a setting that called for prayer, like during chapel or when his Bible study was finishing up. He realizes that his dialogue with God is shallow and selfish most of the time (like today), but he can't seem to work in more conversations with God.

Do you ever wonder what the Creator thinks when He views this kind of prayer life? Isaiah heard it loud and clear: "And so the Lord says, 'These people say they are mine. They honor me with their lips, but their hearts are far from me'" (Isaiah 29:13, NLT). 📖

5. Think about the Google-smashing power of God within you as you prayerfully read Ephesians 3:20. Then go over Kenny's list of ten needs that God's power can meet. Which of these needs are pressuring you right now?

6. How is your prayer life like or unlike Josh's?

7. Kenny says, *"Prayer is the power that fuels the performance of your faith."* What comment, question, or personal experience does this bring to your mind?

👟 EVERY YOUNG MAN'S WALK
(Your Guide to Personal Application)

📖 God is waiting for you to access His awesome strength. Everything is just a prayer away. If you're clueless to the personal benefits of prayer, or in too much of a hurry to slow down and get into the practice of prayer, here's what you need to know: your network card was installed in you at salvation, and talking to God is done wirelessly. So what are you waiting for? 📖

📖 Prayer, for you, is a secret power, an adventure in trusting the living God. When a young man recognizes this privilege, he moves beyond the task of prayer to the treasure of being present with God. As Scripture says, "A single day in your courts is better than a thousand anywhere else!" (Psalm 84:10, NLT) 📖

8. Imagine God *waiting* for you to connect with Him in prayer. Are you mostly…

___ "clueless to the personal benefits of prayer"?

___ "in too much of a hurry to slow down and get into the practice of prayer"?

___ ready to slow down for God in a prayer relationship?

9. How can Kenny call *being present with God* a treasure? What is this treasure's value to you, based on your prayer practices?
10. Rewrite Psalm 84:10 in your own words.
11. What for you was the most meaningful concept or truth in chapter 15 of *Every Young Man, God's Man*? How would you talk this over with God? Write down your response as a prayer to Him. What do you believe God wants you to do in response to this week's study?

👤👤 EVERY YOUNG MAN'S TALK
(Constructive Topics and Questions for Group Discussion)

Key Highlights from the Book for Reading Aloud and Discussing

📖 Josh reviewed how his day was going so far. *Let's see. First the test—no better than a B-minus or C for sure. Then my parents—I'll have to fake like I'm doing good in school. I'll have to work to pay for those Christmas presents—and that Cindy—oh, mama. Not good. What next? How did I get here?* He pocketed his cell phone, took a huge breath, and cupped his face in his hands. Lord, what do I do? 📖

📖 For Jesus, quick connection and quality relationship was an oxymoron—two totally contradictory ideas that don't go together. The message to Martha was simple: *You can't connect with Me on the fly!* He wouldn't cheat Martha's sister, Mary, out of their time together by cutting it short. But I know plenty of young men who have cut Jesus short on prayer because they simply don't know how to slow down, relax, and talk with their Savior about stuff. 📖

📖 Trying to manage your life without praying is like trying to ride a bike with flat tires. It can be done, but life is sure going to be tiring, laborious, and no fun. You certainly can't enjoy the ride or feel the wind in your face. Only a total dork would choose to do that, but that is exactly what you are choosing to do if you neglect the power of prayer. 📖

Discussion Questions

An opening question: Which parts of these chapters were most helpful or encouraging to you? Why?

A. Ever had a day like Josh's? How much do you pray on those kinds of days? on normal days? on good days?
B. Ask one of the guys to read aloud the story of Mary and Martha

in Luke 10:38-42. How deeply has Jesus's message to these women—that *you can't connect with Me on the fly*—sunk into your own heart?

C. Who in your group will admit to living like a dork (according to Kenny's definition)? What could help you repair those flat tires on your prayer bike?

D. A key point in this study session is that Jesus wants to be with you. How does this make you feel?

Section II: focus on chapter 16.

Note: if you're following a twelve-week track,
save the rest of this lesson for the following week.
If you're on the eight-week track...then keep going.

☑ EVERY YOUNG MAN'S CHOICE
(Questions for Personal Reflection and Examination)

📖 After Miss Trench Coat's unexpected appearance, however, I felt like Daniel in a pagan palace asked to swallow food offered to idols. I could not stomach this, nor could I participate in it. But what else could I do? It was just me against a tidal wave of testosterone. 📖

📖 God taught me a powerful lesson that day: pressure is a good thing, because it never leaves you where it finds you. What I mean is that there were only two directions I could have taken. I could have joined in the fun and compromised. Or I could make the best stand under the circumstances and fight with the tools God gave me. In the end, I faced ninety minutes of pressure—from the announcement during dinner to the striptease act, but I received a clear view of God's awesome power. 📖

12. If you had been Kenny in the Miss Trench Coat crisis, what do you think you would have done?

13. What have you learned about pressure so far in your life? How did you learn these things?

14. Kenny says you need God's overpowering strength with you to equalize the pressure being put on you by the world, the dark side, and the devil. Look at the fifteen pressures he lists on page 206. Think: *Which of these are my own pressures and struggles? What pressures would I add to this list? What scriptures in this session could help me apply an equalizer?*

👟 EVERY YOUNG MAN'S WALK
(Your Guide to Personal Application)

📖 When I realized that I led a parade of none, I stomped up to my room on the second floor, my blood boiling and my mind spinning. Part of me wished that I was still on the other side so I wouldn't have this intense battle raging inside. The other part of me said, *Fight!* 📖

📖 When similar situations come your way, think of how God wants to use this pressure to make you a new man. Most young men have a one-sided view of pressure, temptation, and trials—a negative one. But that's how the world, the dark side, and Satan want you to see it. God wants you to see it His way. 📖

15. When have you felt like Kenny as he stomped back to his room? What do you usually do when you are feeling yanked between the other side and the call to fight?

16. What positive results did Kenny experience because of his choices about Miss Trench Coat? What does this tell you about the role of pressure in a guy's life?

17. What for you was the most meaningful concept or truth in chapter 16 of *Every Young Man, God's Man*? How would you talk this over with God? Write down your response as a prayer to Him. What do you believe God wants you to do in response to this week's study?

👦👹 EVERY YOUNG MAN'S TALK

(Constructive Topics and Questions for Group Discussion)

Key Highlights from the Book for Reading Aloud and Discussing

📖 Suddenly, a searing thought landed like a grenade in a foxhole: *Pray Miss Trench Coat out of there.* 📖

📖 God's plan to make you a man doesn't include a provision to remove you from pressure. In fact, He's most likely to *throw* you into pressure-packed situations, because He knows that will increase your faith and grow your character in Christ. More often than not, you'll have to choose God and trust Him with the results. God tests you because you're still growing up. 📖

📖 You'll likely experience ups and downs and the occasional face plant, but that's okay because you aren't perfect (nor am I). Only one man scored a perfect ten on earth, and He's not you! So just chill out

and cut yourself some slack, because God certainly does. Listen to
His encouraging voice speak to your journey…Proverbs 24:16…
Philippians 2:12-13…Philippians 1:6…Proverbs 4:18. 📖

Discussion Questions

An opening question: Which parts of this chapter were most helpful or encouraging to you? Why?

E. Kenny prayed Miss Trench Coat out of the room. Talk about the
    power of prayer for a few minutes. Do you have any personal stories
    to share about this?

F. Name some things that grow stronger under pressure. Then read
    2 Corinthians 12:9-10 and discuss how God's young man can grow
    stronger under pressure.

G. When have you done a face plant under pressure in the past? How
    could Proverbs 24:16, Philippians 2:12-13, Philippians 1:6, and
    Proverbs 4:18 help at a time like that?

H. Kenny tells us that perseverance under pressure pleases God. Then
    he lists nine ways to equalize that pressure. Look at each item on his
    list and tell whether you have ever tried it yourself. What happened?

I. English evangelist Charles H. Spurgeon said: "I owe more to the
    fire and hammer and file than anything else in my Lord's work-
    shop." If Spurgeon were to visit your group right now, would you
    give him a high-five for this statement? Why or why not?

plan the victory; honor the sacrifice

This week's reading assignment:

chapters 17–18 in *Every Young Man, God's Man*

If you're really serious about your relationship to God, then you'll agree that wise planning reduces temptation. When you deal with issues before you're tempted, you enter the battle with a plan versus just showing up clueless about what happens next. When you execute a plan like this, you're counting the cost of what it takes to build a solid spiritual life.

—from chapter 17 in *Every Young Man, God's Man*

EVERY YOUNG MAN'S TRUTH
(Your Personal Journey into God's Word)

First you plan. Then you realize the limits of your plan. Which brings you to the unlimited effectiveness of the Cross. That's what this session is all about: your call to plan for your battles with the dark side and your need to rely, ultimately, on the sacrifice of Christ for your victories.

But really, how important is the Cross to you? Do you realize that without it you would have no hope of eternal life? Do you understand that by the Cross, you were forgiven and made a child of God? If you know these things, how could you respond with anything but gratitude in your daily life? It boils down to this: honor the sacrifice!

> Suppose one of you wants to build a tower. Will he not first sit down
> and estimate the cost to see if he has enough money to complete it?
> For if he lays the foundation and is not able to finish it, everyone
> who sees it will ridicule him, saying, "This fellow began to build
> and was not able to finish." (Luke 14:28-30)

He grew up before him like a tender shoot,
and like a root out of dry ground.
He had no beauty or majesty to attract us
to him,
nothing in his appearance that we should
desire him.
He was despised and rejected by men,
a man of sorrows, and familiar with suffering.
Like one from whom men hide their faces
he was despised, and we esteemed him not.
Surely he took up our infirmities
and carried our sorrows,
yet we considered him stricken by God,
smitten by him, and afflicted.
But he was pierced for our transgressions,
he was crushed for our iniquities;
the punishment that brought us peace was
upon him,
and by his wounds we are healed.

> We all, like sheep, have gone astray,
>> each of us has turned to his own way;
> and the LORD has laid on him
>> the iniquity of us all.
> He was oppressed and afflicted,
>> yet he did not open his mouth;
> he was led like a lamb to the slaughter,
>> and as a sheep before her shearers is silent,
>> so he did not open his mouth.
>> (Isaiah 53:2-7)

And he died for all, that those who live should no longer live for themselves but for him who died for them and was raised again. (2 Corinthians 5:15)

1. When have you left a job unfinished due to poor planning? What did you learn?
2. Some people plan how they will get to heaven. Is it possible to punch your own ticket to the Pearly Gates? Which Scripture truths above help you answer?
3. Carefully read through the Isaiah passage above. How does the idea of substitution come through to you?
4. The Cross is about *dying*, but what does it have to do with *living*?

☑ EVERY YOUNG MAN'S CHOICE
(Questions for Personal Reflection and Examination)

📖 As God's young man, you, too, must have a plan for the key battles in your future. In these circumstances, it helps to think like

General Patton for a second. The following questions are designed to help facilitate your planning process… 📖

📖 Jesus knew how to get a man's attention—and I'm just glad He didn't mention other parts of the male anatomy! What He was saying in blunt language was this:

- Sin is the enemy.
- Cut sin off at the source.
- Keep God and eternity in mind as you make choices.
- Know your weaknesses so that you can cut them out effectively. 📖

5. Think about your plans for righteous living. Go back to the book's list of questions to help facilitate the planning process (under the subhead "Cutting Off and Starving Sin"). Then spend several minutes answering these questions for your own life.

6. Read Mark 9:43-48. How serious is our sin in God's eyes?

7. Kenny says that for every excuse young men may give, there is a bloodstained cross staring back at them. What emotional power does that cross have in your life?

👟 EVERY YOUNG MAN'S WALK
(Your Guide to Personal Application)

📖 Predetermined boundaries may involve cutting off and starving sin in the following ways:

- carving sexy R-rated films out of your cinematic repertoire

- deciding that the bar scene or drinking parties will not be the place where you connect with friends
- refusing to keep sexual secrets that put distance between you and God
- accepting sexual accountability
- inviting people you spiritually respect to ask you the tough questions
- committing to not mentally undressing any woman
- getting software that allows someone to see where you have been on the Net
- committing in writing with a girl you're dating the dos and don'ts of the physical relationship. 📖

📖 Jesus stood in the observation post at one time. He was our forward observer who saw the potential of sin to overwhelm and destroy your life. Then He called for fire directly on His position, saying, in a sense, "Put it all on Me!" And that's when hell and death and sin fell upon Him. Friends protested. "Never, Lord!" said Peter, but Jesus refused to back off. He turned toward His Father and said, "I want your will, not mine" (Luke 22:42, NLT).

How do you honor that kind of sacrifice? By making it a part of your life. 📖

8. Which of the cut-off-and-starve activities hit closest to home?
9. How do you honor the Cross in your life? What qualities are there, in your words and actions, that demonstrate your respect?
10. In quietness, review what you have written and learned in this

week's study. If further thoughts or prayer requests come to your mind and heart, you may want to write them down.

11. What for you was the most meaningful concept or truth in this week's study? How would you talk this over with God? Write down your response as a prayer to Him. What do you believe God wants you to do in response to this week's study?

🙂🙂 EVERY YOUNG MAN'S TALK
(Constructive Topics and Questions for Group Discussion)

Key Highlights from the Book for Reading Aloud and Discussing

📖 One of the reasons so many young men suffer defeat regularly in spiritual warfare is that they fail to engage the Enemy or take a proactive approach to battle. They just show up and expect that's enough to conquer direct attacks against their faith. If Patton thought like that, we might all be speaking German today. 📖

📖 The things that a guy tends to resist—limits, godly boundaries, and rules—are the very things you need to become the man God wants you to be. The dark side, the popular culture, and the devil will attempt to convince you that these commitments are old school and take away your independence. In my experience, most young guys who believe this become slaves to the very attitudes and actions they were told represented freedom. 📖

📖 Charles H. Spurgeon so aptly said, "A dying Savior is the death of sin." 📖

Discussion Questions

An opening question: Which parts of these chapters were most helpful or encouraging to you? Why?

A. What does it mean to be proactive in spiritual warfare?

B. Why do we tend to resist limits, boundaries, and rules? How does this show up in your life?

C. What did Spurgeon mean by his statement about a dying Savior? Answer by explaining your own theology of the Cross.

D. Kenny challenges us to never, ever, ever forget the price that Christ paid for our sin. Do you believe you could ever forget? Why?

E. Since this is your last session together in this study, spend some time talking about what you've learned and how you've changed. Then share prayer requests about your desires for further growth as God's young men.

don't keep it to yourself

If you've just completed the *Every Young Man, God's Man Workbook* on your own, and you found it to be a helpful and valuable experience, we encourage you to consider organizing a group of your peers and helping lead them through the book and workbook together.

You'll find more information about starting such a group in the section titled "Questions You May Have About This Workbook."

about the authors

STEPHEN ARTERBURN is coauthor of the Every Man series, founder of New Life Clinics, host of the daily *New Life Live!* national radio program, a nationally known speaker, a licensed minister, and author of more than forty books.

KENNY LUCK is president and founder of Every Man Ministries and co-author of the best-selling *Every Man, God's Man.* He is the men's pastor of Saddleback Church in Lake Forest, California. He and his wife, Chrissy, have three children and reside in Trabuco Canyon.

MIKE YORKEY is the author, coauthor, and general editor of several books for men, including *"Daddy's Home," The Christian Dad's Answer Book,* and all the books in the Every Man series. He and his wife, Nicole, are the parents of two college-aged children and live in Encinitas, California.